P9-DEO-637

SEP 1 8 2019

Painting by Deirdre Cavanagh

HIVEMIND

The New Science of Tribalism in Our
Divided World

SARAH ROSE CAVANAGH, PHD

GRAND CENTRAL
PUBLISHING

NEW YORK   BOSTON

3817923

Copyright © 2019 by Sarah Rose Cavanagh, PhD

Cover design by Michael Morris
Cover copyright © 2019 by Hachette Book Group, Inc.

Hachette Book Group supports the right to free expression and the value of copyright. The purpose of copyright is to encourage writers and artists to produce the creative works that enrich our culture.

The scanning, uploading, and distribution of this book without permission is a theft of the author's intellectual property. If you would like permission to use material from the book (other than for review purposes), please contact permissions@hbgusa.com. Thank you for your support of the author's rights.

Grand Central Publishing
Hachette Book Group
1290 Avenue of the Americas, New York, NY 10104
grandcentralpublishing.com
twitter.com/grandcentralpub

First edition: September 2019

Grand Central Publishing is a division of Hachette Book Group, Inc. The Grand Central Publishing name and logo is a trademark of Hachette Book Group, Inc.

The publisher is not responsible for websites (or their content) that are not owned by the publisher.

The Hachette Speakers Bureau provides a wide range of authors for speaking events. To find out more, go to www.hachettespeakersbureau.com or call (866) 376-6591.

Library of Congress Cataloging-in-Publication Data

Names: Cavanagh, Sarah Rose, author.
Title: Hivemind : the new science of tribalism in our divided world / Sarah Rose Cavanagh, PhD.
Description: First edition. | New York : Grand Central Publishing, [2019] | Includes index.
Identifiers: LCCN 2019004164 | ISBN 9781538713327 (hardcover) | ISBN 9781549169663 (audio download) | ISBN 9781538713341 (ebook)
Subjects: LCSH: Collective behavior. | Swarm intelligence—Social aspects. | Group values (Sociology)
Classification: LCC HM866 .C38 2019 | DDC 302.3/5—dc23
LC record available at https://lccn.loc.gov/2019004164

ISBNs: 978-1-5387-1332-7 (hardcover), 978-1-5387-1334-1 (ebook)

Printed in the United States of America

LSC-C

10   9   8   7   6   5   4   3   2   1

IN MEMORIAM

Eliza Praetorius,
who taught me to think with
my heart wide open

and

Katherine McLellan Kenworthy,
hand in my pocket

Contents

Preface

A South Carolina textile mill, 1962. A humid June afternoon. Summer was the workshop's busiest season, and everyone had been putting in a lot of hours. This particular week was made more stressful by reports of small, mite-like bugs in the factory, perhaps brought in with a shipment of cloth. As the afternoon wore on, one young woman suddenly complained of feeling a bug bite. Soon after, she fainted dead away.

On Tuesday of the following week, another woman who believed she had been bitten fainted. That afternoon, a third woman. Soon after, four other women reported to the doctor with symptoms of dizziness and nausea. Within eleven days of what would later be known as an epidemic, sixty-two people were medically treated for various physical symptoms due to bug bites. Their reports of the bites were quite specific and detailed. One textile worker claimed, "I felt something bite me on my leg and when I scratched my leg, the little white bug came up under my fingernail. I got weak in the legs and got sick." Tellingly, while this worker recalls a white bug, most other reports described *black* bugs.

Extensive testing by the mill and outside authorities revealed that only a few bugs had been found, the mites were not known to bite humans, and they certainly could not have caused systemic problems like those experienced by the textile workers. But the employees were verifiably losing consciousness, vomiting, and experiencing shakes. Reviewing the available evidence, the doctors and other experts on the case came to the startling conclusion that the maladies suffered by the workers were, at the end of the day, all in their head.[1]

Cases of alarming symptoms spreading rapidly from person to person without being tied to any physical causes occur throughout documented history, from the Salem witch trials to the Bin Laden itch.[2] The term for such occurrences is *hysterical contagion*, which you may know by its more extreme form, mass hysteria. All involve fear of a powerful unknown threat spreading through a close-knit group. A more contemporary example than the june bug story involved a group of teenage girls at a New York high school who began exhibiting symptoms reminiscent of Tourette's syndrome—involuntary twitches and vocalizations called tics. The affected girls were profiled on talk shows, their symptoms were displayed on videos uploaded to YouTube, and their struggles were discussed openly on Facebook. The case was so high-profile that Erin Brockovich, legal clerk and environmental activist (played by Julia Roberts in the eponymous biopic), flew in to help investigate. But exhaustive testing revealed no evidence of any sort of toxin that could explain the girls' symptoms and pointed to the possibility of a mass psychogenic illness, perhaps exacerbated by social and national media attention.[3]

These cases have in common a tight-knit social group with a constrained physical location, the occurrence of a single "index" case that launches the contagion, and the fact that many of the symptoms—among them dizziness and involuntary motor movements—also manifest during states of acute anxiety. Human beings are so social that we can literally make ourselves sick just by observing others, the symptoms spreading from one person to the next by the power of ideas alone.

These hysterical contagions are rare. But vivid instances of emotions and ideas diffusing from one body to another, one mind to another, are not. We are by nature deeply social animals. In this book we'll see just how ingrained that sociality is—to the point where we catch thoughts and moods and, yes, even panic attacks from one another as easily as we exchange cold viruses in midwinter. We synchronize our thoughts, our moods, and our brain activity. In this book we'll tackle both the mechanisms and the implications of this synchronicity using psychology, neuroscience, history, anthropology, literature, and philosophy.

Of course, we don't synchronize with all members of humanity equally; we preferentially harmonize with people who are close to us by birth, location, and shared culture, whether that culture is writ large (at the macro level of entire societies) or small (at the micro level of groups that help form our multilayered identities, for example ethnicity, political party, and even sport fandoms). These tribal tendencies toward forming ingroups can shape our most cherished traditions and moments, but they can also lead to tension with outgroups that can have devastating consequences.

To unite all of this research on our hypersocial, groupish natures, I use the metaphor of the *hivemind*. It is not my metaphor—the notion of a hivemind, a group sort of consciousness and/or collective body of knowledge, has long been discussed in both academic settings and in common parlance. But before we go further, I'd like to spell out what the hivemind means to me in the framework of this book.

For one, the hivemind refers to the extent to which we are capable of entering a state of mind that is more collectively focused, in which we share attention and goals and emotions. At times we may even experience an expansion of our consciousness* to incorporate our social others. As positive psychologist Barbara

---

* Well, depending on your definition of consciousness. They don't call it "the hardest problem" for nothing.

Fredrickson once said: "Emotions are not bounded by skin. It isn't that one person's emotions affect the other...the two people are *sharing* the emotion."*

Second, hivemind also refers to the principle that what we know and feel is not determined in a vacuum of independent experiences and decisions but rather is shaped by the collective. Our synchronicity means that ideas and fashions and ways of interpreting the world have their own sort of life outside the individual people who contribute to it, something eighteenth- to nineteenth-century German philosophers called the zeitgeist, or spirit of the times. We'll discuss a psychological concept called "appraisals," which are interpretations or stories about the world, and we'll see both how the hivemind influences the appraisals we make and how, in turn, the appraisals we choose shape our very reality. The hivemind collectively decides what is true, what is proper, what is normal, what is cool, and what is important. But it isn't just positive and negative judgments that are shaped by the hivemind. Rather, the hivemind is also critical in shaping our perception of the world, in building our consensus reality.

Our deeply entrenched sociality has always been with us, but the advent of both smartphones and social media may be sharply escalating our synchronicity. We are at a watershed moment, for these new technologies have not only allowed us to access a world of information and communication but have also ushered in a revolution in our social functioning. We are suddenly able to access the thoughts and emotions of our social partners at all hours of the day and night, to see their lives unfold in real time—even if they live on the other side of the world. While most think pieces would have you believe that these changes spell irreparable harm to our attention spans and deepest relationships, the truth is much more

---

* As I scribbled this down at a conference talk rather than recording it and transcribing it, my apologies to Barbara Fredrickson if I didn't get the quote exactly right.

nuanced than that. While these new social technologies *are* associated with worrying trends toward echo chambers, radicalization, and societal fragmentation, there is also mounting evidence that, in other ways, they are drawing us closer together, introducing new ways of connecting, and extending our cognitive horizons.

Blaming smartphones and social media for unhappiness is a dominant narrative in our contemporary hivemind. But while feelings of disconnection in our modern age do co-occur with the invention of social technologies, it may be that the latter is not causing the former. As Johann Hari writes in his book *Lost Connections*, "The Internet was born into a world where many people had already lost their sense of connection to each other...our obsessive use of social media is an attempt to fill a hole, a great hollowing, that took place before anyone had a smartphone." In this book I will argue that the true disconnection is not the screens we hold between us but our overemphasis on the individual over the collective, ambition over altruism, personal pleasure over human progress. I will also argue that, ironically, our appraisals of fear surrounding social technology may be creating a self-fulfilling prophecy of anxiety and unhappiness—for us, and for our children.

Moreover, I will propose that *how* you use social technology may be critical for whether social media has a beneficial or detrimental effect on your happiness. We'll build this model together by examining quite a lot of evidence, but for now we can sum it up thus: using social media to actively enhance your existing relationships or to fill gaps in your social support network is likely to result in positive outcomes, but using social technology to supplant face-to-face time with people you love or activities like sleep or exercise (especially if you do so through passive "lurking") is likely to result in negative outcomes. As one major review of the literature put it, "Whether behavior on social network sites is good or bad for well-being depends on whether the behavior advances or thwarts innate human desires for acceptance and belonging."[4] In other words, use social media to *enhance* and augment your social connections, not to *eclipse* them.

I have three aims in writing this book. The first is to explore the extent to which we operate at times more like coordinated honeybees in a hive than lonely, separate individuals, that our thoughts and ideas and emotions spill over and leap from mind to mind. The second is to evaluate the extent to which recent advances in technology—namely, smartphones and social media—may be amplifying these collective tendencies for both good and ill. The third is to take a stab at answering the big question: What now? How can we avoid the worst perils of our hiveminds? How can we do so while also harnessing the marvelous symbiotic power of group action and these powerful new tools we have at our disposal?

I wrote the first proposal for this book in early fall 2015—before Brexit, before the 2016 US presidential election, before Facebook became both complicit in the spread of false information and an emotional minefield of comment feuds among people who previously seemed to like each other quite a lot. I was on sabbatical from my professor job, training for a half marathon, and experimenting with recipes from Haruki Murakami novels. I thought that this book would be fun, a lighthearted romp through some of my favorite research in psychology and neuroscience, a new way of looking at the power and promise of social technologies rather than endlessly wringing our hands over their bevy of distractions.

These are different times, and now this is a different sort of book—one rife with dehumanization and conspiracy theories and political polarization.

It won't be all doom and gloom, though. We're going to go zip lining together, and gambling, and dog watching. We'll hear about some truly amazing science being conducted in laboratories around the globe and talk with people who are working hard on the ground floor of social activism and digital education to try to turn this ship around.

This book is the story of how I came to see that a body of research I've spent most of my career contributing to might offer a solution to the polarized mess we're in. It is also the story of a bit short of a year, a year that I spent reading everything I could get my hands on and talking to everyone I could find who might have light to shed on the nature of our collective selves and how social technologies are impacting our humanity. We're going to drive all over New England and up and down the Atlantic coast, talking to people. We'll talk to people in the canyons of Salt Lake City and by the banyan trees of Tallahassee. We'll talk to them in restaurants and rooftop bars and coffeeshops. You'll hear enough about the food we eat and the libations we imbibe for my writers' group companion to snark, "What do you think you're writing here, *Game of Thrones*?"

In the first section of the book, I'll endeavor to convince you that while you have been living your life to this point as though you are a unique, individual "you" with a personal history, ideas about the world, and set of motivations, you have been operating under a mistaken set of assumptions. This you, the you you probably refer to as "I," is both formed by and intermingled with all of the other people who populate your cultural wing of the human hive. Absent these interactions with your social others, without anyone to give you feedback or to differentiate yourself from, you might not even *have* a sense of self. Turn-of-the-twentieth-century sociologist Charles Horton Cooley argued that influence from our social others "enters into our system of thought as a matter of course, and affects our conduct as surely as water affects the growth of a plant" and called this socially formed identity the looking-glass self.[5] In large part, we source our identity from the reflection our social others hold up to us. He observed that "the mind lives in perpetual conversation"—we spend at least part of every waking hour either conversing with social others or imagining future conversations in our minds.

We'll try to answer the question: How do my thoughts become yours? How do we learn to tap into a cultural hivemind of knowledge and beliefs and biases, our collective library of knowledge? We'll consider the fact that most of what we know about the world (that Earth revolves around the sun, that gasoline turns into energy that our cars use to run, that we get sick when tiny pathogens invisible to the naked eye invade our bloodstream) are facts that most of us have no direct experience with but merely absorbed from our teachers and television shows and conversations with others. Among other interviews, we'll talk with an evolutionary biologist about the intersection of her field of study and fiction, evaluating the degree to which, as historian Kelly Baker writes, "the boundaries between the real and the fictional are ever so porous. We want them to be firm, solid, and impenetrable, but instead, things slide through. . . . Fantasy can stalk our waking hours, too."[6]

We don't treat all human beings equally, feeling a greater kinship to some than to others, welcoming certain people across our thresholds of inclusion and leaving others out in the cold. We'll talk to a biological anthropologist about why this is and how it happens, how we befriend and fall in love with some individuals and not others, how we include people of certain nationalities and personalities and political persuasions in our moral circles and exclude others. At a rooftop bar in the Big Apple, we'll explore the impact of social technology on our well-being—how smartphones and social media can both build us up (by enhancing our existing and creating new social connections) and take us down (through internet shame spirals and harassment).

We'll then travel to the site of the 2017 Charlottesville riots to meet social neuroscientist Jim Coan. Jim believes that on a neurological level, we rely on people being close to us. Soothing behaviors from our close others, like hugs, hand-holding, and reassuring smiles, calm us down in a very physical sense—in terms of reducing blood pressure, stress hormones, and other alarm-related reactions in the body. Absent these interactions, not just our mental health but also our physical health suffers. As Jim says, "Loneliness is tied to being more likely to die at any time of any cause at any phase of life." He thinks his research partially explains this surprising finding. We'll also see what Jim has to say about research on some of the worst of our social human tendencies—our willingness to dehumanize and even demonize people who don't belong to our tribe.

In the darkest chapter of the book we'll talk with historian Kelly Baker, who has written one book about the Ku Klux Klan and its relationship to mainstream Protestant culture in the United States, and another about our fascination with zombies. I'll argue that conspiracy theories, mass movements, and cults all have certain principles in common, and that these characteristic principles have hivemind stamped all over them. Worse, we'll see that the development of the web and social media has allowed adherents of some of these paranoid groups and ways of thinking to fuse in alarming ways.

Feeling decidedly queasy after all of that, we'll begin meeting with people who are determined to appeal to the better angels of our collective souls. During an ice storm we'll meet with clinical psychologist Nnamdi Pole, who will encourage us to consider that people vary in their degree of vulnerability, and we'll adopt that lens to ask whether some people are more susceptible to the negative impacts of social media than others—and consider what we can do to protect them.

In the shadow of the mountains of Salt Lake City we'll consider how our narrative of fear and anxiety surrounding social media may be poisoning our well-being, and how our children may be best served by us taking a deep, calming breath and working with them to develop healthy technology habits.

We will then explore an area of research that I have spent the past decade or two investigating: that of emotion regulation, narrative, and meaning-making. Grounded in our earlier examination of how our understanding of the world and who we are as people is shaped by our collective, we'll investigate how changing the story we tell ourselves can quite literally change our reality—especially when our entire hive buys in. We'll then take this work on emotion regulation and narrative for a test-drive. We'll interview psychologists Keith Maddox and Heather Urry, who are helping college students regulate their anxieties about discussing racial issues in cross-race contexts.

To be sure I don't leave you in despair, we'll end the book by considering one of the greatest unifying forces known to man—puppies. I'll talk to lead trainer Kathy Foreman at NEADS: World Class Service Dogs about how service dogs are taught to meld with their owners, to anticipate their needs before the owners even know of them, to be their eyes and ears and paws. We'll take the lessons from this interview to evaluate the extent to which human happiness may rely on tending to our collective, prosocial natures as much as (if not more than) it does on fulfilling our individualistic goals and desires.

We'll conclude by arguing that it is critically important that we learn to reach outside of our narrow ingroups, that we focus less on our tribal natures and more on our hiveish ones.

WHAT THIS BOOK IS NOT

This book is not a polemic. You won't close it feeling that you know whether social technologies are a net good or bad for humanity. Our relationship with technology and how it intersects with our collective natures is what writer and sociologist Tressie McMillan Cottom and others call a wicked problem, one of the many "tangled, layered and deeply urgent dilemmas" facing modern humanity that cannot be solved by a think piece or one-sided argument. "For if there's one thing I know from studying wicked problems and reading the great writers who wrote into existence our world," Cottom writes, "it is that a smart person avoids certainty."[7] One of the central messages of this book is that our attraction to false binaries, simple stories of good and evil, and quick fixes is among the most dangerous aspects of our hivemind. I refuse to play into that. I *will* present you with research evidence from psychology and neuroscience labs from around the world (including my own), and we'll check in with some of the best thinkers and best writers on the topic. But this is a wicked problem that won't be solved by one person or one book or one perspective.

This book is also not a media sciences book, or a technology book, or a sociology book, and as such won't address many of the problems with social technology that operate on these levels. The social media platforms as they currently exist pose real, present dangers that need fixing both from within (on the part of the technology companies) and without (governmental regulation). A short list of these dangers includes digital monopolies, threats to personal privacy, algorithmic manipulation, propagation of already existing social inequalities, threats to democratic governing, Russian bots, the spread of false information, and organized harassment campaigns.*

There are numerous fantastic people covering these issues, their ramifications, and some possible solutions. To name just three, check out Siva Vaidhyanathan's book *Anti-Social Media: How Facebook Disconnects Us and Undermines Democracy*, Chris Gilliard's scholarship on privacy and how modern technology both exacerbates old and manufactures new inequalities, and Zeynep Tufekci's TED Talk (and related work) called "We're Building a Dystopia Just to Make People Click on Ads."

---

* Uh, and that's the short list.

In a chapter titled "The Problem with Facebook Is Facebook," Vaidhyanathan sums up one of these problems succinctly: "A global system that links 2.2. billion people across hundreds of countries, allows every user to post content indiscriminately, develops algorithms that favor highly charged content, and is dependent on a self-service advertising system that precisely targets ads using massive surveillance and elaborate personal dossiers cannot be reformed at the edges." I urge you to read the work of these scholars and others, and to support legislation (and legislators) willing to make changes to protect our digital and human rights as these platforms spread and are increasingly in the control of just a few hands.

WHAT THIS BOOK IS

This is a psychology book, concerned with the much more personal issue of what happens when you take an ultrasocial animal, with all of its hiveish proclivities and deep desire for human connection, and you give it a slim, handheld screen that conveys the thoughts and emotions of all of its social partners, accessible day and night.

Social media platforms come and go (remember MySpace?), and some of the current giants may fall in the wake of recent privacy and manipulation scandals. There also seems to be a growing transition from more outward-facing, public social sharing (e.g., Facebook) toward more inward-facing, private social sharing (e.g., group texting). But I don't think connecting with one another over digital technologies—whether through texting or Instagram or FaceTime or virtual reality—is going anywhere, at least anytime soon.

This book will tackle what these social technologies mean for the human experience. *Your* experience. I wrote this book in part to write my way into understanding where we are right now as a country, as a Western society, and to a lesser extent as a species. Writing it gave me some level of hope and reassurance. I hope it does the same for you, while also illuminating paths forward to greater collective good.

For a little insight into my approach before we begin: I am an emotion regulation researcher. My research focuses on the strategies people use to manipulate their emotions in order to meet the goals they have. I have studied these strategies by using computerized programs to assess people's behaviors and experiences, psychophysiological recordings to assess their bodily reactions (such as skin sweating and heart rate), and neuroimaging methods to examine their brain function. I have explored whether emotion regulation helps us understand how college students learn new topics in the classroom, why some people with recurrent episodes of depression fully recover and others do not, and why people who have lived through the trauma of a natural disaster experience varying levels of distress afterward.

But even more than I am a researcher, I am a teacher. From the very beginning of my academic career I sought to spend more of my time inside the classroom than out of it. When I teach, my students and I do not ground our intellectual discovery only in the psychological research literature but also in any domain of knowledge that might illuminate our inquiry. I took this teaching-informed approach to writing the book that you hold in your hands. We'll consider quite a bit of psychology, but we're also going to delve into history, anthropology, evolutionary biology, philosophy, and literature. My apologies to my colleagues in these disciplines for any unintentional mischaracterizations or oversimplifications. Feel free to @ me on Twitter.

My third area of expertise, related to the second, is that I have spent a fair bit of time the past few years traveling around the country talking with fellow teachers about how to better our craft. As part of this work, I have done quite a lot of thinking about how one group of people (educators) influence the thoughts and emotions of other people (students) and how we faculty developers can influence the whole collective. This work has certainly shaped how I think about our social natures. Working with faculty across numerous disciplines other than social science also has lent me an appreciation of all of the many ways of knowing about the world.

This book is a work of creative, narrative nonfiction. According to the conventions of the genre, I tweaked the presentation of material slightly to increase clarity and readability and to more thoughtfully draw meaning. The interviews did not all occur in the order in which they are presented in the book (though only a few are shuffled). I recorded all of the interviews and transcribed them, but I did clean up disfluencies and occasionally changed the order of topics to follow a more coherent thread of logic. Anecdotes from my past obviously use reconstructed dialogue, since I didn't have a recorder with me at the time or think to use one if I did.

Since this book is meant to be enjoyed by a general audience rather than an academic one, I didn't litter the text with excessive citations and numerals. I cited specific research studies and new information that I discovered in writing the book—you can find these organized by chapter in a section at the end called Notes. Books I referenced directly you can find in a separate section called Hivemind Reading List. For the most part I trusted the expertise of the book authors and the experts I interviewed, though here and there I inserted additional references where I thought a motivated reader might want to follow up.

As this book is written by an American living in America and interviewing other Americans, it is obviously steeped in an American perspective. Issues of technology and social experience manifest in different ways across the globe, but every book has a page limit and I've focused on what I have seen closest to home.

Without further ado: welcome to the hivemind.

AUTUMN

Chapter One

Welcome to the Hivemind

Deerfield, Massachusetts

On *Star Trek*, one glowing red cybernetic eye connects the Borg to the hivemind of their collective species, the promise of inevitable assimilation. Over on *Doctor Who*, the sinister chrome Cyber-Men similarly wield their capacity for universal domination by absorbing individuals into a mass cooperative, smoothing away individual propensities and desires into one uniform will. Madeleine L'Engle writes in *A Wrinkle in Time* of a spreading blackness taking out the light of the universe. The steadily beating heart of this darkness is a single consciousness who claims that the essential cause of human unhappiness is our insistence on living our "own, separate, individual lives" rather than being subsumed into IT.

Our works of science fiction are filled with harrowing cautionary tales about societies in which the needs of the individual are completely subjugated to the majority. The central premise is that to achieve a successful hivemind, we need to sacrifice individual differences and all think the same, act the same, in lockstep with one another. This tension between our individual and communal natures is ever present in our collective consciousness.

I believe this deep-rooted fear of the collective aspects of human nature stems from the lack of autonomy it suggests, the degree to which accepting our ultrasocial natures means that we surrender the steering wheel of our lives to unconscious influences from without. But the assumption that we are *usually* in conscious control of our own attitudes and feelings and decisions is increasingly suspect, as data from psychology and neuroscience pile up suggesting that our supposedly logical, fully conscious individual selves are not always in the driver's seat of behavior.

Neuroscientist David Eagleman sums up much of this recent research in his book *Incognito: The Secret Lives of the Brain*. A lot of the evidence Eagleman brings to bear has to do with basics of movement and perception, but the really titillating parts of his book tackle more complex behaviors and experiences. For instance, in a section called "Will the True Mel Gibson Please Stand Up?" he references the DUI arrest of the popular 1980s actor, who was caught uttering a series of anti-Semitic slurs on tape. Gibson and many of his friends claimed that these thoughts and feelings were entirely alien to the sober, friendly Gibson and were merely unfortunate drunken ramblings to be ignored; others, pointing to the old saying "in vino veritas" ("in wine, truth") scoffed at the excuse and argued that illicit substances release our usual inhibitions and reveal what's underneath—our "true" feelings. But Eagleman argues that the brain operates more like a democracy of rivals, with multiple subsystems and tendencies, each grappling for control at any given time. Alcohol may dampen one set of selves, the controlled and cautious ones, and allow other prejudices and base desires and selfish impulses to wrest control of behavior. But neither set of tendencies is more or less *you*—each represents different sets of neural circuits.

And even when the controlled, intentional sides of our psyche are at the steering wheel, these other sides of ourselves are still influencing us. Eagleman marshals quite a lot of evidence to this effect—that well-meaning, socially conscious people still hold negative implicit associations about people who belong to other races and genders. Or that our ratings of a person's level of physical attractiveness is influenced by the size of their pupils at the time of rating, which reflects the degree to which they are interested or aroused. Or that people whose job it is to peek at the naughty bits of baby chicks to see if they are male or female (yes, this is a real job) can't describe *how* they know but learn to do their job by standing next to a trained chicken sexer who routinely tells them whether their guesses are accurate or inaccurate.

Our conscious minds may also be too slow to be responsible for most decisions and movements, leading some neuroscientists to speculate that the reason we have consciousness at all is not to make moment-to-moment decisions but to process social and emotional information,[1] to weigh priorities and consider who is friend and who is foe. Eagleman likens the dethronement of the conscious mind to Galileo's discovery that the Earth was not the center of the universe. "To know oneself may require a change of definition 'to know.' Knowing yourself now requires the understanding that the conscious *you* occupies only a small room in the mansion of the brain, and that it has little control over the reality constructed for you." The reality constructed for you by unconscious aspects of perception and predictions based on past experiences, that is—and, as we'll soon see, also the consensus story of reality handed to you by the hivemind.

In *Song of Increase*, beekeeper and writer Jacqueline Freeman waxes lyrical about the cooperative nature of the honeybees, how they exist in harmony not only with one another but also with the flowers and the sun and the changing of the seasons. Each bee exists as an individual, but simultaneously also exists as one unit of a larger collective, one cell of another, larger organism. Freeman invokes the German word *Bien*, which she says incorporates not only this sense of the hive as a larger organism but also the extent to which the hive both relies on and responds to the ecosystem in which it resides.

Like honeybees, human beings may also exist at least in part nestled within a collective, our individual identities both informed by and utterly embedded within our shared existence. While we certainly have separate bodies, separate brains, we share thoughts and emotions and memories—and as we'll see, these shared mental experiences are reflected in a synchronization of our neural activity. These mental phenomena don't respect the physical boundaries of our bodies but diffuse from one mind to another, wiring us up to experience the world in similar ways.

Could we, like the honeybees, be at least partly a collective species? We traveled very different evolutionary paths, but we may have ended up at a cooperative solution that bears some striking similarities.

HUMAN BEINGS: 90 PERCENT CHIMP, 10 PERCENT BEE?

Social psychologist Jonathan Haidt is currently serving as professor of ethical leadership at New York University's Stern School of Business and is the author of both a large body of scientific papers and several popular psychology books. According to Haidt's detailed analysis of psychological and evolutionary evidence, human beings are "90 percent chimp and 10 percent bee."★[2] Like chimpanzees, we are deeply concerned with our own welfare, tribal, and sometimes unafraid to resort to violence to get our way. But at the same time, we also have a more communal, beelike side to our nature. We can be *groupish*, as Haidt puts it. He cites nineteenth-century French sociologist Émile Durkheim, who claimed that human beings should be called *Homo duplex*, a species capable of both individuality and pooled collective identity. Other theorists have similarly proposed that human experience has both an "I-mode" and a "We-mode."[3]

★ Metaphorically speaking, of course.

Our hivelike sides emerge under circumstances that nudge our consciousness into a shared frame of experience, such as dancing in sync to a common rhythm and chanting and singing together. Situational factors that blur the boundaries of our bodies—such as darkness, alcohol, extreme tiredness, shared repetitive movement, and certain drugs—also encourage a more communal than individual level of consciousness. Cult leaders often intentionally foster these conditions to encourage conformity among their followers.[4]

When we sync up both our output (motor movements, vocalizations) and our input (seeing and hearing one another's movements and sounds), we may extend our body's awareness and sense of self to the larger collective. William H. McNeill, professor of history at the University of Chicago and World War II veteran, writes of his experiences of ecstasy while performing rote marching drills with his fellow soldiers: "A sense of pervasive well-being is what I recall; more specifically, a strange sense of personal enlargement; a sort of swelling out, becoming bigger than life, thanks to participation in collective ritual."

In his book *Keeping Together in Time: Dance and Drill in Human History*, McNeill argues that the practice of syncing muscle movements and vocal expressions together in time leads to "boundary loss," or the sense that there are no longer strict divisions between self and other, that one has joined with a larger group consciousness. He believes that this practice enhances group solidarity by affecting human emotions and provides a sort of "muscular bonding" that leads to group cohesion—the keen oneness and kinship many soldiers report feeling for their fellow comrades in arms.

McNeill argues that human beings in all cultures and across time periods have discovered and rediscovered the power of syncing movements and sound in time, from reenacting (and practicing future) successful hunts around campfires to the creation of the pyramids to military drills—all activities in which we sync up and become bigger and more capable than our individual bodies.

Picking up McNeill's mantle, journalist and scholar Barbara Ehrenreich traces the history of ecstatic dancing from prehistoric times through to modernity in the lovely and painstakingly researched book *Dancing in the Streets: A History of Collective Joy*. She draws on anthropological evidence to argue that routinely celebrating with other human beings is a deep part of our heritage. Ritualistic dance and collective celebration crop up again and again in the human historical record, as does frequent backlash, most often by the powerful over the powerless.

Among the oppressed, keeping together in time became a way of ensuring solidarity and developing countercultures. African American people enduring slavery in the United States developed work songs to share oral traditions, help one another cope, and sometimes share coded messages. These songs were frequently sung during repetitive shared movement. In another example, the Native American Ghost Dance spread across the United States in the late nineteenth century with a viral intensity. A circle dance that promised unification with lost loved ones and an end to white colonialization, it was rumored to have mystical properties. Its wide appeal and rapid spread could be tied to the combination of shared ecstatic movement and the promise of power in a time of hopelessness and despair.

Those dominating the dispossessed often see in the shared movement something distasteful, states of barbarism or unrestrained sexuality. But some feel lured into the dance. For instance, Ehrenreich quotes writer Clinton Furness, who in the 1920s attended an African American ring shout, a form of worshipful dance: "I was gripped with the feeling of a mass intelligence, a self-conscious entity, gradually informing the crowd and taking possession of every mind there, including my own...." The dance may whirl one into the hivemind, allow one to release the self and join in a greater collective.

While we may have lost the regular, large, organized ecstatic group rituals of our past, you can find pale shadows of ecstatic group ritual even in modern Western cultures. I would bet if you did a quick scan of your life experience you could find several instances. I can remember feeling the tidal pull while singing Christmas carols in church as a child, feeling the vibration both in my own chest and thrumming all around me from other voices raised in song. I also felt it as a teenager moshing to NIN cover bands, the unexpected sweetness of slamming your body against the hard planes of other people's bodies—especially when one set of hard planes belongs to someone you currently think is cute but who will eventually become your husband and the father of your child.

Every summer, tens of thousands of people converge on the Black Rock Desert in northwest Nevada in a temporary city created for the sole purpose of ecstatic group ritual. An eclectic combination of visual art, music, invention, and "radical inclusion" (and, if rumors are to be believed, quite a bit of better living through pharmaceuticals), Burning Man encourages an intense building of community spirit and collective group ritual.

Even modern-day sports fandoms bear the traces of early ritualistic worship. Fans paint stripes of team colors on their faces, don costumes of sports jerseys and hats and other markers of team belonging, chant, wave, rise, and shout together. In the practice of tailgating, fans also feast and share mind-altering substances, much like their ancient counterparts.

There are likely multiple biological mechanisms underlying various aspects of these hiveish experiences, when our physical divisions seem to break down a bit and we meld our consciousness with one another. Three possible candidates involve the release of endogenous (that is, naturally produced by the body) opioids, the neuropeptide oxytocin, and our capacity for mirroring.

Endogenous opioids may be familiar to you due to their role in the runner's high. It turns out, endogenous opioids are also released when we participate in shared movement and activity as part of a group, for instance during dancing, competitive rowing, and even mutual laughter,[5] which may partially explain why we find these experiences so rewarding and are driven to seek them out.

Oxytocin is a neuropeptide produced in the hypothalamus and released by the pituitary gland during childbirth, breastfeeding, and orgasm. Oxytocin also appears to play a strong role in more indefinite psychological happenings such as bonding and attachment and the development of ingroup solidarity[6]—and its ugly cousin, outgroup hostility.[7] It may have some of its effects on social interaction and attachment by blurring the distinction between self and other.[8] Adorably, it is also released in the brains of both human beings and their dogs when they share long (and presumably adoring) gazes with each other.[9]

In the 1990s, a group of researchers in Italy made a surprising discovery. There were neurons in monkeys' brains that would fire not only when a monkey performed an action (e.g., picked up a peanut) but also when a monkey observed someone else performing that same action (e.g, watched the researcher pick up a peanut).[10] It seemed as though to these neurons, performing an action oneself and watching someone else perform that action was the same thing. In the early days of this research, some people thought these "mirror neurons," as they would come to be dubbed, were specialized types of neurons in a specific part of the brain that were responsible for understanding the worlds of the people we observe, our social partners.[11] Some argued that this mirroring of neuronal activity was the neural basis of empathy.[12]

After this early enthusiasm, the concept of mirror neurons experienced a bit of a backlash. Some people pointed out that the basic phenomena—a single neuron firing both when an organism performed an action and when the organism observed the same action—had only been directly observed in monkeys, not in humans. Others asked how it was that these special types of neurons were structurally and functionally inseparable from other types of neurons.*

Marco Iacoboni is a professor of psychiatry and biobehavioral sciences at UCLA and one of the lead researchers on mirror neurons. He doesn't talk about mirror neurons as separable neurons anymore as much as he talks about "mirroring" as a process.[13] In one of Iacoboni's earliest papers,[14] he had people in a neuroimaging scanner tap their fingers and then watch videos of other people tapping the same finger and observed nearly the same brain activation for both. Neuroimaging picks up on blood flowing to regions of the brain that are more active, so these data are not measuring whether single neurons are firing but rather whether whole regions of the brain are becoming active. These findings reflect the idea of mirroring, of our brains reacting similarly whether we experience something or a social other experiences it—and there are hundreds of such papers at this point. Thus, it seems plausible that mirroring is one of the biological underpinnings of our ultrasociality.

I think of the times that I've felt mirroring on a deep body level. When I lean in behind my daughter and pop the lock on her ski boots with my pole, I can feel in my body my father doing this action for me, how we shift our weight to the outside leg, wrap the arm around, find the notch to press. When I shuck a clam, I can both see and feel my grandfather's weathered hands doing the same, the precise rhythm and tilt of the shell required for the action. When I absentmindedly pluck a leaf of lemon balm, rub it to release its scent, and then sniff it before letting it flutter to the grass, I can feel my mother in my fingertips.

These neural systems and a few others could work together to promote social alignment, a sort of herding at the level of the

---

* Neuroscientist Gregory Hickock went so far as to publish a book called *The Myth of Mirror Neurons: The Real Neuroscience of Communication and Cognition.*

human brain. Rather than flocking like birds or swarming like ants, human beings may synchronize through the processes of emotional contagion and social conformity, producing "shared feelings, shared coordination, and shared identity."[15]

It is not just when part of large crowds or rituals that we sync up, however. Human beings synchronize together all of the time—in pairs, in threesomes, and in groups. When human beings interact face-to-face, they tend to mimic one another's posture and facial expressions,[16] feel similar emotions,[17] fall in step when walking together, and easily share mannerisms and patterns of prosody and even eye gaze patterns.[18] Synchronizing with other people also seems to drive bonding with them. When someone mimics our body movements (posture, gestures), we're more likely to like them and feel rapport with them.

This synchrony and ultrasociality mean we're social when we're completely alone—even thinking is not a solitary activity. For human beings, psychologist Michael Tomasello writes, "thinking is like a jazz musician improvising a novel riff in the privacy of his own room. It is a solitary activity all right, but on an instrument made by others for that general purpose, after years of playing with and learning from other practitioners, in a musical genre with a rich history of legendary riffs, for an imagined audience of jazz aficionados. Human thinking is individual improvisation enmeshed in a sociocultural matrix."[19] Even in the privacy of our own minds we cannot escape our ultrasociality.

We are Homo duplex. We certainly experience much of the world as individuals, but we also have a collective instinct to seek social situations, to sync up together like honeybees in a hive.

SOCIAL ANIMAL, MEET SOCIAL MEDIA

A song comes on in a coffee shop that reminds you of a past lover, and you text him the remembrance, accompanied by a picture of your perfect cappuccino. A crisis strikes in the city where you live, and you check yourself in as safe on Facebook, then upload a video of the aftermath. You are hosting an outer space party and connect with an artist in New Zealand who creates glow-in-the-dark tapestries that recreate parts of the night sky, which you drape around your dorm room to create the illusion of being immersed in a starlit night.

With the advent of social media and smartphones, we have an entire new medium through which we can connect, synchronize, and influence one another. So far we have considered ways we harmonize that involve physical movement and/or in-person presence—but our thoughts and emotions also synchronize over technological mediums. At any time of day or night, you can access not just the thoughts of your social partners (through their texts and status updates and tweets) but also (in the videos and images they share) the world they are seeing unfold before them. Multiple social media platforms now encourage "stories," first-person videos of a tiny sliver of your day that disappear after a delay. These stories slide you right into a few seconds of your friends' lived experience.

Not only has the medium of sharing our experiences changed with the introduction of social media, but so, too, has the reach. It is no longer just our immediate social network that influences us and is influenced by us, but indeed human beings all over the planet. This online spread of ideas and emotions over large groups adopts the language of contagion—videos, articles, ideas go "viral," spread quickly and far.

Consider memes. The word *meme* is short for the word *mimeme*, an ancient Greek word meaning "to imitate." Evolutionary biologist Richard Dawkins coined the term to explain tiny particles of culture (like genes, but for ideas and practices) that are replicated and passed on from one person to the next, across space and over generations.[20] He thought that, like genes, pressures similar to natural selection operated on these ideas, with some spreading with alacrity and having a lasting impact and others sputtering out quickly. The internet age quickly adopted the idea for often-Photoshopped visual images that represent common ways of looking at the world.

Taking our sociality online also means that we have a new way of measuring the degree to which our thoughts and emotions and ideas influence one another because most of what we do online is trackable. For instance, Facebook and some collaborators demonstrated that when it rains in one city, poor moods spread not only throughout that city but also through the social networks of the people living in that city.[21]

Facebook also admitted to intentionally tweaking the content of users' newsfeeds in order to test if they could make people feel slightly better or worse based on the content of their daily dose of friend updates.[22] Controlling people's newsfeeds such that they saw fewer negative or fewer positive posts resulted in people using slightly fewer negative or positive words themselves— seeing one's social network get slightly less positive made you share slightly fewer positively worded posts, and vice versa for negative. While the effect was vanishingly small (the number of positive and negative words used by the two groups was *statistically* different but, practically speaking, was one-tenth of a percent change), it nonetheless suggests that we don't even need to be interacting with our social others in real life to have their moods and thoughts affect us. Social contagion can spread over digital networks as well.

Researchers at the University of Pittsburgh traced the ripples of fear, sympathy, and solidarity spreading through people's social networks following the Boston Marathon bombings.[23] They analyzed geo-information from people's tweets as well as common hashtags about the bombings (e.g., #prayforboston, #bostonstrong) to watch the physical and social spread of emotions and information following the terrorist attacks and subsequent lockdown.

The researchers found strong evidence of contagion in the form of a traceable spread of emotions and use of hashtags across Twitter, leaping from one person to another through interconnected networks. Interestingly, though, the most important predictor of expressions of fear and solidarity was direct experience with Boston. That is, having a number of followers or friends in the Boston area was less predictive of fear and solidarity than recently having visited in the city or having lived there for a time.

In another example, people from Chicago shared more fear than those from Indianapolis, even though the latter city is geographically closer, perhaps because Chicago is an airport hub that frequently interacts with Boston's airport. These findings suggest that "the extent of 'corporeal' social exchange—the number of people who move back and forth between the communities—may reflect a deeper set of social, cultural, and economic ties that go beyond sharing information and other forms of virtual communication to include senses of shared community or identity." What is important is how closely you identify with a region, the extent to which it has gotten under your skin and become part of your identity.

Emotions, too, spread both face-to-face and online, and in fact, sharing emotion with social others may intensify both your affective responses and theirs. At the time of this writing, musician, actor, innovator, and all-over thespian David Bowie has just died of liver cancer at the age of sixty-nine. While 2016 was notoriously full of shocking celebrity deaths, Bowie's was an early and large loss. It evoked a torrent of publicly expressed grief, from man-on-the-street types who found solace in his music, to famous musicians in their own right who felt inspired by his example and shared kismet-tinged stories of encounters with him, to people in the queer community who found in his unconventional approach to gender expression a reassuring reflection of their own experiences and struggles with society's restrictions.

Part of this dramatic outpouring of sentiment was pure Bowie, and well deserved. But I believe part of the intensity could be explained by effects that have been observed in the cold environs of the laboratory, writ large in the big, messy world of social media. It was difficult to feel unaffected by Bowie's death when you couldn't open Facebook or Twitter or turn on CNN without seeing people sharing pictures, stories, quotes, videos; without hearing Lorde and Marilyn Manson and Paul McCartney share touching personal stories about their encounters with the gentle, quixotic artist. Everyone's attention was riveted to these images and stories, in a communal sort of group experience.

Theories about emotional intensification in groups are not new. In 1897 French social psychologist Gustave Le Bon, author of the book *The Crowd: A Study of the Popular Mind*, claimed that merely being part of a group leads to an "exaggeration of the sentiments." Sports fans in crowded stadiums, bullies in the schoolyard, protests that devolve into riots—all are examples of groups seemingly spurring one another on to greater heights of emotion and excess.

Research on people viewing emotional stimuli alone or in groups confirms that viewing them together leads to emotional intensification.[24] Sharing attention with members of your social circle seems to be part of how being in social circumstances can make emotions more intense—you pay greater attention to the emotional stimulus if your friend next to you does, and if you are processing the details to a greater extent and elaborating on the meaning of the stimulus, that is going to increase your affective response to it. Taking these behaviors online could mean that these amplifications may be able to occur more quickly and spread more widely.

In a beautiful illustration of how emotions spread online, a digital arts group named fuse developed an art/data project known as Amygdala.[25] Named after almond-shaped clusters in our brains that are highly attuned to aspects of our world that might hold emotional import, the program analyzes tweets and hashtags, codes them for their emotional content, and then uses them to create a display of light and sound that is played upon forty-one columns. When Bowie died and the internet began its rush of mourning, sadness flooded the Amygdala—and was viewable online, thus creating a fascinating loop of technologically visualized group emotion.

We're synchronous beings, and the contents of our minds spread from one of us to another easily and effortlessly, whether in person or online. Fear and love and hate are infectious, and they spread over new media.

ON HONEYBEES AND HUMANS: AN APIARIST PERSPECTIVE

The morning of my family's annual eleventy-first birthday party, I head toward Western Massachusetts to interview some bees. The day is perfect in the way that only October days in New England can be. The sunlight is warm and buttery but the air contains a bite, and the trees populating the rolling hills around me are every shade of yellow and red and orange. The party is a family ritual inspired by the big birthday bash that launches *The Fellowship of the Ring*, Bilbo Baggins's 111th birthday. While actual wizards are unlikely to make an appearance, there will be a feast and fireworks and more than a few glasses of mead as we toast all the family's autumn birthdays in one big celebration.

I am pretty sure that honeybees don't have holidays or collective rituals. But they certainly do engage in cooperative actions and their behavior informs the central metaphor of this book.* So

---

* Throughout the book I'll occasionally use the shorthand "bees," but I'll be talking about honeybees specifically. There are tens of thousands of bee species, most of which are not the least bit social.

before our autumnal family ritual I pull my car into Warm Colors Apiary to talk with beekeeper Dan Conlon.

The yard is quiet and peaceful. Around the periphery, boxes of hives hum with inner life. They are painted white, pink, blue, and maroon, stacked one on top of the other, spreading off into the distance. The apiary sits in a bit of a valley with more of the same rolling hills of fall foliage as far as the eye can see. Dan awaits me on his deck, dressed in a wolf-howling-at-the-moon tee. People sometimes wear such shirts with ironic detachment, but on Dan it seems perfectly earnest.

Dan's life story is a beautiful one full of fresh starts and following one's passions, but with a steady thrum of bees throughout. He first became enamored of the friendly insects when he was just fourteen years old, working with local farmer and amateur beekeeper Hugh Bell. In the decades that followed, as he transitioned between careers as diverse as traveling musician and high school administrator, he left a trail of hives. Sometimes he'd have just one or two, sometimes up to a hundred, but he was never long without honeycomb. "The only thing Danny ever stuck to," according to his mother, "is those damn bees!"

Around age fifty, Dan began losing steam at his administrative job. When early afternoons hit and the work tangles piled up one on top of the other, instead of staring out the window and dreaming of easing into retirement Dan dreamt of working with his bees. He imagined spending his days outdoors in the warm and the quiet, tending his hives. One particularly dreary afternoon he told himself: Look, Dan, you're still pretty strong, you can still do the work, it's now or never—you're not going to do this when you're seventy. Bless his wife Bonita, when he came home and told her he'd quit his well-paying job with benefits to be a full-time beekeeper, she stuck with him. A few lean years followed—they found themselves asking questions such as "How many jars of honey would a furnace replacement be?"—but now they're thriving, out of debt, and producing tons of honey a year for local universities, businesses, and neighbors.

Given Dan's long history of beekeeping, his successful apiary, and his straddling of bee science, activism, and business, his seems like the perfect brain to pick about the similarities and differences between the ultrasociality of honeybees and human beings.

As soon as we dive into the topic, Dan quickly points out that while he often sees people hold bees up as a perfect model for what humans should strive to be, he thinks this is far from the truth. Bees behave in prosocial ways until you demonstrate a weakness, and then they behave in ways that most human societies wouldn't tolerate. "If you come limping out one morning," he says, "your sisters are likely to gang up on you and throw you out of the hive because you're failing."

I laugh, and Dan laughs back, but a bit ruefully.

But bees will also sacrifice themselves without hesitation for the good of the hive. "One of the saddest and most beautiful things you sometimes see in the spring," Dan says, "is that if the bees run out of food, their cluster of bees is intact because they all die at the same time. They share every bit of food right up until the end." Human beings are capable of this sort of remarkable altruism (e.g., people donating kidneys to strangers, an entirely volunteer-run military), but we also have a profound reverence for the autonomy of individual human life,* and a deep-rooted fear of losing our individuality in the sea of the collective.

Dan points out that honeybees can do many of the seemingly miraculous things that they do because there are so many of them—for one thing, the honey a hive produces represents millions of trips to flowers made by huge numbers of bees. Bees play particular roles in the hive at different stages in their life, from fertilization to hygiene to comb-making to foraging, and

---

* Sometimes. Some lives more than others.

this specialization of tasks allows for a communal benefit, much as human beings specialize in education or plumbing or nursing. No one individual is responsible for all his or her own needs, and it frees up time and energy to advance within one's specialization and for the collective to flourish.

Consider just the past week of your life. How many times did another human being sweep in and get things done for you with skills you don't possess? Pest removal services "diagnosed" the scary-looking nest under your deck as white-headed wasps and effectively removed it; your local middle school teachers taught your daughter how to do math (that you don't remember how to do); your mechanic diagnosed the thumping sound your car was making and fixed it before you were stranded on the way to an important work meeting; your doctor took a tiny snip of your body for some other trained technician to run tests on to be sure you could continue on with your life instead of halting everything and seeking treatment. All these other human beings use their expertise to make your life run seamlessly, and you contribute back your own skills.

Dan points out that much like many areas in our globalized world, American honeybees also represent a melting pot of sorts. The bees buzzing around Western Massachusetts represent seven different strains of bees from seven different parts of the planet. Dan emphasizes: "The healthiest hives are the most diverse." They are a collective, but as with human beings, variation in strengths and skills and propensities allow for the most adaptive and well-functioning sort of collective.

Like humans, honeybees also spend quite a lot of time and energy on communication with one another. In Dan's estimation, honeybees come a close second to humans in their ability for flexible, varied, and accurate communication. He reminds me that it's dark in the hive, so bees are not relying on visual input but rather largely on vibrations and pheromones. For instance, the queen bee has wee pads on her feet that release a pheromone called queen mandibular pheromone. She leaves traces of this chemical signal wherever she walks in the hive. When the other hive members sense the signal, they know how to proceed with their work.

For a long time, scientists suspected that human socioemotional behaviors were not much influenced in a similar manner, that we were a species who for the most part did not rely on chemical messengers released into the environment to impact social behaviors. Part of this reasoning was that unlike other mammals for whom pheromones play a large role in social behavior (like rats), human beings lack a vomeronasal organ, a collection of cells in the nose containing sensory neurons sensitive to chemical signals. However, a few studies suggested that women who spend a great deal of time together—such as living in dorms—tend to synchronize their menstrual cycles. A few others indicated that women preferred the smell of male T-shirts sourced from men with complementary genetic profiles. Studies like these rekindled interest in investigating whether human beings did have some cells in their olfactory system sensitive to pheromones, probably primarily emitted through axillary (armpit sweat) sources.

Psychologist Jasper de Groot and colleagues suspected that at least some of the degree to which human emotions tend to spread through groups might be due to the spread of these so-called "chemosignals" transmitted by human sweat through the air.[26] They decided to test their hypothesis in a manner as controlled and surreptitious as possible. They collected the sweat data from an all-male sample, reasoning that men are smellier (no, really). These men watched a series of videos that were disgusting or terrifying while wearing cotton pads under their arms. These cotton swabs were collected by the researchers and stored for another day. Next, a new, all-female sample of participants sat in a climate-controlled, well-ventilated lab with nasal cannulas under their noses, breathing in the sweat pads. While they did so, the researchers measured the extent to which they tensed the muscles in their foreheads and under their noses. They also measured the number of times they sniffed, and their ability to detect targets on the periphery.

If you're thinking that these are strange ways to measure emotion, you are probably not alone. We tend to think of facial expressions of emotion as being all about social communication. After all, it pays off to have a way to accurately detect that all of the people around you are suddenly very scared, because you probably should start looking around and figuring out what is causing those facial expressions of fear. But many emotion scientists have pointed out that facial expressions may also benefit us by changing how much sensory information we're taking in.

If you are reading this somewhere private, go ahead and make a big fear face—imagine you just rounded a dark corner and saw Pennywise the clown—and observe what happens. When you make a facial expression of fear, you widen nearly all the sensory organs of your face. You open your eyes as much as possible, your pupils dilate to take in more light, you flare your nostrils, you gape your mouth. These effects may help you acquire more sensory information, to see more, smell more, taste more. If something nearby is scary, you need all the information you can get.

Contrast this with a facial expression of disgust—go ahead and make that face. I bet you squinched shut your eyes and ears, wrinkled your nose, and even may have pushed out your tongue. These effects will serve to reject sensory information. Which again makes sense. If there are potential contaminants nearby that could make you sick, close off as many of your orifices as you can.

Counting the number of sniffs and one's ability to detect targets in the periphery similarly aimed to capture the extent to which these sweat pad–sniffing women were demonstrating either heightened sensory acquisition (consistent with fear, widening orifices, sniffing more, and looking for things on the periphery) or sensory rejection (consistent with disgust, closing orifices, sniffing less, and relaxing about things that might be happening in the periphery of your vision).

As hypothesized, the researchers found that women smelling fear sweat from the male volunteers demonstrated evidence of heightened sensory acquisition, and women smelling disgust sweat demonstrated evidence of heightened sensory rejection. What is most fascinating to me about these research findings is that they're not about pure emotional communication—it wasn't that the women were sensing someone else's emotions accurately ("Oh, this man smelled afraid!") but rather that they were smelling evidence of an emotional state and then demonstrating evidence that *the same emotional state* had been recreated in their own bodies—all without them having any awareness that the study was about emotion at all. These findings are evidence of emotional contagion rather than emotional communication.

This research group has replicated their basic finding several times and extended it to other contexts. For instance, they demonstrated that chemosignal transmission of fear was equal to that of audiovisual sensory information (using fearful film clips), and that combining the two (chemosignals with movies, kind of like you may have experienced if you last saw a horror movie in a crowded theater full of sweaty, jumpy humans) led to a stronger emotional contagion effect than either presented alone.[27] In another replication and extension study, they discovered that smelling happy people sweat resulted in not just facial expressions consistent with happy moods but also a more globalized form of attention, which is a cognitive state linked with feeling good.[28]

So maybe honeybees aren't the only ones who share feelings with one another using pheromones.★

Another aspect of behavior and experience that bees and humans share, to an extent, is the degree to which many of our even complicated behaviors operate automatically. Everyone assumes that bees do all that they're able to do based on instincts, on automatic behaviors that are coded in their genes and that unfold from the moment they are born. Dan shares that when baby bees are born, they immediately launch into incredibly complicated maneuvers. They start cleaning up the hive. They grow wax on their abdomens, which they take in their mandibles and shape to make perfect cells, right from the get-go. The bees in charge of ripening nectar into honey meet the foraging bees at the entrance of the hive and share a brief kiss—put their tongues together to transfer the sap so that the house bee can deliver it to the right area of the hive for further processing. The foraging bees also must use the sun as a basis for direction. Dan points to a cluster of trees with red leaves in the distance. "Say some foraging bees have found a great patch of flowers out there—they're going to remember that truck, that green shed, and how the sunlight fell just so...and they seem to have that sort of visual memory. All of these things the bees *just know how to do*, which I find remarkable."

I do, too.

It is easy to pass these convoluted behaviors off as pure instinct, as occurring without any larger sense of awareness or intentional choice, because it is so hard to imagine these tiny insects having anything like mammalian levels of consciousness. "Well, okay,"

★ While emotional communication and contagion via chemosignals has been replicated several times by de Groot's lab and others, there have been failures of replication in menstrual synchrony studies, and many researchers still question the mechanisms by which these chemosignals may transmit. Exactly which chemicals are being released and exactly how are they being detected? Before we have demonstrated a convincing biological mechanism, we should be cautious about concluding for sure that human beings can emit and detect pheromones.

Dan says, eerily stating my own thoughts out loud, "but none of *our* behaviors are similarly guided by instinct, right?"

We opened the chapter considering how much more of human behavior is determined unconsciously, based on instinct and on motivations outside of our awareness, than we may have ever thought before. So probably the largest difference between humans and honeybees isn't whether unconscious impulses drive a lot of behavior—which is likely true of both bees and humans—but rather that we humans have evolved to understand these impulses and act to override some of them. As Eagleman points out, we can model Ulysses and metaphorically latch our more impulsive selves to the ship's mast so that we do not harken to the call of the sirens.

In sum, human beings may be Homo duplex, possessing dual modes of operating in the world: the individualistic and the collective. Dancing ecstatically, scoring goals on a soccer field, or conversing with one another, we may behave more like a superorganism than like single individuals. We begin to line up our movements, our facial expressions, our emotions, and (as we'll soon see) our brain activity—not surprisingly, as brain activity is how we do movement, facial expressions, and emotion.

But the hivemind, it turns out, is not just an in-the-moment phenomenon that occurs when you gather human beings together to dance or sing or fight a common enemy.

Rather, the hivemind is also our collective, consensus sense of reality.

Chapter Two

Our Fiction, Ourselves

Castle Rock, Maine

As I tuck my four-year-old son into bed, he looks up at me with wide eyes and whispers, "Daddy, please check under my bed for monsters." Humoring him, I duck my head down and see him—another him—staring back at me, quivering and whispering, "Daddy, *there's somebody on my bed.*"

This two-sentence horror story goes viral every Halloween. Using just fifty-three words, and ones that aren't even mine,[*] I have inserted my thoughts into your mind and created a mental model that likely evoked two vivid characters, a full, rich setting, and a dread-inducing scenario. Did you see a night-light? Footie pajamas? Did you hear his small, quaking voice? I bet you did.

In Stephen King's wonderful book *On Writing*, he describes writing as an act of telepathy. To demonstrate, he sends his readers an image: a white rabbit in a cage with a blue number 8 painted on his back. Stephen writes on a snowy December morning in the late nineties, but over time and space I receive this image nearly two decades later reading and writing on a July afternoon, my black dog panting at my feet. And now I've passed the image on to

---

[*] In an excellent example of hivemind consciousness, variants of this story are all over the internet with slightly different wording, but I can't seem to find an original source.

you, wherever and whenever you are while you're reading this—in an airport perhaps, or lying on a beach—two, ten, twenty years from my present. But as we'll see in this chapter, the act of transmitting thoughts and images from one mind to another using words isn't just a cute parlor trick. This diffusion of thoughts from one to another to another, hopping across the human hivemind, may be responsible for the vast majority of what we agree upon as reality.

In this chapter I'll endeavor to convince you that while we of course have our own, immediate experiences of the world, the larger weight of our reality is carried by our cultural context. Not only do we synchronize and unite into a collective experience in group settings, as we discussed last chapter, but our sense of truth and how the world works is formed socially, not individually.

We absorb these shared understandings through parenting, conversation, formal education, and consuming online media. But I'd like to begin with one of the most elemental ways in which we absorb our culture's social norms and mental models of reality, and that is through the activity we opened the chapter with—through the telling of stories.

OUR COLLECTIVE LIBRARY

In the slim tome *How to Talk About Books You Haven't Read*, literature professor Pierre Bayard argues that in addition to having personal inner libraries of the books that have been important to us over our lifetimes, we also share a *collective library*. Our collective library consists of the books that we as a culture have decided are important, and the group consensus about them and the connections that are drawn among them are more important than any one book in isolation. Even if you have never read *Romeo and Juliet*, you probably know that it has something to do with a doomed first love and two warring families. The ideas and images and feelings of the story are woven into our fabric of shared meaning.

In an example of this cultural osmosis, writer and performance artist Jade Sylvan posted a challenge to their★ friends and followers on Facebook. The challenge went like this. Followers were to post an image of any *Game of Thrones* character, and Jade would describe the character's name and background despite never having read the books or seen the show, having instead absorbed the details from observed conversations and social media posts. They missed a few names, but not many, and most of the other details were spot-on.

For instance, here is how they responded to a picture of Kit Harrington, who plays Jon Snow in the television series: "Oooh, Jon Snow. People love him because he has dark greasy hair and broods. He's gone north and seen the snow zombies and is FREAKED. He has a big white wolf named Ghost. He died and everyone had meltdowns but then they brought him back, I think because of his magic wolf idk." They had never read a word or seen a scene, but the story entered their consciousness courtesy of the hivemind.

Reading narrative, emotional fiction may have also allowed us to understand that *all* human beings possess interior minds like our own. Historian Lynn Hunt, author of *Inventing Human Rights,* credits the reading of letter-based dramatic stories for the development of our understanding of universal human rights. Fiction in novel form showed us that men and women, rich and poor, dark of skin and light, all had similar feelings and thoughts and anxieties brewing underneath their outward differences. For Hunt, what was critical about this process was the emotional involvement in the storyline and the characters. The literary merit of the works was much less important than how they *moved* people, because it was these emotional heights that reshaped how people saw the world.

★ Jade's preferred pronouns are they, them.

Much to the excitement of bibliophiles, early research studies confirmed positive relationships between time clocked within the covers of novels and various sorts of empathy or interpersonal sensitivity—from scores on questionnaires to the ability to read subtle emotions in the eyes of strangers. For instance, reading a short fictional piece depicting a young Muslim widow in danger led to participants viewing faces as a blend of ethnicities (versus one or the other) and estimating greater genetic overlap between people of varying races, perhaps because "reading a story blurs the boundary line between the self and the other."[1] More recent work has raised questions about whether brief experimental exposures to fiction can nudge people's overall empathy.[2] But I think the jury is still out about prolonged, in-depth exposure over a lifetime, especially since some of these same studies that fail to replicate the effect of brief exposures still find a correlation between lifetime reading and measures of empathy.[3]★

Fictional stories not only enter our collective libraries, but they also then influence our decisions and actions in the real world. A famous example is the movie *Jaws*, which was magic for the box office but deadly to beach tourism the summer following.† It left, as writer Joe O'Connor put it, "bite marks on our psyches," mental wounds severe enough to impact people's summer vacation plans.[4]

Pierre Bayard calls this our *inner book*: the set of understandings and theories about how the world works that pin both our culture and our collective library together. I would argue that we have inner books not just for our fictional works but also for

---

★ The problem with the lifetime correlations is that, of course, it could also be that people with higher empathy are more likely to read a lot.

† In a very hivemind sort of way, I can find numerous articles claiming that beach tourism was down significantly the summer following *Jaws* but can't seem to trace down an actual statistic or research study. Is the original finding lost to the sands of time, or did we just collectively decide it must have happened?

science, politics, history—all of our domains of knowledge are informed by our cultural hiveminds.

For instance, for a long time the field of economics developed their theories based on the assumption that human beings behave rationally and according to their best interests. Papers, conferences, theories all worked within this hivemind framework, and the research questions that were asked and answered assumed it to be true. But psychologists and economists began investigating the many reasoning blind spots human beings have—the ways in which we rely on emotions and often-faulty rules of thumb to make decisions rather than thinking everything through carefully.[5] The field of behavioral economics was born, shifting the economic hivemind and in the process earning a couple of Nobel prizes.

HIVEMIND FAILS

Sometimes the narrative we've absorbed from the hivemind fails; when it does, it reveals the degree to which our knowledge of the world relies more on the collective story of how things work than on our direct experience—that while you might be able to talk about books you haven't read, you may occasionally reveal your ignorance. For example, editor in chief of online magazine *Electric Literature* Jess Zimmerman shared on Twitter that her boyfriend thought ponies were baby horses. After a few people replied with their own amusing misconceptions about how the world worked, she asked her Twitter followers to share their own stories of ridiculous misunderstandings.

The ensuing hilarity revealed such treasures as husbands believing babies were born with full sets of teeth, friends who grew up thinking Pennsylvania and Transylvania were the same locale, and men convinced that skirts and dresses referred to the same item of clothing that varied only in length. For some reason, a surprising number of contributions had to do with mayonnaise—that it was a dairy product, that if you mixed it with mustard it would turn to poison, that it was a product born of older potatoes when they were cracked open. These factoids are good for a chuckle but they also show the bones of the truth: most of what we know is secondhand, is gist-based collective knowledge, and is often wrong.

Another way that collective knowledge fails us is when errors persist despite the best evidence, just because the story is so compelling or because it confirms other aspects of our worldview, our biases and fears and assumptions. There are many examples of this phenomenon—that routine vaccinations cause autism, that we only use 10 percent of our brains, that the healthiest way to eat is how people ate in Paleolithic times, just to name a few—but let's start here with one that blew my mind because I had no idea.

In health scientist Emily Nagoski's book *Come as You Are: The Surprising New Science That Will Transform Your Sex Life* she shares the information that hymens do not typically break and are not a marker of virginity. The hymen is a thin membrane that stretches across the lower edge of the vaginal opening. Like most other aspects of human genitalia, there is remarkable variation in hymens—some cisgender★ women don't have them at all, some disappear during the adolescence years, some persist into middle age and beyond. But according to Nagoski, hymens don't break like a seal, and the presence or absence of a hymen does not tell you whether a woman is a virgin. Hymens can tear or bruise, but like many other body parts, they can also heal. They also don't typically bleed—blood in first-time penetrative sex is more commonly due to vaginal abrasions—and the hymen's size doesn't vary depending on whether the vagina has been penetrated.

But the *story* of hymens persists. That they are a onetime marker of virginity, that losing one's virginity is "popping the cherry," that women with intact hymens could not have been

---

★ Women whose gender identity conforms to their chromosomal sex.

raped. To this day, there are parts of the world that use virginity tests in which a doctor evaluates the presence or absence of a hymen, and the "wrong" result can result in violence or death.[6] There are even plastic surgeons willing to surgically replace missing hymens.

This particular hivemind myth is spread through literature, religious practices, schoolyard sex rumors, and word of mouth. This is how the hivemind enters our understanding of the world, without our knowledge or volition, shaping our sense of reality under the hood.

THIS IS HOW WE DO IT: SOCIAL NORMS

Another way that the hivemind impacts our behavior is by shaping how we believe we are allowed to act. These behavioral rules based on shared social understanding are called social norms. While some social norms are codified quite explicitly in the form of laws—these are the sorts of people you can marry, these are the places you can relieve yourself without getting into trouble—most are communicated more subtly, in an informal way that is highly consistent with other messages we receive from the hivemind about how the world works. When you enter an elevator you all face forward. You whisper in a library but shout at a rock concert. When greeting your grandmother or childhood best friend, you wrap your arms around them and squeeze, but you do not greet your high school principal or your opposite-sex coworker in this way.

We are exquisitely in tune with how our social others behave, and we tweak our own behavior to meet these expectations. We notice that the shiny pretty people on television increasingly have long wavy hair, and we start growing our hair and buy a hot iron to make long waves. Half of our Facebook feed is filled with videos of both celebrities and close friends pouring buckets of ice water over their heads, and we are filled with the irrepressible urge to pour buckets of ice water over our own heads. We fall in line.

Interestingly, the actual norms (what most people *do*) are often less important for governing people's behaviors than are the subjective perceptions of the norms or how people think most people behave.[7] That is, it matters less how many people in your neighborhood are actually recycling than how many people in your neighborhood you *think* are recycling.

Collectively, these norms form the backbone of what we call culture. Michael Tomasello, a linguist and psychologist at Duke University, argues that culture arose as we began cooperating in increasingly larger groups.[8] We first developed what he calls "shared intentionality," the ability to work together with other human beings and understand our mutual goals and intentions. Over time our shared intentionality evolved into "collective intentionality," the norms and morals of our particular group becoming absorbed and automatic. For as our collaborative groups got larger, we could no longer keep track of individual other human beings and whether we could trust them or not. We needed markers of the humans who belonged to our tribe and not the tribe next door—and so distinctively human culture was born, the ways of eating and dressing and worshipping and speaking that marked someone of your group versus someone of another group. This is how *we* capture prey, this is how *we* build a shelter. In other words, our social norms.

Relatedly, rather than people being influenced by how they think most people in the entire culture behave, they are more influenced by how they perceive people belonging to their particular ingroup or subculture behave.[9] If more people in your social network rolled their eyes at the ice bucket challenge than posted videos, you'd be more likely to share a sarcastic status about lemmings than a teeth-chattering video.

Provocatively, social neuroscientist Matthew Lieberman argues that social norms influence our behavior by convincing us that we are the ones who thought of curling our hair or dumping the ice bucket in the first place. He provides extensive behavioral and neuroscientific evidence suggesting that our sense of self is a Trojan horse of sorts that allows the values of our shared culture to sneak in and influence our behavior, convincing us that it was our idea all along. "It is not enough for us to recognize what the group believes and values," he writes. "We have to adopt the beliefs and values as our own if they are to guide our behavior.... Much of what makes up our sense of self was snuck in from the outside, under the cover of darkness."[10]

Finally, we are also more easily influenced by people with whom we share personal connections, and by idealized others—leaders and celebrities.[11] The latter fact is well known to folks in advertising and marketing, who pander to people with large followings on social platforms like Instagram (so-called influencers), sending them free products and even free vacations at resorts so that they will then pepper their feed with references to and images of their products in use.

What does it take for social norms to shift? It turns out, small groups of people can have very large impacts, especially if they have elevated status in the group. A set of researchers cleverly set up an experiment to test how many people need to adopt a new social norm in order for it to be accepted by the whole group.[12] They found that the tipping point for an abandonment of one social norm in favor of another was a surprisingly low 25 percent—when about a quarter of the group endorsed the new norm. Anything below, and the norm didn't shift. Anything above, and it did. This number conformed to mathematical modeling predictions by other social scientists, and data from other sources such as case studies of business practices.[13]

Writing about this experiment in the *Atlantic*,[14] science communicator Ed Yong reflects, "Small groups of people can indeed flip firmly established social conventions, as long as they reach a certain critical mass. When that happens, what was once acceptable can quickly become unacceptable, and vice versa," noting American views on gay marriage, public smoking bans, and the legalization of marijuana as examples. The social norm in this experiment was an arbitrary, relatively neutral one, and most social norms are much more laden with history and politics and identity. But even when heavily incentivized to stick with the status quo, the tipping point budged only to about 30 percent.

Businesses have begun implementing strategies that specifically tap into consumers' perceived social norms in order to influence their behavior. For instance, your electric company may send you reports on how much electricity you are using compared to your neighbors, with little happy or sad faces indicating whether you are meeting the social norm for energy consumption. Their hope is that they can nudge you into behaving differently (i.e., using less electricity) by tweaking your perception of how your behavior fits in with the rest of the hive.

These social nudges can sometimes backfire depending on how they're being presented. One study found that a sign shaming people for removing petrified wood from a forest actually *increased* rates of petrified wood theft. The authors concluded, "Within the statement 'Look at all the people who are doing this undesirable thing' lurks the powerful and undercutting normative message 'Look at all the people who are doing it.'"[15] In this case, chastising people for behaving in antisocial ways was inadvertently conveying a social norm for antisocial behavior.

Our ideas about the world spread through the hivemind, affecting not just the people in our individual social network but also people we may never meet face-to-face. As Nicholas Christakis and James Fowler write in their book *Connected: How Your Friends' Friends' Friends Affect Everything You Feel, Think, and Do,*

"It is as if we can feel the pulse of the social world around us and respond to its persistent rhythms. As part of a social network, we transcend ourselves, for good or ill, and become a part of something much larger. We are connected."

Part of how we establish these connections is through the stories we tell.

STORIES: OUR MOST NATURAL FORM OF THOUGHT

Social norms are communicated by institutional laws, by our perception of the average behaviors of our social others, and by examples from leaders and celebrities. Our social norms are also shaped by the stories we read and hear and watch, the morals of our fiction. One of the most primitive, basic ways that we understand the world is through stories, through narratives.

Psychologists Roger Schank and Robert Abelson argue that stories are our "most natural form of thought."[16] They argue that verbal knowledge exists in order to remember the past, to understand the present, to project oneself into the future, and to share information with others.

Verbal knowledge exists to *tell*.

In every introductory psychology class, students new to psychology are taught that there are distinct types of memories. The first big subdivision is between implicit and explicit memory. Implicit memories are those that influence your behavior in ways that aren't accessible to your waking mind. The precise changes in your musculature involved in balancing on a bike are implicit, as is the rush of warm emotions you feel when you smell your grandmother's perfume. Explicit memory, on the other hand, is subdivided into episodic memories (autobiographical memory) and semantic memory (memory for facts). When I teach this difference, I put up an image of a big tree and tell my students that episodic memory would be your memory for the day you were married under a particular tree, and semantic memory would be your memory for the difference between evergreen trees and deciduous trees. Remembering what you did last Valentine's Day is an episodic memory, remembering who St. Valentine was is a semantic memory.

Except Schank and Abelson argue that this basic tenet of cognitive psychology is actually wrong, that there is in fact *no such thing as semantic memory*. Even memories that seem "factual" are actually made up of stories, are part of autobiographical memory. When you say, for instance, "I was born in New York," you are recalling a story that you were told by your parents. While we're at it, what is New York? There are no natural boundaries of New York as a state. We agree upon the story of New York, that there is a line demarcating the borders of this land, that the people who live within these borders can decide upon certain ways of governance that are slightly different from people just a few feet on the other side of the border. We agree upon this story largely because of historical precedence. And what is history but a long set of interlocking stories?

I was once at a large family party to celebrate my brother's engagement when a particularly liberal friend happened to ask a small girl at our table what she was studying in school. She responded that they were memorizing the states. He replied, much to her consternation, "Oh, honey, there is no such things as states." Which at the time I found hilarious and odd, but when you really stop to think about it, *there is no such thing as states*—the entire concept of states is caught up in the shared mental models of our hivemind, our laws and agreed-upon governments and social practices.

We also tell ourselves stories about the kind of people who live in New York. Telling someone you grew up in New York versus Nebraska changes their predictions and estimations about the kind of person you are, even though there are likely huge differences between a woman working in finance on Wall Street and a male Reiki practitioner living in Woodstock. Even knowing these additional facts about these two people, we still know nothing about who they are as individuals. Many of the stories that we tell ourselves about our social others are stereotypes, or assumptions about the characteristics of people based on their belonging to social groupings.

We develop stereotypes because in our collective libraries of television shows and novels and commercials, these groupings have been reliably associated with certain characteristics. In our fictional stories, lawyers are always ruthless and sharply dressed, blond women are low in intelligence but high in desirability, and gay men are frivolous but funny. Many of the associations we carry about social groupings are even more pernicious than these examples, for instance reliably associating people of certain races with violence or lack of motivation. These characteristics become implicitly associated with people who belong to these groups,[17] then impact how the people belonging to these social groups are treated when they're applying for jobs and mortgages and trying to date.[18] We carry our implicit associations into all of our social interactions, and they become woven into the structure of the world we share.

Our political beliefs, too, are largely stories we tell ourselves about how the world is constructed and which sorts of values should be held preeminent. As Schank and Abelson put it, "There are good guys and bad guys, and the bad guys, using illegitimate methods, are trying to bring about an evil state of affairs. This can only be averted if the good guys mobilize their forces, recruit people from the sidelines (who are in danger of being seduced by the bad guys), and press forward to glorious victory." Do me a favor and remember this particular skeleton of a story, because it is going to come back at us again and again in the pages that follow.

How did this come to be? How did we evolve to be what

beloved fantasy author Terry Pratchett called *pans narrans*, the storytelling ape? Next we'll check in with an evolutionary biologist to attempt to answer just that question.

EVOLUTION, FICTION, AND THE HIVEMIND

One afternoon in my first year of graduate school, I got home and fired up my email. I deleted a bunch of spam and university announcements and then noticed a personal email from a name I didn't recognize, Kimberly Norris Russell. I clicked it open and read what would turn out to be a famous line in our now decade-plus friendship. The email began: "I'm not ordinarily in the habit of emailing complete strangers, but these are desperate times."

Kim went on to say that we shared a mutual friend, and that the two of them would spend hours dissecting the latest episodes of the cult television show *Buffy the Vampire Slayer*. This mutual friend had recently stopped watching, and Kim ached for a new conversation partner. Kim's friend directed her to me, a fellow fan.

We struck up a correspondence, to put it mildly. We marshaled evidence, we waxed eloquent, we probably could have solved several intractable global conflicts in the time we dedicated to these trivial pursuits. In the midst of all of this discussion and episode rehashing, Kim and I became close friends. *Buffy* went off the air after six successful seasons,★ and we transitioned from young academics in training to mothers with full-time careers. Out of time for lengthy email binges but wanting to stay in touch, Kim and I started exchanging voice memos (we call them "audios") that we use to catch up on the minutiae of our daily lives but also to have rousing debates about topics like screen use and parenting, whether *Game of Thrones* is at its heart a feminist tale or a misogynistic mess, and the extent to which sex differences are innate or

---

★ I don't acknowledge the seventh season.

the product of culture. At one point we even turned one of these conversations into a blog post—after the publication of journalist Daniel Bergner's *What Do Women Want? Adventures in the Science of Female Desire* we took our conversation to the pages of *Psychology Today*. It remains my most-read blog post of all time.

When deciding whom to interview for this chapter, I thought of Kim not just because our friendship origin story involves new connections via social technology but also because Kim is an evolutionary biologist and thus a fantastic person with whom to discuss our evolved sociality. Over a series of audios, I asked Kim for her evolutionary biology perspective: What is it about stories that so thoroughly engages human curiosity and cognitive processing? How does binge-watching tie in to our social natures, our evolution into Homo duplex?

Kim points out that there are very few human traits or abilities that you can't observe elsewhere in the animal kingdom, but that one exception is our degree of sociality, reciprocity, and understanding of one another's mental worlds. In psychology we often refer to this ability as "theory of mind." It allows us to understand the lived experiences of another, to appreciate that not everyone has the same perceptions and knowledge and sets of biases. We can theorize about the minds of others. This ability underpins much of what makes our society tick: it allows us to empathize, to want to reduce suffering. In terms of how and why this ability may have evolved, Kim refers me to anthropologist and primatologist Sarah Blaffer Hrdy's research and book *Mothers and Others: The Evolutionary Origins of Mutual Understanding*.

Agreeing with several other experts we'll encounter in this book, Hrdy takes issue with claims that we evolved to be violently tribal. She points out that in times of sharply limited resources, it would have been much less costly for hominid groups to up and move home than to engage in lengthy battles over land and other resources. She also sees in the anthropological record little physical evidence of extensive warfare in our early evolutionary history, and points to modern hunter-gatherer societies, which are marked by "being fiercely egalitarian and going to great lengths to downplay competition and forestall ruptures in the social fabric, for reflexively shunning, humiliating, even ostracizing or executing those who behave in stingy, boastful, or antisocial ways." Hrdy argues that we developed networks of sharing and mutual support, a web of social connections that could catch us if we fell—in our ability to procure food, to care for our young, to seek shelter.

To evaluate how our social tendencies may have evolved, both chimpanzees and bonobos are good candidates for examining shared ancestry with humans. Both species are approximately equal in their genetic proximity to human beings, and all three of us share a common ancestor from an estimated six million years ago. Hrdy points out that evolutionary accounts have focused most on chimpanzees, seeing possible early mirrors of us in their tribal nature, their propensity for competition and violence, and their carefully maintained dominance hierarchies. Less attention is paid to bonobos, and so we know less about them. But what we do know suggests that they are much more cooperative and egalitarian than their chimpanzee counterparts, more open to new members of competing tribes, more willing to share food, and more openly sexual. If we use bonobos as a model for our shared ancestor, then the narrative about our evolutionary history shifts quite a bit—and here we are again, restricted in our understanding by the narrative the hivemind dubs superior.

But whether we look to chimpanzees or bonobos for models of what our ancient ancestors may have been like, at some point along the way we evolved to become exponentially more socioemotionally complex than either of these, and presumably more than our common ancestor. What truly set human beings on their own path?

Hrdy's reading of the evidence is that we began raising our young in large groups, cooperating with one another to shoulder the task of raising vulnerable infants into thriving adults, something she calls "alloparenting." She draws from wide-ranging sources of evidence, from the genetic to the endocrine to the archaeological, to argue that the origins of human sociality and our incredibly sophisticated theory of mind may be integrally tied to the human practice of turning to multiple caregivers for support. Whether this need for extraparental care was a driving force in the development of theory of mind or not, the ability to both understand and care about the underlying motivations of other members of our species is certainly a deeply human trait.

It is also just this critical human ability that Kim credits for our drive to fictional stories—our desire to not just read or watch these stories but also to analyze, to critique, to discuss, to rehash. She argues that we probably did this first around campfires, then in common squares, then over watercoolers, and now on the web. It teaches us how to empathize, how to understand the motivations not just of the fictional characters but also of the characters who populate our lives. Because when we are transported into a story, we become the characters, we feel what they feel, we do what they do.

"If the character's choices as written by the author don't feel genuine to us, that's our critique—I don't think that imaginary character in this imaginary situation would do that imaginary thing." Kim laughs. "I mean, that's a uniquely human thing to think!" We get upset when characters that exist only in our shared imagination with the writer behave in ways that we feel are inconsistent with their fictional values and fictional understanding of the world.

This practice may be particularly key for humans because many of our achievements and abilities are tied to the unusual fact that we are capable of both biological and cultural learning. We are born with the neurological mechanisms to process empathy, to project ourselves into others, and to perceive that information and make use of it. But *how* to make use of that information, in which precise ways, we need to instill in the young through the processes of culture. "The tools we're born with are honed and fine-tuned," Kim says, "by the hearing and interpretation of stories, by storytelling."

Early human cultures who were able to accomplish this fantastical fine-tuning might have been better able to interact with others and had more stable social systems, which may have given them an evolutionary benefit. Among the Filipino hunter-gatherer population called the Agta, members who are proficient storytellers are preferred as social partners (even above good foragers, who presumably bring more food in) and enjoy greater reproductive success.[19] The content of the stories commonly told by the Agta also prioritize social sharing of resources and equality. One example: Wild Pig and Seacow were best friends and enjoyed racing each other for fun until Seacow suffered an injury to his legs and could no longer run. Wild Pig was so unhappy at the loss of his treasured playtime with his friend that he carried Seacow to the sea, where they could race again—Wild Pig on land and Seacow in the waves. Like this one, most of the stories of the Agta focus on cooperation and even the reversal of social inequalities.

Stories act as one mechanism by which groups establish and reinforce their social norms and cultural values.

STORYTELLERS BY DEFAULT: A SPECIALIZED BRAIN NETWORK FOR NARRATIVE?

How might this evolutionary pressure have nudged us in the direction of constantly fine-tuning our narrative abilities? Well, perhaps we began to dedicate an entire network of brain regions to support the activity. Matthew Lieberman, social neuroscientist and author of *Social: Why Our Brains Are Wired to Connect*, asks us to consider the fact that whenever we disconnect from the tasks of daily living, our brains tend to revert to social musings: that recent crush, that upcoming party, the perfect comeback to that coworker's slight—had you only thought of it in time.

In his book, he provides quite a lot of evidence that we use a specific set of brain regions coactivating as a network to enact this social rumination. The network is somewhat strangely named "the default mode network" (DMN for short) and is so named because it was discovered when neuroscientists began examining what brains tended to do when they stopped working on a specific task. In other words, these are the regions that leap into (mental) action the moment you *stop* leaping into focused (mental) action. The network that activates by default.

The activities we tend to engage in during this off-time, so-called spontaneous cognition, comprise activities like day-dreaming, remembering, and simulating future social interactions. All of these activities have in common the fact that they are mentally processing events separate from the present moment, either consolidating memories of the past or speculating into uncertain futures[20]—in other words, telling stories.

Indeed, studies that ask participants to listen to, watch, or otherwise perceive narrative stories observe activation in this network.[21] The brain regions involved in the DMN share quite a bit of overlap with the brain regions social neuroscientists find to be critical for social cognition, or thinking about other people. Originally, Lieberman thought that we must turn on the DMN whenever we get a spare second because we are so innately interested in our social worlds. But examining all of the evidence and thinking deeply about it, he realized that the evidence actually better supported the reverse causality: "We are interested in the social world because we are built to turn on the default mode network during our free time." That is, this neuroscientist is echoing Kim's evolutionary biologist perspective about evolving to dedicate our neural free time to stories, to vignettes about people.

When we engage in social processing, we're telling little stories to ourselves—whom we like, who likes us, who might be friend or foe or ally, and how interactions with these people might pan out. When we consolidate memories, we take the events of our lives and turn them into neat little stories for future rehashing. Stories are the stuff of thought, one of the most basic and most important aspects of human cognition, and we may have evolved an entire network of brain regions to hone our story telling abilities.

Fascinatingly, neuroimaging studies of what happens in the brain when we read stories indicates that we may use the same circuits for both literal experience and metaphorical experience.[22] That is, when you read about a character running in the forest, you may activate regions of the brain involved in motor movement and visual perception—the same regions you'd activate if you were actually running through the forest. As B. J. Catling writes in his novel *The Vorrh*: "He instinctively knew that memory and imagination share the same ghost quarters in the brain, that they are like impressions in loose sand, footfalls in snow."

Like the dreams of our nighttime slumber, reading fiction may be one way that we simulate possible futures, that we practice experience. This may be why fiction feels so personal even though it is secondhand.

APPRAISALS: THE LITTLEST STORIES

Before we leave this chapter and our deep dive into how our narratives shape our consensus reality, I'd like to introduce you to a term that we're going to consider frequently in the pages that follow.

That term is *appraisal*.[23] An appraisal is a teeny-tiny little story you tell yourself about the meaning of an event or situation, your interpretation of its significance or novelty or impact on your goals.

We engage in appraisals all the time. Is the herb cilantro a pleasant, lemony addition to fish tacos or a noxious weed that tastes like old dishwater? Does the length of your supervisor's response on the "areas for growth" section indicate her investment in your future or her contempt for you as a person? Are social technologies malicious forces in society or are they innocuous tools? These are all appraisals, and the appraisals we make determine how we react—whether we spit out the cilantro, whether we ruminate over our performance evaluation, whether we toss our child's smartphone in the garbage bin and force him to use landlines and pass handwritten notes instead.

What determines which appraisals we make and which we don't? So many things. To some extent, appraisals may be influenced by genetics—for instance, we know that personality traits like extraversion and neuroticism are highly heritable. People with neurotic tendencies may be more likely to appraise the supervisor's feedback as negative than people with extroverted tendencies. Parenting makes a difference, certainly. If you grew up watching your mother lock the car doors anytime she drove past someone with a different skin color, that is going to influence how you appraise people from racial backgrounds different from yours. Education has an impact, reading fiction has an impact, conversations with friends, too—much like any other aspect of our personality or understanding of the world, appraisals are to a large degree socially determined.

You can even feel your shifting appraisals and the resulting changes in your emotions if you pay attention to them. For instance, most fights between couples and between friends involve two competing sets of appraisals, and once you talk things out and understand your social other's competing sets of appraisals your anger melts away.

Stories are the stuff of thought, and thought presages and determines behavior.

As we'll see, the hivemind plays an enormous role in the appraisals that we make.

Chapter Three

Thresholds of Inclusion

Providence, Rhode Island

The development of intimacy with another human being involves a relaxing of barriers, a lowering of drawbridges, a dismantling of walls. In becoming close to another person, we allow them access to elements of our experience and emotions that we don't share with most people. We typically invite only a handful of other beings into the most private parts of our being, both physical and mental, and we call this expansion of the threshold of our interior love.

Moving one step out from this most cherished inner circle, we have our relationships with people who might not have unfettered access to our interior but for whom we don't need to put on a brave front or a polished face—they've seen us tired, they've seen us sick, they've seen us at our best and our worst. They know and appreciate our quirks and offer support when we need it. We call this friendship.

Step out again and we have our more general social network, the people we know and are known by, the people we'd sidle up to in a bar if we spotted them through the crowded room. One more step out and we have those people we might not know personally but with whom we share a sense of meaning and an approach to the world. We all belong to different subgroups of gender and ethnicity and region and philosophical outlooks and political parties and popular cultural preferences. We preferentially source a sense of identity with these people, forming an "us" that is different from "them."

In this chapter we'll consider what happens when people form preferences and ingroups, when instead of embracing humanity as a holistic hive, we instead splinter into tribes. We'll start large, with whole cultures, and then winnow down a bit to friendship networks, and then to the romantic couple.

But first, let's travel to the smallest state in the union to talk to someone who has written a lot more than I have about this crazy little thing called love.

THE WATER WE SWIM IN: AN ANTHROPOLOGICAL VIEW OF THE HIVEMIND

"More bees!" I exclaim.

I'm peering into a display case of Kamba drinking gourds at the Haffenreffer Museum of Anthropology at Brown University in Providence, Rhode Island. The Kamba people, sometimes also called Akamba or Wakamba, live in Kenya, Africa, and in Paraguay, South America.

The drinking gourds are beautiful, carved in rich wood with intricate patterns, presented before a background of honeycomb. According to the accompanying text, a beer made from honey (called *uki*) plays a large role in traditional Kamba ceremonies such as marriages and coming-of-age celebrations. Traditionally, only the elders of the society were allowed to drink *uki*—and only men, since it was a marker of masculine status—or to own a honey box (*kihembe*).

I've come to the museum not just to explore the artifacts but also to grab an Indian buffet with biological anthropologist Patrick Clarkin. Patrick is a professor at the University of Massachusetts

Boston. He researches the effects of war and displacement on biological markers such as body composition and chronic disease, studying populations such as the Hmong, Lao, and Khmer living in French Guiana and the United States. Today marks the first time Patrick and I have met in real life, but we've followed each other on Twitter for quite some time; a click-through quiz once dubbed us "Twitter valentines," probably using some algorithm of mutual follows/followers and number of times we've liked each other's tweets. We're here today to talk about an anthropological take on matters hivemind.

Or at least, one anthropologist's take.

We start with one of our themes from the previous chapter—that of social norms and the development of culture.

"When you take Cultural Anthropology 101," Patrick says, "you hear about all of these things that seem bizarre to you but that other people around the world accept as normal. It works the same for us, but we're so embedded in it that we don't see it. It is like that bit from David Foster Wallace about the fish and the water, right? Do you know it?"

I do. It goes like this: "There are these two young fish swimming along and they happen to meet an older fish swimming the other way, who nods at them and says, 'Morning, boys. How's the water?' And the two young fish swim on for a bit, and then eventually one of them looks over at the other and goes, 'What the hell is water?'"[1]

We chuckle together.

According to Patrick, comparative psychologist Michael Tomasello (who told us last chapter about shared intentionality) says that fish are born expecting water and humans are born expecting culture. It is the air we breathe, the gravity that keeps us grounded, and just as invisible as both of these.

Patrick's perspective on the essential nature of human beings is more in line with Sarah Blaffer Hrdy's view than with a focus on the evils of our warlike natures. He believes that larger conflicts probably only arose once we developed agriculture, began settling onto plots of land, and started defending them from others. Yet another expert suggesting that we're more hiveish than tribal.

"We've tumbled into this level of conflict and violence over the last twelve thousand years," Patrick says. "That's still relatively new on a human scale."

I can't help but marvel at this perspective: twelve thousand years as a short period of time!

Patrick smiles ruefully. He acknowledges that this perspective on time is not typical of how most people think. But when you are used to looking at the entire span of human evolution, anything on the order of thousands of years seems fairly short.

"When you start thinking in deeper timescales," he continues, "you can see more possibilities for the ways that humans can behave." In US culture, Patrick sees a nostalgia for a way of living—nuclear families raising 2.5 children, father working and mother at home, two-story house with a lawn—that is reflective of a short-lived period of time in the middle of the twentieth century and only shared by people in suburban, largely white, middle- and upper-class communities. He feels that to some people, it is as if a handful of decades in a single subculture in a single country are all that ever was.

Our own cultural practices are likely to seem alienating and unnatural to other societies in the world. To most human beings over the span of history, the practice of taking a tiny infant and forcing it to sleep on its back, alone in a wooden cage far from its parents and siblings, would have been considered at best odd and at worst barbaric. Our lack of physical activity, our tendency to move far from our families and friends for work, even (possibly—it's up for debate) our insistence on lifelong monogamy as an ideal are all cultural practices out of step with much of human history.

In contrast, Patrick offers the example of fraternal polyandry, where one woman marries a couple of brothers so they can keep the family farm together. In contemporary Western culture we can't imagine that the situation wouldn't end in bloodshed or at the very least misery—but to some other cultures, it is a reasonable solution to a difficult problem.

Not only does the anthropological perspective yield a sense of the great expanse of human evolution and culture, it also allows you to see how flexible human experience can be, how shaped by context and appraisals and the chosen narrative of the hivemind.

Patrick asks, "Have you ever seen the Frans de Waal video of the monkeys with the grapes?"

I have not. I've paraphrased Patrick's description below but the real deal is pretty entertaining if you want to pick up your phone and do a quick google.

De Waal is a primatologist at Emory University. He set up an experiment where he trained South American capuchin monkeys how to use "money." Their form of money is a rock. If the monkey gives a rock to the researcher, the researcher will respond by giving the monkey a reward. In the video, there are two monkeys in separate cages, side by side, so they can observe each other. The first monkey gives the researcher a rock and gets a cucumber in return. The second monkey gives the researcher his rock and this monkey gets a grape. To capuchins, grapes are way yummier than cucumbers. The researcher goes back to the first monkey, who has seen all of this go down. She refuses the cucumber from that point on; she'll wait for the grape, thank you very much. The monkeys are making appraisals about what is fair and telling themselves little stories about what they deserve.* The social context changed, and suddenly a cucumber, previously quite tasty and desired, was no good.

---

* Neither Patrick nor I is suggesting that these appraisals are conscious and/or verbal in nature. But neither, probably, are many of the appraisals that human beings make.

Human beings are even more tuned in to their social environments and the changing meaning of what is good, fair, and right. Writing about college students rather than monkeys, author and educator John Warner points out that two critical appraisals shaping what we think of as fair are *scarcity* and *precarity*.[2] An appraisal of scarcity leads to the perception that resources are limited, that one might need to compete and to scramble. An appraisal of precarity leads to the perception that one's current standing is vulnerable, that the slightest wind could topple you. There are not enough grapes to go around (scarcity) and you have a grape coming to you but its arrival is not guaranteed, it could be snatched away at any moment (precarity).

Warner sees these appraisals at work in the current high rates of mental health problems among college students. Scarcity is real, especially among those not in the highest income brackets: only so many people can get into and stay in college and succeed there, and many students must make sacrifices such as tremendous financial debt and missed meals to do it.[3] Precarity is also real in this age of politicians scraping away the safety net and everyone and their uncle running GoFundMe drives to pay for their heart surgery. In the presence of scarcity and precarity, competition and selfishness and accusations of resource hoarding and freeloading can escalate. So, too, might depression and anxiety, Warner reasons, pointing out that when national surveys ask students what they worry about, they point to future employment and finances and their grades (which translate into employment and finances and social standing in the future). Much like de Waal's monkeys, our conception of the world relies to a large degree on our perceptions and observations of our social others.

"I wish I was good at animation or drawing," Patrick says, "because I have this idea for an animation. It would depict a human being with a thought cloud above her head. All her thoughts are spinning in a certain direction. Then she walks past another human being with his thought cloud—but his thoughts are going in the opposite direction. The two people crash into each other and so do their thought bubbles, which combine a bit and influence each other." Our thoughts don't just stay in our heads, they spread out and influence each other.

This interpenetration and social spread of thoughts is also one of the driving forces behind Patrick's blog writing. When he perceives a discouraging negative trend in the hivemind, he sends a positive blog post out into the world, his own thought cloud hopefully colliding with a few other clouds and spinning them in a positive direction. His posts aren't naive cheerleading—they're grounded in anthropological science and empirical research—but they do try to nudge the hivemind narrative a bit in a hopeful direction.

One of my favorite blog posts of Patrick's is titled "Thresholds of Inclusion."[4] In the post, Patrick refers again to primatologist and grape dispenser Frans de Waal, who has described human empathy as existing in "moral circles."[5] The tightest circle, for whose denizens you have the greatest empathy, consists only of yourself. One step out is family. Next, village. Next, ethnic group. Next, nation, and so on until you reach humanity, and then perhaps all living beings.

But as Patrick points out, a lot of these definitions are arbitrary. You are not the same you, static through time. Friends can become like family, what Sarah Blaffer Hrdy calls "as-if kin." For some people, nationality trumps ethnic identity. Research shows that if you prime one aspect of identity or another or manipulate people's beliefs about the biological versus social construction of race, these manipulations shift participants' level of bias against outgroups.[6]

We compare our experiences in the world to those of others

and form expectations and resentments in relation to how we perceive others are doing. It is yet again all about context and appraisals, the story we tell ourselves.

This metaphor of thresholds of inclusion is not just a metaphor, however. When we spend time with our social others, we begin to synchronize with them, to line up not just our mannerisms and our actions but also how we perceive the world—to literally include them in our sense of self. Research on how our brains harmonize with the brains of people in our inner circles is called neural synchrony, and it is (in my humble opinion) some of the most fascinating research currently being conducted in psychology.

TUNING IN: NEURAL SYNCHRONY

Social neuroscientist Thalia Wheatley has spent the past several years spying on first-year students at the Dartmouth Business School. Dartmouth is situated in Hanover, New Hampshire, which is far from a metropolitan mecca. Wheatley likes to joke that the tree/person ratio is quite lopsided, with the leafy denizens easily outnumbering the bipedal ones. The business program has its own building on campus, where students spend most of their time taking classes, eating together in the dining hall, and living together in dorms. Thus, Wheatley has access to a group of human beings new to one another settling into a shared social endeavor for several years, spending nearly all of their time working and learning and sharing with one another. It is as close as a social psychologist might get to a controlled experiment, with the ability to observe social networks forming in real time. Even better, every fall the experiment begins anew with a new crop of students. It also allows for one of the gold standards of great research: longitudinal designs, where you can assess groups of people at one point in time and then follow them forward into the future to observe changes.

Together with fellow psychologist Carolyn Parkinson and some other collaborators, Wheatley has started answering sophisticated questions about the degree to which we experience the world similarly to our friends at the level of the brain[7]—and whether we seek out friends who think like us. She calls this work "neural homophily," where homophily refers to attraction to sameness.

She and her lab created a series of video clips that were designed to include "engaging but divisive," content that would evoke a variety of positive and negative responses depending on who was watching. Think snippets of political speeches, comedy routines, mockumentaries. She had one cohort of the Dartmouth Business students watch these videos while in the fMRI scanner and observed how eighty different areas in their brains reacted to these video clips. Because they were a cohort, she was also able to measure their entire social network. For each person she could see not just whom they were connected to through friendship but also who was connected to them—so not just who were friends but also friends of friends and friends of friends of friends. She then took their brain responses to the videos and examined them to see how closely they did or did not seem to covary, to activate and deactivate similar regions of the brain and at similar time points.

What Wheatley and her collaborators found was that friends of friends of friends did not have similar neural reactions to the videos. But once you moved one step closer to real connection, the brain activity started lining up. Friends of friends exhibited changes in brain activation that were significantly correlated (related), and first-degree friends much more so.

At the level of the brain, we react to the world similarly to our friends. While this specific study only examined brain activity, the overarching idea is that friendship involves a sharing of experience: the same things make us laugh, make us feel disgusted, make us pay attention or become bored.

There are at least two compelling possibilities for why Wheatley and her colleagues observed these results. For one, it could be that the brain-based correlations are due to common, shared life experiences, that part of the development of friendship is a tuning or synchronizing of our brain activity and reactions to the world. If this is true, you should see that these correlations grow stronger over the course of the friendship, as the months and years experiencing life together pile up. On the other hand, it could be that we are attracted initially to people who react to the world in a similar manner. If this hypothesis is true, then you should observe the correlations between two likely friendship candidates before they ever become friends. Moreover, you should be able to use brain activation patterns to predict who, in the future, will choose whom for shared fun and venting and Netflix bingeing. (And of course, it could well be that the truth is that both are true to some extent.) Wheatley and her team are actively testing all the possibilities.

They aren't the only researchers investigating neural synchrony. In an innovative brain-imaging study of how shared memories might work at the level of the brain, a group of researchers out of Princeton University asked some research participants to watch an episode of BBC's show *Sherlock* while in the scanner.[8] Once out of the scanner, the participants were asked to describe the show, much as one would having just watched with a friend. The researchers compared how similar (or different) people's brain activation was when they were viewing and when they were remembering the various scenes of the television show. Remarkably, people's brain activation when retelling the events of the episode was more similar to someone else retelling the story than it was to their own brain activation when they first experienced Sherlock and Watson's antics. In an interview with the website DeepStuff.org,[9] lead researcher Janice Chen interprets these findings as showing that there are "fundamental similarities between the brains of different people as they perceive and remember the real world. That gives us good groundwork for understanding each other." In other words, these similarities in how we experience the world allow for our interpretations and recollections to line up and become similar, to synchronize.

In another example, some Finnish scientists asked people to lie in an fMRI scanner and watch short film clips from popular movies, selected to induce various positive and negative emotions (e.g., *When Harry Met Sally, The Godfather*).[10] After having their brains scanned, participants watched the movies again, this time rating their emotional ups and downs as they viewed them. The researchers then looked at all of the subjects' data together, paying special attention to when the participants exhibited similar patterns of brain activation and how these times of synchronized activity were associated with the emotional highs and lows of the film clips. Their results indicated that when the participants felt intense negative emotion, their brain activity showed remarkable similarities, particularly in areas known to be involved in the processing of emotion. "Through this kind of mind-simulation," the authors write, "we may estimate others' goals and needs more accurately and tune our own behavior accordingly, thus supporting social interaction and coherence." Intense emotional experiences may direct people's attention to similar features in the environment and synchronize their brain activity, allowing the experience to be lived in similar ways and thus enabling a shared understanding of the content of another's mind.

These are all examples of synchrony that involves similarities in brain activation patterns during shared mental states, a lining up. On the other hand, two people in conversation with each other might show something more like an improvisational jazz trading, with one person's verbal areas lighting up and then quieting down as the other takes his turn to speak and vice versa.

Research on just this latter topic got a lot of press when the scientists observed that your word production brain regions light up a few seconds in advance of you speaking, leading to all sorts of headlines about "listening is just taking turns preparing to speak."[11] It's possible to interpret this research to mean that we don't really care what the other person is saying, that we're just getting ready for our turn to talk. But rather than demonstrating inattention to what the person is saying, these overlaps may illustrate how conversation involves a mutual experience where your thoughts can influence one another. As social neuroscientist Beau Sievers once said in a conference talk, "conversation is neurofeedback," your brain activity influencing someone else's brain activity and then the interaction looping back to affect you again.

As I'm speaking, you are anticipating what I am going to say next, and you are preparing your response—so even the moments when I'm talking and you're quiet, we're both still contributing. There is also evidence that this predictive synchronization is associated with better comprehension—that is, if your brain activity was similar to Jeb's while you were thinking about what he'd say next, you'd be more likely to easily understand his next utterance.[12] Listening is a sort of rudimentary mind reading.

We are one in conversation together.

Together, this body of research increasingly suggests that the famous quote, "You are the average of the five people you spend the most time with"* is on the right track. The number is suspect, and of course we all vary in the degree to which we are susceptible to influence. But the general idea that your close social others impact how you process the world, the appraisals you make and emotions you have, is supported by this body of work on neural synchrony. If you spend most of your time with other people who tend to make appraisals about a cutthroat world where everyone cheats to get ahead, you'll probably start seeing examples of selfishness everywhere and questioning everyone's motives. If you

---

* This quote is most often attributed to motivational speaker Jim Rohn but appears to be one of those meme-y quotes whose original source is not entirely clear.

spend time with people who care and are kind, recycle and volunteer, you might find yourself a more generous person.

I know who I'd want more as friends anyway.

THE ULTIMATE SYNCHRONIZATION: ROMANTIC LOVE

Before we wrap up, I can't help but ask Patrick about the series he wrote on romantic love: *Humans Are (Blank)-ogamous.*

Patrick unpacked the science of mating and bonding and romantic love to ask: Are we shaped by an evolutionary quest for one true love to bear or help raise our young, or are we instead born to be promiscuous opportunists, craving novelty? What is our "true" nature when it comes to that most basic of collective groups, the first step toward a hive: the romantic couple?

The answer: it's complicated.

According to Patrick, a lot of the answer will probably rely on how we frame our questioning of romantic love. If we're asking whether it is easy and natural for human beings to bond with a single partner who meets all of their sexual, romantic, and companionship needs over the course of an entire lifetime, then the answer is almost undoubtedly no. But if the question is framed instead as whether human beings evolved to be naturally drawn to attractive mating partners, focus attention wholly on them long enough to bond, intertwine their lives and goals, often procreate, and then enjoy the process of early heady intoxication settling down into a warm, supportive companionship, at least for some stretch of time? Then the evidence seems to point to the fact that we likely are, as advice columnist Dan Savage once put it, "monogamish."

This is an intriguing question to me as well, but I am more curious about how romantic love affects our minds and brains in hivemind-like ways, the melding and synchronization that makes us feel like we have literally become one with another. In other words, how it occurs that as novelist David Mitchell writes in *The Bone Clocks*: "Love is a blurring of pronouns."

For the nature of love may be elusive, but instances of it are not—it is an experience found in nearly every culture on the planet. Passionate love is characterized by an obsessive focus of mental attention on another individual, a driving need for physical closeness, feeling like you have a map to the other's mind, and an overidealization of both the partner's attributes and how similar you are to each other. There is also a common sense of involuntariness, of being driven to this person, combined with a desperate sense of temporality to the feelings. As Patrick writes, "Love would not be very good at its job if it was left to rational choice, or if we knew where the off switch was. Instead, it is much more effective because it seems to grab us by the throat." One must act.

All of these experiences indicate a breakdown in the boundaries between self and treasured other, a merging of one's thoughts, goals, time, and priorities, and yes, even a literal dismantling of the physical boundary between self and other. For what are sexual acts but a blurring of the strict confines of one's physical self, a jubilant (if temporary) ceasing of the separate, lonely self, dissolved into blissful union with another?

For a clue to *this* mystery, we can check the *New York Times* op-ed section. A bit before Valentine's Day 2015, the *Times* published an about-to-be-viral essay by Mandy Len Catron called "To Fall in Love with Anyone, Do This."★ In the article, Catron shares that she used a technique studied by famous psychologist Art Aron in 1997 to artificially generate intimacy between strangers. The technique involves pairing off with a partner and asking him or her thirty-six questions that start with the impersonal (*Before making a telephone call, do you ever rehearse what you are going to say?*) and

---

★ Now in book form—called *How to Fall in Love with Anyone: A Memoir in Essays.*

then introduce increasing degrees of intimacy (*If you were to die this evening with no opportunity to communicate with anyone, what would you most regret not having told someone? Why haven't you told them yet?*) A number of the questions also prompt the partners to compliment one another with increasing levels of detail, and to state several "we" statements, for instance, "We are both in a crowded room feeling quite hot."

At the end of the thirty-six questions, the partners are instructed to stare into each other's eyes for four minutes. In typical one-on-one interactions, people tend to repetitively meet eyes and then look away, with the average length of each eye contact episode averaging three to five seconds. Couples who are physically attracted to each other tend to hold each other's gaze both more frequently and for longer periods of time, but still on the order of under ten seconds. As my favorite psychology professor, Michael Fleming, once told our classroom of rapt freshmen, "If someone holds your gaze for longer than a few seconds, watch out—they either want to f$ck you or they want to kill you." So you can imagine that holding a gaze for 240 seconds is . . . intense.

Art Aron performed many versions of this essential research paradigm over the years, and lore has it that two couples from his studies, strangers when they walked into the lab, eventually married. Catron herself ends up in a committed relationship with the friend she dragged into the activity with her.

Accepting for a moment that we believe the strong form of the argument here—that using these thirty-six questions and the eye contact could, in fact, make any two people fall in love—let's consider what the mechanism could be. That is, how could answering a series of questions and awkwardly maintaining eye contact with someone trigger such a complicated hormonal/motivational/emotional/cognitive experience as romantic love, something so vast and complicated that it is steps away from magic?

Turns out, the questions are expertly designed—by expert

Aron and his colleagues, that is—to intentionally begin blurring the boundaries between you and the other person, to serve up on a platter your innermost wishes and memories and fears. They take thoughts and memories and emotions that are usually held inside and only shared with oneself or the closest of the others (*When was the last time you cried by yourself?*) and put them in the hands of this intriguing other, who is in turn sharing his or her innermost thoughts with *you*.

The "we" statements are icing on the cake. Those explicitly ask you to merge your identities and discuss your experiences as if you were one person. "We are feeling hot in this room." There is nothing mystical about these questions. They simply nudge a couple along the way toward developing the blurring of boundaries, the synchronization of thoughts and desires, that would occur much more slowly and naturally in the wild. We could think about these questions through the frame of Patrick's thought clouds. Instead of allowing thought clouds to naturally collide now and then by happenstance, the questions explicitly merge the thought clouds and bind them together for a time, long enough for some degree of melding to take place.

Romantic love, then, may be the extreme version of the same sorts of neural synchronization Thalia Wheatley and others are investigating as the basis of friendship and familiarity with social others.

BIRDS OF A FEATHER

The development of human culture facilitated cooperation with ingroup members. We tend toward homophily—like attracts like—in cultural background, demographics, and perhaps even in how our brains perceive the world. We not only prefer people from our cultural ingroups but also specific people within that ingroup. We choose friends who see the world in similar ways, synchronizing with them. Romantic love may be the peak of this synchronization as we dissolve into each other, no longer separate beings.

But these ingroups are not set in stone. Our ingroups are influenced, as is everything else, by the appraisals we make, the stories we tell ourselves. We may feel more kinship toward the people who share our love of science fiction than the family we grew up in or the religion we were raised in. The ties that bind us to a group that perfectly mirrors our identities at one age may fray as we get older and our interests change. Our appraisals of inclusion, our moral circles, are open to manipulation.

As we'll see next, social media may be having both beneficial and pernicious effects on these social tendencies. They can both build us up and take us down, augmenting both the positives and the negatives of our ultrasocial natures, and the negatives are indeed quite negative.

Winter is here.

WINTER

Chapter Four

Building Us Up and Taking Us Down

Brooklyn, New York

As I approach my hotel, I can't help but notice a swarm of teenage girls a few years older than my daughter milling around outside. They smile and laugh but hold themselves in space with a fraught tension that makes my heart ache. Entering the hotel, I am drawn up short by a bodyguard in a black suit standing stiffly with his arms crossed. I ask him lightly what the deal is with the young crowd. He reluctantly admits that they are there because his client is staying at the hotel, but he can't divulge who that client might be.

I raise an eyebrow and reflect that the young women must have seen on Instagram or Twitter that their idol, whomever he or she may be, was spotted at this locale. What a wonder of this age, that one can track every move of one's celebrity heartthrob through space, see what the celebrity is eating for breakfast and what he or she is sipping at the club and which other shiny famous people are in the celebrity's group selfies. I have one of those "in my day…" moments and roll my eyes at myself.

Of course, one doesn't need social media to encounter celebrities in New York City. On one visit to the city I met a friend for dinner and we unknowingly plunked ourselves down two tables away from the actress who plays Piper on *Orange Is the New Black*.

But I'm here today not to meet a singer or actor but Rana

LaPine, currently project coordinator at First Nations Development Institute. Because she is someone working on collective action and is a millennial who grew up with social technologies, I thought Rana's perspective might be valuable on those topics— particularly because, as you'll see, she is a delightfully sharp contrast from what we've been led to believe is a selfie-obsessed, narcissistic generation. She is also a great example of someone who embodies our principle of *enhance, don't eclipse* in her social media usage. Finally, I knew she had found a rich community online and was active on what she calls "Native Twitter." I was eager to hear her thoughts on Twitter's call-out culture, or the practice of calling people out publicly when their behavior steps outside social norms.

I'm excited for lunch after an early morning wake-up and long drive into the city, and so Rana and I meet up in the hotel restaurant. Her shiny black hair is even longer than I remembered, settling around her waist in a curve, but her warm smile and penchant for dramatic beaded earrings haven't changed at all.

I ask Rana what it was like growing up as a millennial, both in terms of the perception of her generation as "digital natives" and the challenges of coming of age with social media.

Rana tells me that she is often frustrated with the perception of her generation as not working as hard as previous generations, because this theme has recurred as long as there have been generations following one after the other. "I'm sure that in ancient Egypt parents said things like, 'Oh, now that we have papyrus, it is too easy for these kids,'" she says, "'because they don't have to work chiseling rock like I did.'" But Rana also has to admit that she sometimes looks at younger children on their iPads and, before she can squelch it, has a knee-jerk reaction about the fact that at that age she used to work with crayons and paper. I reflect on my thoughts about celebrity Instagram just a few moments earlier and smile.

As we discussed in chapter 2, stereotypes are stories we tell ourselves about people who belong to certain social groups. We have stereotypes about generations as much as we do about other social groupings, an unpleasant side effect of our tendency toward story making.

But part of our hypersociality is also our capacity for community building, and taking our lives online means that we have another medium through which to accomplish the development of these networks.

BUILDING US UP: ENHANCING EXISTING RELATIONSHIPS

Smartphones and social media can build community by drawing us closer to people we already share real-life connections with and by introducing us to whole new communities. We can remain close with our social others even when they are no longer part of our face-to-face lives due to the constraints of physical distance or circumstance. It has been about ten years since I have visited with a married couple I became close to in my graduate school years, but I have felt part of their journey as they moved from spot to spot, started new careers, lost parents, and began a new chapter of their lives as adoptive parents of two beautiful foster children. Before social media, our lives would have diverged instead a decade ago.

Clive Thompson is a journalist and author of *Smarter Than You Think: How Technology Is Changing Our Minds for the Better*, which argues, well, that we're smarter than we think and that technology is changing our minds for the better. He focuses on many topics, from how Google is affecting our memories to how some pioneers are using tiny video recorders to create permanent records of their lives. But most relevant for our concerns is his consideration of how social media changes our understanding of each other.

Thompson points out that one of the easiest and most

prevalent criticisms of social media is that it increases narcissism—
"Honestly, who cares what you had for breakfast?" But contrary
to popular wisdom, Thompson argues that you can't isolate single status updates and judge their value. For their value lies in
the landscape they plot out for you, in the sense of the "ambient
awareness" we develop of the rhythms of our friends' lives. When
we post what we had for breakfast—and what articles we're reading and our frustrations with our commutes—we are establishing a map of our lives and sharing it with our social network.
Thompson says these "ambient tools weave this knowledge into
a tapestry you can glance at, which makes the picture both more
complete and more inviting." It also allows us to notice disrup-
tions in a friend's feed and reach out to them if they are strug-
gling, or to note that a friend has had a lot of successes lately and
arrange to celebrate in person.

A common criticism of social technology and smartphones is
that our mobile devices draw us away from the people we are
with, leaving us not truly present. A viral project by photographer
Eric Pickersgill called *Removed* depicts people in their daily lives
physically present with their friends and families but emotionally
removed due to their attention to their smartphones and other
devices. To drive home the point about physical presence accompanied by emotional absence, he digitally removed the smartphones and devices so that people were ignoring each other to
peer at nothing: a couple in bed lie in rumpled sheets, backs to
each other, staring blankly at their cupped hands; a mom and her
daughter sit on a couch together, empty faces peering down at
their empty laps. The pictures have an eerie resonance, and it is a
fair critique of smartphones and social media. But it is also missing a critical element—what is happening on the smartphone. For
smartphones may remove us from the people we're with, but they
can also connect us with the people we're *not* with. We could take
a competing set of photographs—a grandmother beams down at

a video she just received of her grandchild's first steps, a stressed-looking woman is interrupted in her harried day by a text that makes her stop and blush and bite her lip, a college student bursts out laughing at a meme just sent by a friend.

Friendship and love have always involved an overlapping of our mental interiors. With the ambient awareness that social media brings, we can have an ever-present awareness of our friends and lovers moving through their separate real-life space, eating and creating and thinking and feeling. Indeed, research shows that frequently interacting with social others who are not part of our daily lives can shore up our sense of shared intimacy, acceptance, and belonging.[1] A study of college students in the early days of Facebook found that heavier users had more "social capital," a broad term that refers to resources provided by having social support,[2] and using social media intentionally to connect with people has been found to be associated positively with measures of well-being.[3]

What you do online matters. A large review of this research concluded that *passive* use of social media—so-called lurking, only viewing others' posts and not commenting on them or contributing your own—is negatively associated with well-being.[4] However, *active* use of social media—posting, commenting, sharing—is positively associated with well-being. The negative effects of passive use are tied to envy and social comparison, whereas the positive effects of active use are tied to feelings of social connectedness. Even not all active use is created equal: receiving personalized content (e.g., sharing photos, links, memories) from close friends is predictive of well-being, whereas neither lurking nor receiving "one-click feedback" (that is, "likes" or "favorites") is predictive of well-being.[5]

One of my favorite quotes is from writer Louis Adamic: "My grandfather always said that living is like licking honey off a thorn." I think that our hivemind narrative surrounding smartphones and

71

social media is so focused on the thorn that we have forgotten that the honey exists at all. I recently took a day and tracked all of the social benefits granted me by my smartphone—from my two-year-old niece sending me an audio file telling me that she loved me to organizing a team of six friends to take shifts visiting my dog during my vacation to ordering Mother's Day gifts while in line at the grocery store. With a few clicks we have unprecedented access to vast stores of human knowledge, can engage with scholars and celebrities on Twitter, and are able to maintain social connections despite limitations of time and space. These benefits absolutely come with thorns, many of which we've touched on already and many more of which we'll spend our other winter chapters considering in depth.

But I think it worthwhile to stop now and then to lick the honey.

BUILDING US UP: AUGMENTING

The second way that social technology can build us up is by connecting us to new communities online that we don't have access to in our everyday lives. These communities can fill gaps that exist for any number of reasons, including a lack of people with similar interests around you, sudden moves for work or school, introversion, depression, or other personal attributes that may make it difficult for you to form in-person connections.

Rana has had just this experience. Social media played a large role in helping her form a deeper connection to her cultural heritage as a Native American woman. Both of her grandparents on her father's side are Mohawk and French Canadian, their families having emigrated from Canada a few generations back. Given the cultural climate at the time and the fact that they could pass for white, they lost touch with many of their cultural traditions and instead focused on assimilation and avoiding discrimination.

But through Facebook and Twitter, Rana sought out a network of people who could connect her to those traditions. She found a huge amount of support from other Native people who were happy to answer her questions, link her with resources, and expand her knowledge of her people's history.

"Social media has some real creeps," Rana says, "but you also have elder Native women on Twitter who reach out and teach you about your heritage."

Rana isn't the only person to have found a rich community online, a way of building up her belongingness. Another good friend of mine has similarly found online a social network of supportive others. Her name is Teri Clarke, and she is a speculative fiction writer who sometimes writes under the moniker Zin E. Rocklyn. Teri credits social media for both her current career and for being a lifesaver. "In addition to support and help I've gotten from friends that I've made in real life," Teri told me, "growing up, there was always one definition of blackness that I never really fit into. I was targeted or ignored because of this mismatch between what I was and what was expected of me. But online I found a community of black women who shared my way of looking at the world and who also loved to write horror." Through these social media connections, Teri has been published in an award-nominated anthology called *Sycorax's Daughters*, earned a fellowship to a prestigious writer's workshop, and made connections that directly and indirectly yielded conference presentations, publications in essay collections, and financial support for her work.

Both Rana and Teri's stories reflect an idealized version of what we were promised from the internet and social media—a potential for community building across time and space, allowing for these connections to build based on mutual interest rather than geography or demographics or chance. The popular site called Meetup is designed for just this purpose, to allow strangers with shared interests and hobbies to link up. At its launch, the founders anticipated that most of the linkages would be those involving pretty traditional tastes—dinner parties, touch football games, board games. Instead, the top fifteen interest groups, at least a few years ago, included witches, people raised as Jehovah's Witnesses who had left the religion, and *Star Trek* fans.[6] These are all groups that might identify as countercultural and who may have trouble finding like-minded others in their face-to-face communities. The internet and social media allow for the development of these communities, nestling people who might otherwise be isolated and misunderstood within collectives that understand them.

And as we'll discuss in greater length in the chapters to follow, a sense of belonging is critical to human happiness.

"To some extent," Rana says, "that sense of belongingness to a group is the strongest thing in my life. When I talk to other Native people, there is this underlying reassuring thought that no matter what else happens, you still have your sense of group identity. And it's layered, right? Being Mohawk, and then Haudenosaunee, and then Native American, and then indigenous, and a woman, and young...these identities are in circles. There are moments when I'm really upset about life, or don't want to put the work in, when this sense of being part of something larger gets me out of bed in the morning." We all have our own intersecting identities that shape our experience of the world.

Haudenosaunee or Iroquois culture explicitly asks you to live your entire life considering how everything you do will impact seven generations from now, from how much sugar you put in your tea to what sort of car you drive. It lends an almost exponential sense of belonging that echoes both into the past and into the future.

"That hive mentality, applied to generations seven generations out," Rana says, "gives you a sense of responsibility but it also gives you a sense of hope and belonging. I think that's probably how we survive, right? As bad as things get, all of our ancestors, no matter where you're from, have gone through so much worse. They dealt with colonialism, and with the Holocaust, and with the Khmer Rouge. People are dealing with awful things right now. We get past it somehow, with this sense of community."

Its capacity for community strengthening is an assuredly good aspect of social media, a way that it can build us up.

But can it go too far?

BUILDING US UP TOO MUCH: ECHOING EACH OTHER

An echo chamber forms when we self-sort into groups with members who all share similar opinions, and begin repeating the same ideas back and forth to one another in a way that strengthens those opinions and makes them stronger. One of the most serious problems with never encountering other opinions is that you'll never have cause to question your own beliefs. Confronting counterevidence, weighing it, evaluating it, and then either disregarding it or accommodating your belief systems is the essence of critical thinking.

Cass Sunstein is a legal scholar who worked for several years in the Obama administration and authored several books, including his most recent, *#Republic: Divided Democracy in the Age of Social Media*. Sunstein worries that, increasingly, we don't have enough opportunities to engage with people outside our ingroups, to be challenged by opinions and experiences divergent from our own.

Sunstein points out that we used to have more opportunities for encounters with people from other ages, classes, races, and political parties in the form of public gatherings—through religious organizations, public squares, school events, and so on. But as we increasingly settle into geographical areas with like-minded people, we only ever encounter other versions of ourselves. Social media forces us further into an "architecture of control," something Sunstein calls "a Daily Me." News, friend updates, advertisements: all tailored for you individually. This tailoring happens in part because of your intentional choices—you choose to follow people and celebrities and news organizations who share your views. But the tailoring also happens behind the scenes and without your volition. All of the major social media platforms spend quite a bit of effort developing algorithms whose sole job it is to figure out what you want to see before you see it, because if that sleuthing is successful, you're more likely to click, to hit "like," and to add items to your shopping cart. Together, these volitional and nonvolitional forces increasingly curate our online experiences so that we see just a narrow sliver of the world.

Additionally, in the past most Americans had a common base of shared experiences—in the days of fewer television channels and less programming and no internet, everyone imbibed similar entertainment and similar news, and the fact that the news networks served everyone rather than a targeted political viewpoint meant that news was much more objective. People's reaction to the news certainly still varied, but they weren't fed a steady diet of biased takes; additionally, everyone could talk about what was happening on *M*A*S*H*, *ER*, or *Seinfeld* because everyone had to watch it in real time, and there were only a few channels to choose from.

Sunstein credits these shared experiences as deeply vital to a national sense that although our backgrounds and experiences might be diverse, we are still part of the same community. "Any well-functioning society depends on relationships of trust and reciprocity," he writes, "in which people see their fellow citizens as potential allies, willing to help and deserving of help when help is needed." Now, though, we tend to share experiences only with a small segment of the population whose interests and worldviews mirror our own.

The problem with endlessly associating with people who share your beliefs is a well-demonstrated phenomenon known as group polarization.[7] Group polarization is just like it sounds: groups becoming more polarized over time as a result of their association. If you walk into a town hall or a class meeting and engage in a discussion where everyone is echoing your opinions back at you, you will walk out of that space with a more extreme opinion than when you walked in.

Even worse, as group consensus builds, people stop feeling comfortable expressing a more nuanced or complex take on the issue. People with weaker or opposing opinions sense the leanings of the group and opt for silence rather than risk censure or damage to their reputations. This silence convinces the group at large that there are no opposing beliefs, and everyone moves closer to the loudly vocal opinion through the processes of conformity.

Group polarization is encouraged by a sense of loyalty to group identity. Polarization is both more likely and more extreme if the group shares an identity, a common cause, and/or a sense of solidarity, as seems to be occurring in the United States within our political parties. The feeling that we're dividing further into camps of right and left with nothing but animosity is backed up by polling. In 1960, Sunstein reports, the number of people who would be displeased if their child married outside their political party was 5 percent for Republicans and 4 percent for Democrats—political views just didn't weigh in strongly in terms of life values. In 2010, those numbers had risen to 49 percent of Republicans and 33 percent of Democrats. One can only imagine that the 2016 presidential election has sharply increased the upward trend.

Echo chambers and group polarization present real challenges, but they are still in essence ways that we build community.

But social media doesn't just build us up—it also takes us down.

TAKING US DOWN

From anonymous harassment to call out or take down or outrage culture (shaming people for real or perceived slights or betrayals of social norms) to cyberbullying, the ways that social media can take us down are as varied as the ways it can build us up.

The anonymity that accompanies much of what goes on online can lead to a disinhibition of impulses, a freedom from consequences. This disinhibition can be benign, such as when you work through the stresses in your life by sharing personal reflective essays on a blog; it can also be toxic, such as making hateful comments on social media that you would never utter face-to-face.[8]

Several factors may fuel appalling behavior online. Our online activities can be easily dissociated from our everyday reality, particularly if we are using pseudonyms. There are no consequences, no need to dial back from strong opinions for fear of hurting others when you never have to deal with their responses—you often don't even see their reactions. Later in the book we'll interview clinical psychologist Nnamdi Pole. He refers to how puppies learn to control the strength of their bite through playing with siblings—take a puppy away from its brood too early and it may have biting issues. A similar thing may happen online, where we can bite without ever hearing the resulting yelp.

Second, the asynchronicity of much of what happens online means that even if someone responds with displeasure, it is not immediate and does not influence what you say next. "In a continuous feedback loop that reinforces some behaviors and extinguishes others," psychologist John Suler writes, "moment-by-moment responses from others powerfully shape the ongoing flow of self-disclosure and behavioral expression, usually in the direction of conforming to social norms."[9] As we know, we are deeply synchronous beings—the asynchronicity of the internet can interfere with this natural way of interacting. We depend on subtle cues like frowns, sighs, and head tilts, and adjust what we say next based on this feedback. These cues are entirely lacking online.

Whole online communities can become infected with social norms toward greater aggressiveness through all of the processes we've already reviewed about the development and influence of social norms. They can become part of "how we behave" in this particular group or community.[10]

As an adolescent, Rana and her classmates would log on to a social media site that allowed for anonymous contributions and ask point-blank for honest evaluations of their physical appearance, coolness, and character. The post would be circulated among their classmates, and they would leave anonymous evaluations—often unrelentingly cruel ones. Malice seemed to be the norm, almost the whole point of the exercise. These sites were incredibly popular across the country. I just couldn't wrap my head around why someone would voluntarily subject him- or herself to such animosity.

Rana can't really explain it either. "You know it's going to be bad, right? You know people are going to say all these messed up things, but you just do it anyway…." She shakes her head in recollection. She got the responses she feared. The viciousness of the resulting comments about her appearance and personality weighed her down, made her reevaluate her self-confidence. A close friend of Rana's assured her that the cruelty probably just had to do with internal politics and cliques at their school, that just because people in her class didn't think she was "cute" didn't mean that she wasn't.

This friend convinced Rana to let her post a picture on her public Yahoo Answers account with the question: Do you think my friend is pretty?

I wince in anticipation.

Scores of responses poured in, telling Rana she was disgusting, that she looked like a horse, like a man, that she should seek surgery to alter her appearance. One man took the time to download the pictures, photoshopped them how he thought she should be altered to be prettier, and emailed them to her with the advice to seek a plastic surgeon.

She was in eighth grade.

At thirteen, she didn't have the context of knowing that the only people logging onto Yahoo Answers looking to evaluate the hotness of preteens are disturbed trolls making themselves feel higher status by lowering the status of someone else.

As an adult, Rana now has that perspective. But it took her a long time to get there.

"Even in college, I would randomly remember and feel all of those emotions again. Like—oh, my god. Over sixty people on the internet took the time to tell me I was a hideous monster." She takes a sip of coffee and shrugs. "When you are young, you somehow falsely believe that the internet will be a nice place. And then you get older and you get death threats on Twitter and you think: All right. I know now this isn't a kind space."

I feel queasy. Rana is too close to a surrogate daughter for me to feel anything else.

But Rana seems to have reached some acceptance of the event. While it does still sting a bit, she doesn't seem any more upset by the memory than I am when I recall my preteen crush saying at a party with the entire junior high present, "Sure, I'll play Spin the Bottle, but not if it lands on Sarah," or when another cute boy rushed me off the high diving board at our local pool by snarking, "Hurry it up, Tubs." We could spend all night tracing one another's scars from what Barbara Ehrenreich calls the crushing weight of other people's judgments. Online or off, part of our hypersociality is the pain we inevitably inflict upon each other.

Of course, both Rana's and my experiences were mostly isolated incidents in our childhood. Organized, ongoing cyberbullying campaigns can cause devastating harm[11]—as can face-to-face bullying.

Along with cyberbullying, another way that social media can take us down is when we become targets of public outrage. Moral outrage is an intriguing phenomenon, and one that has clear hive-mind signposts. It serves to underscore and reinforce social norms and also to cement ingroup bonding. When the target is deserving of moral outrage (that is, has committed a social wrong that is harmful to another person or to the group), the shaming associated with moral outrage can benefit cooperation among the group, and the person who initiated the shaming can experience a boost in status.[12]

What has happened with the advent of social media, of course, is that all of these aspects of the outrage—its scope, the shame, the consequences, and the boost in status—can be massive, can go viral, sometimes with truly destructive consequences.

Expressing outrage in person and following through with physical or social consequences requires being physically proximal to the person being shamed, and also requires a fair application of effort. Not so online, where shaming is just a few keystrokes away and one does not have to observe the ramifications on the shamed, who remain just an avatar.[13] These developments have led some to speculate that outrage begets outrage, and that people are more and more willing to indulge, leading to the Twitter joke "So, what are we angry about today?"[14]

The more outraged a person gets, the farther and wider his or her message might spread through social networks, which might reinforce people to default to extremes. Social psychologist Jay Van Bavel and his research team gathered a huge database of social media posts about polarizing political issues (e.g., same-sex marriage, gun control) and found that using moral-emotional words increased the tendency for the message to spread, with a 20 percent boost for each moral-emotional word used.[15] They labeled this a "moral contagion" effect. Unsurprisingly, the moral contagion appeared to be restricted to within groups rather than across them—moral outrage among liberals stayed within liberal networks, and the same for conservative outrage.

Fascinatingly, other research indicates that when presented with viral comments condemning an individual post, people begin to rate the shamed less negatively and the people doing the shaming less positively, as they apparently begin to sympathize with the person being piled upon.[16]

So really, no one makes it out of an internet shame spiral for the better.

I ask Rana if she'll talk a bit about call-out culture on Twitter, the encouragement of tweets that take people down or shame them, calling them out for poor behavior.

In terms of people who have crossed serious lines, offended in ways that are explicit or intentionally malicious, Rana views call outs as part of how a society functions. "People saying and doing racist things and losing their jobs and scholarships because of it," she reflects, "I think is just a lesson in paying consequences." Often the people who commit these acts have to that point led a life of few such consequences. We have social norms surrounding certain behaviors—including racism and dehumanization and sexual harassment—to protect people, and these social norms being enforced are part and parcel of being a community.

On the other hand, Rana has observed cases where someone has made a mistake and is willing to learn from it, but the internet mob refuses to allow room for that growth. Some of it gets pretty ugly pretty quickly, including threats of violence; often threats will include "doxing" the offended, which means revealing their identity and personal contact information for more targeted harassment.

In 2015, popular actress Kerry Washington of *Scandal* and *Django Unchained* fame tweeted that fellow actress Kate Winslet was her "spirit animal." Rana replied directly to Kerry's tweet, letting her know that the term referred to an ancient Native spiritual tradition and that using it colloquially and jokingly could be construed as offensive to indigenous beliefs.

Kerry responded to Rana in a friendly and open manner. The rest of Twitter was not so friendly and open. People labeled Rana a snowflake, assumed she was a white woman speaking for Natives, and accused her of being antiblack. People threatened to find her in real life and visit violence upon her. She had to make her Twitter profile private. She still gets messages about that one tweet, years later.

She doesn't view her tweet as a call out, but rather as a respectful interchange. She didn't post Kerry's tweet to any message boards, or quote-tweet it, or otherwise call attention to it. She merely tried to offer ingroup expertise to someone who had unintentionally crossed a line many Native people aren't comfortable with.

People with good intentions nonetheless come into conflict with players who have ugly intentions. Twitter in particular is plagued by noxious people spending their leisure time making other people miserable (and bots programmed to mimic them). These trolls disproportionately target women and people of color, and women of color most of all. Several celebrities have been chased off Twitter after long and exceptionally hateful campaigns against them—for example, Leslie Jones after receiving racist, sexist, death threat–filled targeted harassment for her role in the all-female reboot of *Ghostbusters*, and Kelly Marie Tran after she played Rose in *The Last Jedi*. Incidents like these have led many to feel that Twitter is broken in essential ways, and that the platform is responding too slowly to address deep programmatic issues that threaten their users' safety and well-being.

In addition to echo chambers and viral shame spirals and harassment, false information spreading on social media is another disadvantage in taking our social lives online. We could spend a whole book on the topic. But since we have other concerns and many other people have indeed written books on the topic, let's consider the issue briefly here by checking back in with our earlier expert, Kimberly Norris Russell of evolutionary biology fame.

One of the challenges of being a cooperative species—where "I scratch your back if you'll scratch mine" reciprocity is the norm—is dealing with those who either hoard (take an unfair share of the resources; see liberal attacks on "the 1 percent") or freeload (take benefits without contributing work; see conservative attacks on people abusing social services). Kim explains that in most cooperative species, like vampire bats and wasps, cheaters are actively recognized and punished and so the system remains stable.

Recognition and punishment of cheaters requires recognition of individuals and also repeated interactions with people within a group. But social technologies have us writing our culture on a global scale, anonymously, with very few consequences for those who violate the rules of the cooperative system. Social media has ushered in an era where the mechanisms by which to evaluate and judge information and to punish perpetrators of false information haven't grown apace with the expansion of our social networks.

I ask Kim about our capacity to adapt to this new medium.

"It's not that technology is bad or that we can't adapt," Kim says, "but there is a time lag between new developments and our adaptation." We evolved systems for detecting and punishing cheaters and also for evaluating trustworthiness in others (e.g., facial expressions, perhaps even smell), but these tools are reliant on face-to-face interactions in small-scale societies. They didn't evolve for Twitter. Kim believes that false information benefiting certain groups is a form of cheating, and as such lying typically would be punished in a reciprocity-based social system.

"If you don't have safeguards to weed out liars and cheaters," Kim says, "you are ripe for invasion by self-interested parties—they will win. They can manipulate or even topple the entire system."

Yikes.

Some of these problems need to be solved by the tech companies themselves, and they will probably only do so if enough people in their user communities make noise and demand—or legislate—change. We have failed to develop regulatory safeguards to protect ourselves in the face of the rapid growth of our social networks, and since the social networks are unlikely to go anywhere, we need to act quickly and decisively in order to protect people. An encouraging example is that at the time of this writing, YouTube declared that they will no longer recommend videos that advance conspiracy theories, even though they make more money when they do so. We need major companies to make these sorts of pro-social decisions even when it hurts the bottom dollar.

In the meantime, there's no denying the stark ugliness that lurks in some of the dark corners of the digital world.

Considered collectively, the ways that social technology can both build us up and take us down suggest that taking our social communities online holds the potential to amplify all of our existing social tendencies, both the prosocial and the antisocial.

Summing up the existing literature on online technology and sociability and echoing our *enhance, don't eclipse* principle, psychologists Adam Waytz and Kurt Gray write, "Online technology enhances sociability when people use it to bolster or create relationships with prospective or existing offline friends, but it is associated with diminished sociability when used excessively—unless face-to-face engagement does not come easily."[17]

We'll revisit that surprising last point in chapter 7—as well as the question of whether for some people, excessive use of social media could pose a host of personal problems, from depression to addiction to distraction.

HIVING TOGETHER, HIVING APART

As we head out, Rana thinks to ask the young crowd still waiting for a glimpse of their celebrity whom they are waiting for, and a few girls enthusiastically share that it is singer Shawn Mendes. True to the day's generational theme, I have never heard of their idol.

We meet up that evening with some friends at a rooftop bar. The enclosed part of the bar has floor-to-ceiling glass windows that show a marvelous view of the surrounding city, all tall sky-scrapers and twinkly lights reflected in the river. We order some drinks and take them outside, the air surprisingly warm for it being early winter.

Our friend Jeff asks if any of us have visited the World Trade Center memorial. None of us have. He gestures to the horizon in the direction of the memorial. "It is surprisingly moving," he muses. "I had seen pictures of it beforehand but seeing it in person was another thing entirely." He says the water flows continuously into two pools with voids at the center, creating a feeling of loss that never ends. He pauses, frowns. "But somehow, the steadiness of the water also creates a profound sense of peace."

I watch the lights of the skyline sparkle in the general direc-tion of the memorial and reflect on the tragedies that occur when we split into warring tribes. I think of a quote I love from biolo-gist and writer Adam Rutherford's book *A Brief History of Every-one Who Ever Lived*, which is an impressive overview of human genetics and ancestry:

> The truth is that we all are a bit of everything, and we come from all over. Even if you live in the most remote parts of the Hebrides, or the edge of the Greek Aegean, we share an ancestor only a few hundred years ago. A thou-sand years ago, we Europeans share all our ancestry. Triple that time and we share all our ancestry with everyone on Earth. We are all cousins, to some degree. I find this pleas-ing, a warm light for all mankind to share. Our DNA threads through all of us.

How can we appraise ourselves as one giant hive rather than a collection of fractious clans? How can we achieve an appraisal like Rutherford's while also appreciating the sense of belonging and cherished cultural traditions that our ingroups lend us, of the sort that Rana has experienced? I wonder if it is pure naïveté to think we can have both, that we can embrace our moral circles, our thresholds of inclusion, without ostracizing or treating poorly those not in our inner circles of inclusion.

To start to answer these questions, I head south to a site of clashing ingroups that famously ended in tragedy: Charlottesville, Virginia.

Chapter Five

Selfing and Othering

Charlottesville, Virginia

During the first snowfall of the year, I lace up my sneakers and head out for a run in Charlottesville, Virginia. I'm several states away from my home state of Massachusetts, but I know from social media that snow is falling back home, too, as well as in many other spots. It feels unifying to know that people from so many different parts of the country are looking out their windows to the same soft, drifting flakes.

Charlottesville is a quintessential college town, and so it seems like every other shop I run by sells roasted coffee or craft beer, with a few dumpling shops thrown in for good measure. I am out for a run for the usual reasons of death-avoidance and contin-ued jeans-fitting, but I also have an ulterior motive. I slow down as I approach Emancipation Park, recently renamed from its past moniker of Lee Park. The dual names for the park exemplify the so-called culture war plaguing America. The park was a hot spot during a recent period of unrest and violence in this usually tran-quil town.

In tension affecting multiple parts of the Southern United States, communities struggled with deciding whether or not to remove war memorials lionizing Civil War figures who had fought to hold on to a way of life that included slavery. Some people in these communities felt that these statues were part of the South's history and that to remove them was to attempt an erasure of this history. Others felt that to pepper one's town with memorials dedicated to people who fought to keep their fellow human beings as slaves was essentially enshrining white supremacy.

In the midst of this ongoing controversy, the Charlottesville City Council voted to remove two statues of generals who had risen to fame fighting for the confederacy: Robert E. Lee and Thomas "Stonewall" Jackson. One local resident and white nationalist, Jason Kessler, became particularly fired up. He teamed up with Richard Spencer, a national figure proudly advocating white supremacy and a spokesperson for the alt-right movement. Following a few smaller, earlier events and also some candlelit vigils organized by counterprotesters, Kessler began organizing an August rally that he dubbed Unite the Right, under the auspices of staging a protest in support of the Lee statue.

The Friday night before the rally at Emancipation Park, the Unite the Right group held an illegal march at the University of Virginia. Across the nation, and I imagine the world, we watched in disbelief as images of young white men in khakis and polo shirts carrying torches spread across the web, their faces contorted in rage as they shouted Nazi slogans such as "Blood and soil" and "You will not replace us; Jews will not replace us." In response, a group of antifascist activists linked arms and shouted their own slogans in return. The two groups began taunting each other and wrestling over the torches. People began to punch, to kick, to use their bodies to bruise and scrape and harm the bodies of their opposition. Police eventually disbanded the groups until the next morning.

Since the Saturday event was preplanned and had gained such national attention, representatives from the alt-right and the antifascist movement descended on Charlottesville. Notoriously, the event quickly devolved into tragedy. Multiple people suffered injuries, and activist Heather Heyer was mowed down and killed by a car driven by a member of the alt-right. Viewing the horrific images in the national press, one is left with the disquieting feeling that human beings are naturally savage, that crowds of oppositional belief systems are destined to erupt in violence, that our loyalty to our personal ideological tribes does indeed put us in opposition to other ideological tribes.

But the independent report on the events commissioned by the city of Charlottesville is full of surprising details in which both sides of the conflagration seemed eager to avoid violence and unrest.[1] At multiple points, activists from both sides openly implored the police to intervene. Alt-right national organizer Chris Cantwell told Kessler that he would not participate in the event unless local law enforcement was apprised of their plans. The report seems to lay a large part of the blame on local law enforcement and its leadership, who were quoted by a witness as saying that the quicker things degenerated into violence, the sooner they could declare the event an unlawful gathering and end it.

This snowy morning, the infamous statue of Robert E. Lee is covered in a black tarp that looks like a giant's trash bag and surrounded by orange temporary fencing. I can almost see overlaid on the quiet park the opposing crowds of alt-right and antifa, the clouds of pepper spray that periodically plumed through the air, the too-passive police presence arranged around the periphery, the ugly shouting and kicking and hatred.

But I didn't come to Charlottesville to visit this site.

Rather, I came to interview someone who might help us understand it.

SELFING

I meet Jim Coan, social neuroscientist and professor of psychology at the University of Virginia, in a local coffeeshop. Jim is dressed casually, which is also how he dresses for the big conference talks I've seen him give—warm sweater, blondish-grayish hair back in a ponytail, worn-in Converse sneakers that remind me of my favorite incarnation of *Doctor Who*.

Outside, the snow falls gently. Inside, silent University of Virginia students tap away at their computers and flip through notes, preparing for final exams. As we settle in, Jim shares that it has been an especially busy week, in part because he just received a large grant to fund a new wing of his research. He expresses mixed feelings about receiving the grant. "I'm just so lazy," he says. "I just want to play with my kids and work on my podcast."

It takes me a minute to reply because I'm a little stunned. To prepare for this interview I had spent some time reviewing Jim's website to download his latest scientific papers. His bio on the front page made my mouth go dry with jealousy. Professor, neuroscientist, consultant. Recipient of early career awards from several major scientific organizations. Author of books and edited series and more than eighty scientific publications. Work covered in *Science*, *Nature*, and the *New York Times* and on NPR. All that and the kids and the podcast, too. On what planet could this man be perceived as *lazy*?

But then I recall an insight I had years ago about human beings. Namely, that our greatest fear about ourselves is most often actually our greatest strength. My most disciplined friend's greatest fear is that she is undisciplined. My most competent friend's greatest fear is that he is incompetent. I once told this pet theory to my sister-in-law Kathie while spending the weekend at her house with my cousin Elizabeth. I asked my sister-in-law what *her* greatest fear about herself was and she hardly had to think for a second before responding, "I worry that I'm a f$cking asshole." My cousin and I laughed out loud at her, it was so ridiculous. Later that night we nestled the kids into bed and then settled out on the porch, drinking wine and watching the stars and telling old family stories. It was late August and the night air held a bite that heralded the coming autumn. Kathie ducked inside the house, retrieved two down camping blankets, and returned to wordlessly tuck them around me and Eliz, taking extra care to cover our bare toes. "You are such a f$cking asshole," I told her, and the three of us sailed into helpless giggles.

I have no data to support this theory, but my suspicion is that we spend endless resources and time trying to convince ourselves and the world that we *aren't* our greatest fear. All of this time and these resources mean that we shore up that very side of ourselves until it becomes one of our greatest virtues, almost like a clam worries away at an irritant until it forms a lustrous pearl.

The podcast Jim longs to work on full-time is called *Circle of Willis*, after the arterial circuit at the base of the brain that supplies it with blood and that looks for all the world like a little cartoon man. Jim's goal for the podcast is to humanize scientists—giving them space to tell their life stories, and him space to query their latest passions and to laugh with them frequently. His delight is evident in pretty much every moment of every episode.

The research that takes up some of Jim's podcast time considers how our close social others become absorbed into our sense of self at the level of the brain. Jim believes that when we reach a certain level of familiarity with our close social others, to some extent our neurons don't know the difference between ourselves and other people. He calls this his Social Baseline Theory, and it argues that human beings evolved not to be alone but to be together.[2] He believes that one problem with much of psychological research is that we spend so much time studying individuals. We cleave people from their social networks and put them in research studies in which we assume we're studying the basic level of humanness, but we are incorrect. We have as a result of this cleaving already introduced a level of artificiality to the proceedings.

One of the reasons we see strong ties between social isolation and poor health measured in all sorts of ways (heart disease, cancer, depression, hypertension...the list goes on and on) is that our brains rely on those social resources to be present and to provide resources. Our brains do this, Jim argues, by including familiar others in our neural representations of self, in our brains' mapping of what is self and what is other, what is us and what is our friends.

It all sounds very sweet and touchy-feely—our brains bundling beloved others into our very neural map of our own bodies—but Jim developed his theory in a less than endearing way. Namely, he started sticking people in long, dark, metal tubes and electroshocking them. He wanted to create a situation in which his participants were truly under threat, so that he could activate those regions of the brain that respond when you are experiencing physical and mental duress. Threat of shock seemed like a method that would get his participants' brains into the right zone, as it were.

In Jim's classic research, while the participants lay in the neuroimaging scanner, they viewed a series of Xs and Os on a screen.[3] When a blue O appeared, they knew they were safe from shock. When a red X appeared, they knew there was a 20 percent chance that they would experience a slight electric shock to their ankle. Critically, in some of these trials, the participants' hands were held either by their spouse or by a stranger. Jim found that when he compared the threatening trials with and without handholding, the neural regions associated with threat processing were significantly less active in the handholding condition, and particularly less so for spouse handholding than stranger handholding.

Jim has since replicated in several subsequent studies this essential finding that handholding of loved ones is linked to reduced threat processing, and in some of the studies the social partners were not touching the participant but merely present. Collectively, this research suggests that when our loved ones are near, we react less to stress—and critically, we are less likely to activate structures in the brain that govern our release of stress hormones.

In his book *Tribe: On Homecoming and Belonging* journalist Sebastian Junger draws on anthropology and psychology and his own experiences living with soldiers in battle to argue that human beings crave working in groups on collective efforts. He argues that many aspects of modern human societies neglect this deep need. This neglect, he believes, is the root cause of the perplexing growth of poor physical and mental health in Western societies as they grow wealthier and cover more of their members' basic needs for food and shelter—their physical needs are met, but the growing focus on individualism means their psychological needs are left unfulfilled. Junger reviews data that suicide rates go down when countries go to war and that people living through natural disasters report unexpected bonding and a feeling of immediacy and oneness. He argues that veterans coming back from war suffer less because of the trauma of their war experiences and more from the loss of social connectedness and purpose that greets their transition back to ordinary living.★

A modern soldier returning from combat—or a survivor of Sarajevo—goes from the kind of close-knit group that humans evolved for, back into a society where most people work outside the home, children are educated by strangers, families are isolated from wider communities, and personal gain almost completely eclipses collective good.... Whatever the technological advances of modern society—and they're nearly miraculous—the individualized lifestyles that those technologies spawn seem to be deeply brutalizing to the human spirit.

★ My friend and research psychologist Terri Krangel Pogoda studies traumatic brain injury in veterans, and she might disagree that lack of connection is the *primary* cause of depression and PTSD in veterans.

This raises a natural question in my mind. Since Jim has only ever studied pairs of people, how does he see his work pertaining to the larger collective? Are some of the group phenomena we've discussed so far—social contagion, ecstatic group ritual, neural synchrony—subserved by the same sorts of processes that yield one-to-one influence?

Jim thinks that his work on dyads informs a lot of group phenomena and that the underlying emotional, cognitive, and neural processes are likely the same. He believes it all comes down to understanding how the brain does *familiarity*. Or as he puts it to me, "Why are you not just some hermit crab to me? Why are you familiar?" Familiar, that is, both as a fellow human being—versus a crawly critter—and as a specific human being whom he knows personally and has some degree of warm feelings about.

We take the concept of familiarity for granted. You know that when you encounter another human being a few times, you will remember them and can predict at some level how they'll react to you. But familiarity goes much deeper than that and is intimately intertwined with how our brains construe a sense of self. How an organism determines what is *self* and what is *other* is an essential problem that an organism needs to solve, and not just at the level of the brain.

Jim continues: "I think that there is a principle here. The biological organism has to exist out in the world where it can't control things, so it has to draw boundaries. Human beings have this expanded, fluid, flexible way of determining what is self and what is other. We experience that subjectively as familiarity, and as preference."

Sometimes we do become familiar with someone and reject them, perceive them both as familiar and unliked. But this is pretty rare. In fact, a classic experience in basic psychology is called the mere exposure effect, and its definition is right in its name: merely being exposed to something a few times influences your feelings about it so that you are more likely to rate it positively—even if you have no recollection of having encountered it before.[4]

All of this research seems really encouraging and optimistic, the sunnier side of human social psychology, and I'm almost reluctant to ask Jim about the nastier stuff. But as we're swamped daily with news of hate crimes and modern-day genocide, of systems that close in to protect the powerful when they've committed crimes, of the multitude of horrors enacted when we become "us" versus "them," the conversation seems unavoidable. Because, of course, another appraisal we can make is that a person is outside of our moral circles, our thresholds of inclusion.

That they are Other.

When we form social identities, part of defining who we are is defining who we are not. If you think about it, even the simple act of defining a social group excludes other people from that group. Defining (biological) family leaves out people lacking shared genes, marrying someone traditionally declares all other people to be excluded from your sexual life, and joining a sports team declares your opposition to other athletes in your league.[5]

We are more likely to point the finger of blame at people from outgroups versus people from ingroups, to scapegoat them. Research shows that temporarily frustrating people leads to their willingness to disparage another, and that activating people's terror about death tends to amplify ingroup tendencies (like patriotism) and also amplify outgroup hostility (like xenophobia).[6]

Even more worryingly, if we appraise someone as Other, we risk going one step further and indulging in the darkest appraisal of all.

THE DARKEST APPRAISAL: DEHUMANIZATION

Dehumanization refers to a very specific appraisal that has been integrally tied to the worst acts committed by humanity. It occurs when we perceive people belonging to another social group as being less than human, not possessing the full mental capacities we associate with humanness. Dehumanization depicts the outgroup as having lower intellect, less ability to empathize, poorer control over behavior, more aggressive impulses, and/or more "bestial" qualities. These appraisals can lead to visceral dislike—it is no coincidence that dehumanizing language often associates the outgroup with things that disgust us, like cockroaches and excrement—but it also can lead to a casual indifference, a lack of empathy. If these other beings aren't like us, if they're as removed from us as flies, then what does it matter if we swat them out of existence? As playwright George Bernard Shaw reportedly once wrote, "The worst sin toward our fellow creatures is not to hate them, but to be indifferent to them. That's the essence of inhumanity."

Scour the vilest moments in human history and you will find dehumanizing language, talk that likens entire social groups to rodents or insects or creatures we associate with decay and disease and dirty conditions. A Spanish colonizer: "I took no more notice of a hundred armed Indians than I would have of a handful of flies."[7] An English bushranger would just "as leave shoot [Tasmanians] as so many sparrows."[8] In Nazi Germany, the government justified mass extermination of more than six million human beings because they were *lebensunwetes Leben*—"lives unworthy of living."[9] In Rwanda, prior to the mass genocide that left an estimated half a million to a million Tutsi people dead, the victims were compared to tall trees needing to be mowed down.[10]

But dehumanization is not isolated to extreme points in our history. It is an active process at work in contemporary society. Nour Kteily is a psychologist at Northwestern University who finds that a shocking number of Americans are all too willing to endorse the idea that some human beings are more human than others.[11] He and his collaborators use a tool called the "Ascent of Man," and you can check it out below. In a series of studies, they asked participants to move a slider to indicate where they felt different groups of human beings rate in their humanness on a scale of 0 to 100.

Fig. 1. The "ascent of humans" measure of blatant dehumanization. Scores are provided using a slider scale ranging from 0 to 100, with 0 corresponding to the left side of the image (i.e., quadrupedal human ancestor) and 100 corresponding to the right side of the image ("full" modern-day human). Although this popular image is not a scientifically accurate representation of how evolution works, it nevertheless captures lay conceptions of evolution as linear progression. This figure was originally published in Kteily, Bruneau, Waytz, & Cotterill (2015).

Nour Kteily

Typically, Americans rate other "Americans" and also "Europeans" pretty highly in their evolved humanness, with average scores in the 90s. But the same groups of participants are all too willing to give some other groups lower scores, especially Muslims and Mexican immigrants, rating them as less evolved, less human. For Muslims, Kteily's lab sees scores typically in the 70s, with about a quarter of the sample rating them lower than 60 percent evolved.

Not content with demonstrating that dehumanization occurs, Kteily and colleagues also investigated the implications of these lower ratings of humanness. Not surprisingly, people who are willing to slide the lever lower for Muslim people are more likely to blame the entire group for the actions of a few extremists, more desiring to restrict immigration, and more likely to favor societies where some groups have more power than others. They are also more willing to endorse extreme, xenophobic statements such as "Muslims are a potential cancer to this country" and "The attacks on San Bernardino prove it: Muslims are a threat to people from this country."

All of this research explains why psychologists are so alarmed when the so-called leader of the free world frequently engages in dehumanizing language, characterizes entire countries as "shit-holes," calls black women "dogs," claims that illegal immigrants "infest" our country, or says of gang members, "These aren't people. These are animals." (One should note that dehuman-izing language is not restricted to the right side of the political spectrum: Hillary Rodham Clinton was also sharply criticized for her depiction in the 1990s of young black men in inner cities as "super-predators.") This concern is not politically correct nit-picking: it reflects a profound desire to avoid new eras of atrocity in our own country.

More subtle mechanisms within social bonding can encourage dehumanization. In one research study, participants who were assigned to walk in step (e.g., synchronize) with the experimenter were more willing to kill insects when instructed to than those who hadn't engaged in such motor synchrony,[12] and those who were assigned to shuffle plastic cups in time with other partici-pants were more likely to follow similar instructions to blast a group with painful noises.[13] Psychologist Mina Cikara sums up this body of research: "When people in groups coordinate their behavior, individuals often end up doing and saying things that violate their personal beliefs, desires, and moral standards."[14] Supporting this view, research indicates that genocide and out-group violence happens more often in cultures where obedience to authority and conformity are high, where people are more bee-minded.[15]

I remind Jim of this research and ask him for his take on how it fits in with his Social Baseline Theory—whether he believes that getting closer to those who are more like us, our ingroups, can actually make us *less* tolerant, more divided, to increase the extent to which we view outgroup members as less than human.

Jim has been shaking his head as I speak. "I am going to say something potentially controversial here," he begins. "I think that is mostly a folk theory. I don't think the data over the past several decades actually do much to support it. In fact, what you see as outgroup dehumanization is usually a reframing of an ingroup preference. When you pit groups against each other and then introduce a sense of danger, people *don't* tend to devote resources to going after the outgroup. What they actually tend to do is to devote more resources to their ingroup. So they become more groupish, but it is more inwardly focused than outwardly focused." Remember, our ingroups not only are how we socially identify ourselves, they become incorporated into our brain's sense of what is self and what is other. For this reason, when others within our group feel threatened, we do, too—this idea will come back to us in a few chapters, when we consider the effect of hate crimes on marginalized groups.

I'm intrigued but still unconvinced. I ask Jim specifically about some work by his fellow social neuroscientist Lasana Harris, author of *Invisible Mind: Flexible Social Cognition and Dehumanization*. Harris argues that we flexibly either attribute or withhold "social cognition" (thoughts, feelings, complex motivations) to or from different social groups. Harris was curious about the extent to which people vary in their activation of regions of the brain known to facilitate thinking about other people and their interior mental lives when asked to consider different categories of human beings. For instance, might a middle-class person activate these regions less at the sight of a homeless person crumpled on the sidewalk than they would at the sight of someone upright and dressed like them, or someone who appeared to be a drug addict?[16] Harris's data answered yes.

Research by other investigators asked participants in a neuroimaging scanner to watch hands being either stabbed or touched. These hands were described as belonging to people of various religious belief systems—Christian, Muslim, Jewish, Hindu, Scientologist, and atheist. As the authors hypothesized, areas of the brain related to empathy activated less when watching people of other faith groups than the participants' own being harmed.[17] Critically, though, this effect was observed even for the atheists—so it really isn't about thinking your particular group is somehow special in the eyes of your deity. It is all about ingroups.

"Right!" Jim exclaims, victoriously. I'm confused until he continues: "But that's *not* dehumanizing. That's de-selfing."

It isn't that the person under threat is less human than you, it is just that they don't belong to your identity in the same way that someone from your ingroup does. Jim's appraisal of these results flip them on their head: you aren't actively excluding some people—you just *are* actively including some select others. It is a subtle but important difference from Harris's perspective, which is more that we selectively reward certain human beings with full humanity and social cognitive skills and deny those fully human attributes to others. Here, Jim argues that we see everyone as human, yet we see only select humans as actively part of our own selves.

Jim's thoughts here echo those of Sarah Blaffer Hrdy and Patrick Clarkin—that our evolved natures are deeply cooperative and push us toward the development of ingroups, but that outgroup hostility and violence is much more recent, and perhaps more of a cultural invention than an evolved biological one. Human beings are most certainly capable of great violence and hostility. But perhaps this tendency is not coded into our essential nature—perhaps it has more to do with our culture, our appraisals, than our instincts.

THE CLOAK OF ANONYMITY AND THE LIMITATIONS OF SUNLIGHT

As we discussed in the previous chapter, anonymity online and off can encourage the sense that we are free from the possible social consequences of our behavior, and may make us even more susceptible to the influence of social context. These factors probably influenced the decision making of the white nationalists who swarmed into Charlottesville in 2017.

But in this connected age, our perceived anonymity is often the thinnest of veils.

Witness the experience of University of Nevada student Peter Cytanovic. In the most famous of the images to come out of the Charlottesville march, he was the central figure, his firelit face contorted in rage as he shouted along with racist slogans, torch in hand. According to interviews he gave after the event, he felt that his motivations in going to the rally were good.[18] He thought it would be "lighthearted" and affirmational, underscoring "white pride"—he claims that he is "pro-white" without being anti any other group. When people started chanting, he reports that he was simply unintentionally swept up by the group's energy, part of the overall motivated collective. Likely, Cytanovic felt divorced from his ordinary everyday self. "I hope that the people sharing the photo are willing to listen," he told a reporter from a local TV station, "that I'm not the angry racist they see in that photo." This, despite the fact that he was at a white nationalist rally holding a torch and shouting Nazi slogans.

Twitter quickly went to work and identified him and many of the others in the photos, and moral outrage and social norm enforcement did their jobs. Reportedly, one depicted supremacist lost his job, another was disowned by family, and Cytanovic himself became a frequent target of protests at his university. But the state university worked hard to keep him on campus, protecting what they saw as his First Amendment rights. In a TEDx event on free speech,[19] Nevada deputy district attorney Orrin Johnson explained their rationale: "His ideas, like all disgusting things, only grow and thrive in dark, dank and hidden-away places. We want to hear his ideas put up against better ones, because sunlight is the best disinfectant. Seeing it, exposing it, examining it, laughing at it, that's how you make ideas like this lose power."

But is it?

Maybe. Or could it be that like the people stealing petrified wood from the forest because they realized that other people were doing it, exposing these ideas to sunlight means that more of the dark, disgusting creature-thoughts slither out of their dank places?

Next we're going to travel even farther south to Tallahassee and talk to someone whose take on ingroups and outgroups is a little more pessimistic than Jim's—perhaps because she is a historian rather than a psychologist.

Chapter Six

The Enemy Inside

Tallahassee, Florida

Confession: I'm afraid of the dark. Always have been. You don't know what might be lurking in that inky absence. It is a vacuum that my mind tends to fill with shadowy others with malign intent, possibly with preternaturally long teeth and a sharp weapon, and almost definitely a grin that is just a bit too filled with glee.

I've long been fascinated by what our fears tell us about our humanity. In graduate school a friend and I taught a series of college classes on the psychology of popular film, and through that work I started to suspect that most horror isn't actually about the scary stuff on the surface at all—the serial killers, the madman in a mask, the vengeful dead—but rather about our deep-seated fear of insanity. Specifically, the form of insanity in which our reality becomes somehow unhinged from the hivemind, from consensus reality.

I noticed that nearly every horror movie I could find had a strikingly similar moment about two-thirds of the way through when the protagonist, bedeviled by whatever particular flavor of devil was haunting them, sought out a friend or lover or sibling and uttered some variant of the line, "I know this sounds crazy, but—" But I can talk to the dead. But I think my child may be the Antichrist. But there is a burned man with a metal claw chasing me in my dreams, and I think he can kill me there. Most often, the main character is not believed by this supportive but highly skeptical significant other. Most often, that main character goes on feeling paranoid and alone, ostracized from the hive.

I also think that while the primary fear underlying all of this horror is actually our fear of losing touch with reality, the choice of monster still holds symbolic meaning.* Aliens are, easily enough, about our xenophobia. Ghosts about our fear of death and the afterlife. Vampires about our fear of our own bodily appetites.

The symbolic meaning of zombies always eluded me, though. They always just seemed...sort of gross. Oozing everywhere, craving brains.

But in early February, while the bitter cold still has its grip on New England, I head south to Tallahassee, Florida, to talk with Kelly Baker, a religious historian. I am here principally to talk with her about her research on the Ku Klux Klan and how it can inform our understanding of ingroups and outgroups, dehumanization, and social media's role in exacerbating extremism—but as it turns out, she is also a zombie expert. I have followed Kelly for some time on Twitter, mostly due to her role as editor of the online publication *Women in Higher Education*. In addition to her book on the Klan and one on zombies, she is the author of two well-received and thoughtful books about her complicated relationship with academia and some of the systemic problems the academy faces.

Kelly joins me at my hotel, a funky spot in downtown Tallahassee with dewdrop chandeliers and slate walls. To my winter-weary delight, the lodging also has a rooftop bar that serves food. We head up there, and I'm momentarily unable to focus because the feel of sun and a gentle wind on my bare skin is almost deliriously

---

* Much like my theory about our greatest fears turning into our greatest strengths, these ideas are all playful thought experiments, unbacked by any actual data.

wonderful. We order up some Malbec and tapas. Throughout the interview that follows, I'm struck by the disjointedness of the casual beauty of the setting and the raw ugliness of the topics we discuss.

We start with zombies, because why not.

Kelly laughs. "They're a great way to think about contagion, right?"

Contagion, but also dehumanization. Zombies have never been more popular: zombie entertainment and paraphernalia represent a five-billion-dollar industry. From *The Walking Dead* to the video game *Plants vs. Zombies*, zombies have been creeping slowly out of the horror genre and into the mainstream for years now.

Now is an interesting time for zombies to be on the rise. They are often trotted out as a metaphor for mindless human behavior, everything from consumerism to terrorism to addicted smartphone users. Zombies stem from a voodoo legend about corpses reanimated by shamans. Early depictions involved a master leading a mindless hoard, again echoing our fears of our hiveish natures, our terror of being dissolved into a mass collective. More recent zombie narratives drop the master and instead focus on a more viral explanation for their dysfunction.[1]

Doomsday prepper clubs and conferences regularly discuss how to prepare for a zombie apocalypse. The gun and ammo industry, no slouch for new marketing opportunities, sells special clips and other supplies targeted at these zombie aficionados; they also sell life-size zombie targets that realistically shed flesh as you shoot them.[2]

"What is most unnerving to me about the zombie media," Kelly says, "is the sort of glee evoked by talking about destroying them. It is also about what kind of people make us nervous. What sort of people is it acceptable to torture, or shoot in the face? A lot of people ask me how I go from white supremacists to zombies. It is actually a pretty easy switch."

At the end of the day, zombies and racism are both about the dehumanization of beings who appear like us on the surface but who don't fully "count" as human in the same way. Are these others somehow less conscious, less discerning, less capable of the full range of human emotion? If so, perhaps they are less deserving of the full panoply of human rights and opportunities—or, even, are like zombies we should double-tap.

The most dangerous appraisal, indeed.

Which leads us, of course, away from fictional creatures and back to the idea that people can begin to see other humans as less human as they increasingly leave them out of their thresholds of inclusion. It also leads us straight into Kelly's more academic interests, which have to do with an organization that unites white people under the banner of racial superiority—the Ku Klux Klan.[3]

Over America's history, the Klan's story is one of waves. The most recent waves were in the 1960s, commonly viewed as a backlash against the civil rights movement, and in the 1980s. Like some of the earlier waves, the 1960s and '80s waves were poorly organized, highly emotional, and mostly about intimidation of outgroups rather than people collected tightly around an ingroup. The 1920s Klan, on the other hand, was much more organized and focused, rising in prominence to a peak of four million American members in 1924.

In the 1920s, there was a lot of anxiety surrounding what it meant to be white. Much like today, immigration was a focus of this anxiety. But unlike our current time, most immigration was of people who were white but still considered "other," in that they were Catholic and Jewish. The Klan decided that neither group could be assimilated into American culture: the Catholics because of their suspicious allegiance to the pope and the Jewish people because of their loyalty to one another. "True" Americans were both white and made of preferred immigrant stock, from places like England and Scotland. Though notoriously, while official

Klan writing focused on immigration, local acts of hate and the most bald-faced aggression provoked by their rhetoric landed on the backs of the black community.

That was then, this is now—but now looks dismayingly like then. In 2016, the Klan literally took to the streets and started marching again. Alt-right provocateurs launched media tours talking about the need for America to intentionally become a white nation.

Suddenly, everyone wanted to talk to Kelly.

"It was the weirdest moment for me," she says, "because suddenly I became relevant. I had these moments in 2016 where I'd feel—wow, I wasn't wrong. We really are living in the Klan's America. This is a terrible thing to be right about."

Reading Kelly's book, the echoing between the Klan's rhetoric and some of the language used by those on the alt-right is haunting. In the 1920s Klan, white Christian men and women in America felt threatened by a trifecta of changes in society: escalating modernization of jobs, increasing diversity and attention paid to the problematic ways that race and gender were limiting factors in society, and changing social norms surrounding what was considered acceptable language and behavior. They banded together for collective change. They defined "real Americans" as white, Christian, and almost militantly patriotic. They gathered together in marches and parades and on college campuses, sometimes marching with banners that read "America First."

Kelly feels strongly that one of the largest mistakes the popular media, journalists, and even academics make with the Klan is to assume that its members are either unpolished, uneducated hicks or looming specters of evil. Racism is often both sophisticated and prosaic, and threaded throughout mainstream culture; to assume otherwise is to allow major aspects of racism to go unexamined. If you only point to a "hillbilly" with a noose and call that racism, then you don't have to look closely at your own choices or tendencies. You don't have to wonder why major news networks feature attractive talking heads who echo the language of the ugliest periods of our history. You don't have to examine the ways in which our education system and employment system and legal system are engineered to offer more opportunities to some people over others, and how these structural forms of racism may have benefited you and deprived others.

"We always get close to that conversation and then veer off," Kelly observes, "because if you can use the Klan as your signpost, that allows you to say—well, I'm not burning crosses in someone's yard. And I'm like, that's our metric? Please don't let that be our metric."

Kelly presented some of her work on the Klan to a faculty seminar at the university she was working at, emphasizing Klan rhetoric about the importance of nation and faith, about the need to preserve a certain way of life that was white and Protestant, that longed nostalgically for a past of more traditional approaches to life, that questioned the value of diversity and emphasized nationalism. One of the faculty members said, point-blank, that he didn't believe Kelly's work could be true because so much of the rhetoric sounded "too much like a lot of the Methodists I know"; another said that her work was dangerous because it illustrated the degree to which Klansmen and Klanswomen were similar to regular white people.

Kelly shakes her head. "That was the point!" she says. "The Klan *are* regular folks who meet those markers of how we determine ordinariness. They're middle class, and educated, and men and women, and they're very much involved in this white supremacist way of thinking. But the reaction from white audiences has been, 'No, they're too similar to us.' I'm trying to drive a point home, and the audience is really doing everything they can not to hear it."

Today's white nationalists don't parade around in sheets that make it easy for us to identify them. And they couch their racism not in explicit antiblack or anti-Jewish rhetoric, but in patriotism and pride in their own heritage. They play rhetorical games— "We're not anti anyone else, we're just pro white." Many of them cleverly sidestep the implications of their speech, and they have made effective use of meme culture, images, and catchphrases that spread like wildfire among the hivemind of the internet— remember the research we reviewed on moral contagion in social media posts. These potent little visuals succeed in eliciting emotions without encouraging any analysis.

One way that the 1920s Klan was so effective was that they offered their followers a ready-made community. They gathered over family picnics, they did volunteer work in the community together, they held parades that probably tapped into ecstatic group ritual—essentially, they appealed to the collective side of Homo duplex. Followers were welcomed into a tribe of shared meaning. Klan writing and speeches also emphasized being absorbed into a collective identity. While we often think of the hoods and robes as ways of allowing members to be secret about belonging to a brotherhood that most of society viewed as abhorrent, the cloth also served to deindividuate members, allowing them to forget their independent selves in the larger body of the group. To immerse themselves into the larger movement. Part of this dissolving is putting one's personal identity aside and allowing the collective will to take responsibility for the outcome.

"I do think they had some moments when it really did work," Kelly reflects. "Klan members wrote about [the group dynamic] working in a weirdly poetic way. They're writing about fiery crosses and how it feels to be Klansmen surrounded by your brothers in a way that really carries an emotional punch. And rituals make bodies do things, and ingrain in the body the memory so that you continue to do these things."

These practices also call to my mind an amazing little book called *The True Believer: Thoughts on the Nature of Mass Movements*, published by Eric Hoffer in 1951. In the book Hoffer puts in his sights all mass movements, all collective surges for societal change, and makes no differentiations based on the content of the movement, whether the desired change is political, religious, nationalist, cultural, or creative. He considers Nazis and American revolutionists alike, Christians and cultists, and questions what historically these movements have in common.

Hoffer argues, essentially, that mass movements occur when a swell of people are discontent with their individual lots and long to shed their identities and dissolve into the collective. He writes:

> If they join the movement as full converts they are reborn to a new life in its close-knit collective body, or if attracted as sympathizers they find elements of pride, confidence, and purpose by identifying themselves with the efforts, achievements and prospects of the movement.... The vigor and growth of a rising mass movement depend on its capacity to evoke and satisfy the passion for self-renunciation.

Followers eagerly relinquish what they see as a burden of free choice. Hoffer writes that the "sense of liberation comes from having escaped the burdens, fears and hopelessness of an untenable individual existence," and quotes an early Nazi about the delight of "being freed from freedom." This attraction may be particularly potent for people who have tried and failed to live up to their own expectations of themselves and those of their families or their societies. Much better to be a thread in an overall tapestry than an individual who didn't pass muster.

What social media has done for the current white nationalist movements is allow people to find what Kelly calls affinity groups or kindred spirits. Certainly, the Klan in the 1920s managed to find one another without the aid of digital media, but now the ease, reach, and power is greatly magnified, and writ on a global scale. It has also allowed previously distinct groups to cluster under the alt-right label—white supremacy, men opposed to women's rights, and so on. They can express shared nervousness about losing cultural dominance, and fears that the groups opposed to them could themselves align and enact revenge. The Klan explicitly called themselves knights and painted themselves as militant. But these new collective movements similarly use the language of needing to defend themselves, needing to wage war against the forces that resist them or wish to dissolve them.

"Have you read Michael Barkun's book on conspiracy theories?" Kelly asks me.

I tell her I haven't and take the opportunity to slide some Manchego onto a cracker.

"He is a political scientist writing about mostly religious conspiracy theories," Kelly continues. "I used to teach his book because it was fabulous—he takes people's beliefs very seriously and objectively presents some of their religious beliefs. And the students are good, they're right with him until he gets to the reptoids...."

I choke on my cheese a bit. "Sorry, reptoids?"

Kelly nods. "Then my students are like 'Wait a second,' right? 'There are folks who believe in lizard people?' And I'm like, '*Yes*, this is a true thing.'"

My research has taken me down some strange and unexpected paths, educated me about some truly unimaginable and appalling beliefs held by unexpectedly large groups of people, but lizard people?

I'm a little stunned.

HIVEMIND AMPLIFIED: CULTS AND CONSPIRACY THEORIES

When I pick up Barkun's book *A Culture of Conspiracy: Apocalyptic Visions in Contemporary America*, I see numerous connections between his research on conspiracy theories and what I've been reading about collective movements and cults. All three share some common underlying hivemind principles, taking advantage of both the slippery social nature of how we construct reality and our craving for belongingness and certainty. As we'll see, it isn't just my academic take on these topics that unite them: increasingly, people who believe in these various ideas are beginning to find each other online and to band together in sometimes strange and alarming ways—white supremacists uniting with incels* uniting with people who think reptoids control the American government. Where in the past these various groups used to operate in isolation, they now have blogs and Reddit and 4chan—twenty-four-hour access to voices reaffirming and even escalating their existing beliefs through the processes of group polarization.

A note on cults specifically before we get started: many academics take issue with the word *cult*, instead preferring a more value-neutral term like "new religious movement." Traditionally, *cult* was used to describe a movement that demanded utmost obedience and required that its members sacrifice their individuality to join the mass collective; often, such groups also took advantage of their members financially and/or sexually. Not all intense groups collected around a shared identity and way of living meet these criteria. After all, most religions have mystical stories about the origins of the world and humankind, prescriptions for how to live, meetings in which officials of the religion lead collective songs and chants, and opportunities to donate money to the organization. Just because some are ancient and some are modern doesn't mean that the latter should get the term *cult* slapped on them, the thinking goes. Just because they are freshly invented doesn't mean that they deserve scorn. I appreciate this point. But as scholar Janja Lalich points out, on the other hand not all destructive closed social

---

* Short for "involuntary celibates," men who believe they are owed sex with women, and of course specifically women they deem extremely attractive.

groups are religious—strong, closed groups can form around secular topics like health practices, business, and exercise.[4] So "new religious movement" doesn't work terribly well either.

I am going to use the word *cult* but will only review research relevant to those organizations that have been documented as threatening to people's autonomy (e.g., Heaven's Gate), leaving aside what to do about the wide gray zone that exists between seemingly healthy collectives and fringe groups whose leaders demand extreme acts of self-renunciation and even violence from their followers.

The term *conspiracy theory* has its own murky problems. For one, actual conspiracies do happen in the real world. As the old saying goes, just because you are paranoid doesn't mean they're not out to get you. In the twentieth century, the US government *did* for decades deny treatment to African American men with syphilis while conducting research on them.[5] In the 1950s and '60s, the Central Intelligence Agency *did* dose unknowing people with LSD in an attempt to explore its possibilities as a mind control agent.[6] And of course there are actual terrorist conspiracies that aim to harm our country—and our own government carries out convoluted plots to topple foreign administrations deemed unfriendly to our self-interests. Outlandish things do happen and do get covered up.

How to know which are true, and which are fantasy? It turns out, we have only our biased, gist-based hiveminds to rely on, and so we often don't do so well. We are surrounded by people— you may be one yourself—who hold stock in beliefs that seem to contradict both common wisdom and experimental evidence. For instance, that vaccinations are a harmful conspiracy to make Big Pharma richer, that there are mediums who can read the minds of the deceased, that the government covered up what "really" happened on the eleventh day of September, 2001.

I openly admit that some of the "conspiracy theories" I review in this book could one day turn out to be true. But I think we have to start somewhere if we're going to talk about this topic at all.

Before we get to some of the common hivemind principles that underlie conspiracy theories, mass movements, and cults, I'd like to first discuss one of the animating forces behind their success—our tendency toward paranoia and persecution, seeing people out to get us behind every corner.

THE POWER OF PERSECUTION

In his fascinating book *The United States of Paranoia: A Conspiracy Theory*, writer and editor Jesse Walker traces conspiracy thinking in the United States back to the country's founding, demonstrating that paranoid worries about secretive others working against us have been with us since our very first days. There may be no faster way to create a strong ingroup than to tell a group of people that their shared community is under attack and must be defended. The idea of a dominant enemy can become a preoccupation: from fearing Native American chieftains with superpowers to the undetected "second shooter" at the JFK assassination to President Obama being an al-Qaeda operative. This enemy can be looming outside of the group or lurking within it, but all of the visages of the enemy serve to mobilize the collective against a person or outgroup who threatens life as we know it.

The first face of the enemy is the Enemy Outside. These enemies, according to Walker, are those human beings who are not like you, who do not eat the foods that you eat or wear the types of clothes you wear or worship the same god as you do. They are other, foreign, and therefore highly suspicious.

Here, Walker describes the Enemy Outside:

There is the image of the world outside your gates as an unfriendly wilderness where evil forces dwell. There is the proclivity to see those forces as a centralized conspiracy guided by a puppet master or a small cabal. There is the fear of the border zone where the cultures mix, the suspicion that aliens at home are agents of a foreign power, and the fear that your community might be remade in the enemy's image. And there is the tendency to see this conflict in terms of a grand, apocalyptic struggle—if not literally against Satan, then against something deeply evil.

It doesn't take much creative thinking to see in this description multiple Enemies Outside during the course of US history: Germans during World War II, Russians during the Cold War, ISIL in our current time. Stoking fear of the Enemy Outside serves to increase outgroup hostility, which can help curry public favor for restrictive political policies (e.g., war support efforts, curtailing immigration, lack of resistance to governmental surveillance).

Not all enemies are outside your gates, however. Perhaps even more pernicious is the Enemy Within. They eat your foods and wear your clothes and worship your god . . . or at least they appear to do so. But secretly they are still Other, still opposed to your interests, working internally to bring you to ruin. The Russian spy, the witch, the closeted Communist are all enemies of this sort. When the Enemy Within is waxing, no one is safe from suspicion. This Enemy is calling from inside the house.

In the 1950s, when fears of both hidden Communists and being targeted by McCarthyism rose, movies like *Invasion of the Body Snatchers* gripped the public imagination. In these movies, human beings who looked ordinary and trustworthy were actually alien others underneath their normal-looking exterior. These particular fears all centered around concerns about being absorbed into a conformist collective, losing one's individuality in the mass collective. "When the fear of the Enemy Within is at its strongest," Walker writes, "even the physical world might feel inauthentic, like a fragile shell obscuring a hidden realm."

When the Enemy Within is surging, the potential is high for it to sow distrust among communities, such as during the McCarthy hearings, the Salem Witch trials, and the 1980s daycare paranoia. Neighbors can turn against one another, and innocent people may be persecuted.

The Enemies Outside and Within are all about individuality versus collectivity and allegiance—who belongs and does not belong to our trustworthy tribe. The next two themes have to do more with status in society, ways in which those above or below you in status might be working against you.

Those who are low in social power but might overthrow those above them and upset the whole social order are the Enemy Below. The Enemy Below are often the poor or other powerless groups, who are thought to be at risk of massing together, no longer satisfied with their lot, and revolting against the rest of society. Of course, many social movements for positive change are sourced from oppressed groups fighting to create a more equitable world, but the paranoid aspects of the Enemy Below exaggerate the danger and dehumanize the marginalized.

The Enemy Below "is a bestial force with monstrous appetites: a collective id eager to rape, burn, loot, and massacre." In other words, racism and classism and all of the ugliest of our tendencies to believe the worst of one another, especially of those we're at the same time actively oppressing. The open wound of America's history of slavery means that this version of the enemy is weaponized against people of color in our country; racism against black men in particular emphasizes their supposed aggressive nature and danger, and with devastating regularity the implications can be deadly. Witness Officer Darren Wilson's testimony in his shooting of Michael Brown of Ferguson, Missouri—that holding on to his arm was like being a small child holding on to Hulk Hogan, that Brown appeared to him to be like a giant "demon."[7]

Walker observes that the group identified as the enemy shifts over time, as can the sort of enemy that they are—for instance, as Irish immigrants assimilated into American culture, they transitioned from the Enemy Outside to the Enemy Below. No longer a menace because they were alien outsiders allegiant to the suspicious foreign pope, they were now dangerous because they were ruthless criminals. This transition from one type of enemy to another demonstrates yet another way that our appraisals shape our reality, but also how this equation works in reverse—we can shape our appraisals to fit the changing circumstances, performing a sort of mental gymnastics to never have to question our prejudices.

Finally, the Enemy Above involves conspiracies centered on the people with *more* power than we have. The government controlling people with subliminal advertising or by dousing our drinking water with chemicals, pharmaceutical companies causing autism with mercury in vaccinations, insurance companies holding "death panels" are all examples of conspiracies from above. Interestingly, these conspiracy theories centering around the Enemy Above seem to tend to attract more people from the left side of the political spectrum than the right.

Now that we have a grip on the animating principle fueling a lot of conspiracist thinking, let's consider some of the mechanics by which one succumbs to it and to other forms of dramatic collective thinking.

YOU ARE WELCOMED TO A READY-MADE COLLECTIVE, AND RESISTANCE IS FUTILE

Rarely does one jump headfirst into full immersion in a cult or a conspiracy theory. The acclimation is gradual, whether through slippery slopes of research on the internet or through more controlled exposure at the hands of a recruiter. One often begins with a first meeting or a first reading about a somewhat suspicious action of a government agency or a group opposed to your own interests. Next you are offered a sense of community, or a deeper dive into the topics. Inch by inch you slide in.

Research on who might be vulnerable to cultic recruitment reveals that one of the strongest predictors of vulnerability is feeling isolated or unmoored from one's social support systems.[8] People whose social fabrics have been disrupted are particularly at risk. College students away from home for the first time. New widows or widowers. Someone who just moved across the country for work. In the laboratory, experimentally induced feelings of ostracism lead to participants being more willing to endorse extreme views and acts.[9]

Uncertainty, especially uncertainty regarding one's self-identity, appears to motivate identification with groups, especially groups with strong beliefs and internal characteristics.[10] One theoretical framework for how uncertainty leads to extremism is called the "uncertainty-identity theory."[11] This theory argues that when people are feeling uncertain about who they are and how they should behave, they are motivated to resolve this uncertainty, and that one primary way through which they accomplish this resolution is by identifying with a social group, particularly those with strong identities and proscriptions for behavior and how to view the world.

Scientology reportedly has a specific model for approaching new people in which the recruiter first makes friendly contact, attempting to disarm potentially antagonistic responses.[12] The next step in recruitment is to "find the ruin" or the life problem most plaguing potential recruits. Perhaps they never felt like they measured up to their parents' expectations. Or they fear they will never find true love. The job of the Scientology recruiter is to find this ruin and then suggest that Scientology can solve or heal this psychic wound.

Initially, a lot of the beliefs that a group subscribes to may seem reasonable, comforting, and logical. These gateway beliefs are what make it harder to question the accepted knowledge of the new group as you are pulled farther afield from consensus reality. In many instances, this is a carefully cultivated experience.

In *Bounded Choice: True Believers and Charismatic Cults* Janja Lalich chronicles two cults—the famed suicide cult Heaven's Gate and also the Marxist group Democratic Workers Party, of which she was for many years a member. As one gets deeper and deeper into the belief system, "one drifts further and further from the shore of common understanding," more and more detached from the rest of the hive.

Lalich argues that what cults offer is the idea of personal fulfillment, the very best *you* that you can imagine, while at the same time allowing for complete self-*renunciation*, an absorption of the lonely self into the group collective, which you may recall Hoffer also argued was the appeal of mass movements. As Lalich writes, "Members experienced the personal joy of having found an expression for their innermost desires—to have a life filled with purpose and meaning and to be part of a group."

In many instances, your original social network gets quietly pruned as you're becoming gradually immersed in the new group's way of thinking. You are encouraged to cut off all ties with nonbelievers until the members of this new group are all of your social support, all of your connections. And then you are threatened with isolation and shunning if you step outside the group's belief systems or codes of behavior. For instance, in Scientology, social others who are skeptical about the group's beliefs or hold on the person are called "Suppressive Persons," or "SPs" for short. If a person within Scientology gets close to an SP, they may be labeled a "Potential Trouble Source" (PTS) and be denied access to training and services.[13]

In the Democratic Workers Party, one of the first things you did upon recruitment was to choose a new name and abandon your old one. It is hard to conceive of a more basic way of cutting someone off from their previous ties than taking the name that has represented you since infancy and replacing it with another, shedding the old skin to adopt this new one. Members of the Peoples Temple wrote false confessions that cult leader Jim Jones kept on file as a way of blackmailing anyone who wanted to leave.[14]

According to Hoffer, for mass movements it always goes like this: the present is unbearable and terrible, nothing like the wonders of the past and the glories of the future to come. People must join the movement to bring to fruition this glorious future, and in doing so they join a grand purpose, unlike the meaningless day-to-day struggle to exist and jostle for status. They join the movement in front of an audience: the future to come, the history books yet to be written.

The battle is against not just abstract forces that threaten to move the world in the wrong direction, but also a specific enemy. The devil, the immigrant, the Jew, the atheist, the Russian or the American, the East Coast elitist, the Islamic terrorist—the devil differs for these movements, cults, and conspiracy theories, but there is always a devil. As we learned earlier, it is not at all difficult to convince people of a devil. We are always on the lookout for enemies above, below, outside, and within.

It may seem like this epic battle is better suited to cults and collective movements, but conspiracy theories traffic in its themes as well. Indeed, Barkun claims that the very essence of conspiracy is to delineate evil, to know its shape and give it meaningful form. This evil shifts and morphs but is always located outside of what is viewed as the "true" community.

For cults and mass movements in particular, there is usually a charismatic leader. The best leaders for these movements, Hoffer believes, are absolutely certain, bombastically confident, willing to play fast and loose with facts, demonstrate a "joy in defiance," and employ mass spectacles and rituals like rallies.* The leader "articulates and justifies the resentment dammed up in the souls of the frustrated." Intriguingly, Hoffer writes that those frustrated are most often not the truly destitute but the bored, aimless, unsuccessful people who are just out of reach of success or power.

Perhaps the most tantalizing gift that cults, mass movements, and conspiracy theories offer is the gift of absolute certainty, of finally knowing the answer to life's nagging questions.

As Doris Lessing once wrote,

People...crave certainty, they seek certainty, and great resounding truths. They like to be part of some movement equipped with these truths and certainties, and if there are rebels and heretics, that is even more satisfying, because this structure is so deep in all of us.[15]

Importantly, the answer to life, the universe, and everything is not the capricious randomness that we deeply fear but rather a simple, reassuring order and design. The doctrine of these movements must be absolute and certain—joining the movement means that you remove all doubt. Conspiracies are so convoluted and all-encompassing in part because they are supposed to explain everything, to remove all uncertainty.

Part of the certainty, especially for cults, is that choices are removed. The rituals and norms of the group seem geared to develop a sense of mindlessness and automaticity, an ultimate freedom from choice. In the Heaven's Gate cult, elaborate manuals spelled out every decision, no matter how minute, from the exact diameter of morning pancakes to the amount of toothpaste to dollop on your brush.[16] Scientology calls their complicated

---

* Ring any bells?

chain of progression through the layers of their self-improvement system the Bridge to Total Freedom.

So there we have it—an offering of coveted belonginess and social acceptance, a gradual immersion, a pruning of your existing support networks, a sense that you have been recruited into an epic battle against a terrible evil, and finally, absolute certainty, a remedy for your personal ruin, a salve for all of your crushing doubts and nagging fears and deepest anxieties.

It is kind of a wonder we don't all succumb.

THE STIGMATIZATION OF KNOWLEDGE

The Facts About Fluoride the Government Doesn't Want You to Know. What Is Hidden in Area 51. The 20-year National Network of 'Smiley Face Serial Killers' That No One Will Investigate.

Conspiracy theories, cults, and mass movements all share a deep skepticism regarding authority, institutions, and academic experts, and enshrine something Barkun calls stigmatized knowledge.[17] Indeed, the stigmatized nature of the information seems to be both a point of pride and part of the draw. People drawn to conspiracies and cults appear to revel in knowing things that other people don't know and even enjoy their ideas being rejected by mainstream society.

This stigmatization of knowledge can even work in a reinforcing cycle, where the believer points to the mainstream rejection as further evidence of the conspiracy—"Look, they're silencing us! We must be onto something!" And of course, mainstream society *does* stigmatize certain kinds of knowledge or beliefs. Few people take seriously talk of fairies, of ghosts, of secret government cabals.

Conspiracy theories in particular are marked by an extensive pseudoscholarship that intentionally models itself after mainstream scholarship. The knowledge is stigmatized, but an elaborate body of work is developed in order to support it—you can find extensive articles about the vaccine/autism link or about major seed companies hiding evidence of the dangers of genetically modified foods. Even though mainstream academia is maligned by the group or the movement, its adherents nonetheless put on a big show of bibliographies and citations. A few sources are often repeated over and over, often in specialist journals created by the cause. It doesn't help that most of the populace does not have the skills to differentiate between authentic, peer-reviewed science and works mocked up to appear to be so.

It might seem curious that so much conspiracy thinking eschews academic thinking and science while also embracing and mirroring its practices. But this simultaneous rejection and embrace, envy and revulsion, marks much of this world. Historian Richard Hofstadter wrote a famous essay called *The Paranoid Style in American Politics* in 1964 that notes this tension: "The enemy seems to be on many counts a projection of the self: both the ideal and the unacceptable aspects of the self are attributed to him. A fundamental paradox of the paranoid style is the imitation of the enemy."[18] It reminds me of the classic Freudian defense mechanism called reaction formation.* Reaction formation involves wanting what one loathes and loathing what one wants, covering up for shamed feelings with an overdone reversal—bullies hiding same-sex attraction under a mask of overt homophobia and mothers concealing their ambivalence toward their children by smothering them in affection.

It is possible to combat people's attraction to conspiracy, to defuse the hostility, and create cracks in problematic narratives. It is work that takes sensitivity and strategy, though, and we're going to tackle it in chapters 9 and 10.

---

* As a modern-day psychologist I'm not supposed to talk about Freud.

THE SPLINTERING OF CONSENSUS REALITY

And tackle it we must, because dismayingly, more and more of us seemingly *are* succumbing, and it has implications for consensus reality. As we have discussed right from the first pages of this book, our society, our understanding of the world, and probably our well-being all rest on the idea that there is a reality we can agree on. We do not directly experience much of the world, and we rely on education and popular culture to develop and maintain a web of facts and relationships between them that make up the world as we know it. We weren't there when Neil Armstrong took his steps on the Moon, we haven't personally spelunked the caverns of Salt Lake City to see if there are reptoids there, we have neither observed nor have the chemical knowledge to understand how the round white pill we just swallowed works to take away our headache. We rely on a basic sense of trust—of experts, of the world being a benign place more of the time than not, of people like me having done the research to support ourselves in saying things like "there is no evidence that vaccinations can cause autistic symptoms."[19]

We are witnessing an unprecedented melding of previously isolated fringe groups gathering together under the same banners online. Much like Kelly Baker warned is happening on the alt-right (e.g., men's rights groups joining forces with white supremacists), conspiracy theories are melding into a conglomerate of paranoia, globalists in league with the Illuminati in league with the reptoids in league with Hollywood elites. Barkun calls this melding "improvisational millennialism" or "fusion paranoia."*

This fusion is highly problematic because it allows groups that have been shunned and isolated from the mainstream to grow in

---

* The latter term was coined by journalist Michael Kelly.

strength and to collect new followers as they go, to snowball. The more they collect together, the more of the world the conspiracy theory may explain, and the greater the attraction due to certainty grows. Even more worryingly, ideas that used to fester on the outskirts are making their way into common parlance, encouraged by meme culture and skepticism about experts.

Barkun notes that prior to the wide-scale adoption of the web, conspiracy thinking seemed to be limited to militant antigovernment conservative groups and Christian fundamentalists who believed that the Antichrist was on his way. The ideas of these groups largely stayed fringe and did not taint the larger hivemind. But the advent of the internet and the use of "core conspiracist themes" in popular shows like *The X-Files* both popularized all of these ideas and allowed for them to merge. Barkun lays quite a lot of blame at the feet of the mainstream news media treating seriously the claims of the "birther" conspiracy that President Obama was not born in the United States.

Mainstreaming conspiracy theories both gives them an aura of legitimacy—if they're debating the birther conspiracy on the standard nightly news, there must be some legitimacy to the possibility of the claim—and introduces the ideas to new audiences who probably otherwise would have never been exposed.

Concluding the second edition of his book on conspiracies in 2013, Barkun seems worried:

We are not yet in a situation of radical epistemological pluralism in which different groups espouse completely different ideas of what is real. Even those involved in bitterly contested "culture wars" over issues such as abortion still inhabit the same mental universe where other matters are concerned. . . .

As indicated earlier, there have always been some genuine outsiders who contest everyday notions of reality. They

have been effectively marginalized as eccentrics or tolerated in small groups. . . .

The measures once taken to contain them might not be
appropriate much longer. . . .

[A] degree of boundary permeability unlike any that has
existed in the recent past. . . .

Barkun shared these ominous thoughts about a half decade
before, in my estimation, everything started going really south.
Before famous celebrities came out as flat-earthers. Before a White
House representative used the term "alternative facts" to describe
the administration's string of falsehoods. That these sorts of illegitimate, conspiracy-style arguments have become mainstream
has wide-ranging possible implications for our democracy, for our
social functioning, and for our ability to work together as a society.

There are even worse risks. Already diseases we long ago con-
quered through vaccination have begun a resurgence, claiming
lives of the most vulnerable, as more and more people decide to
sacrifice our immunity based on pseudoscience. As novelist Emily
St. John Mandel writes in her luminous novel *Station Eleven*, "If
you are the light, if your enemies are darkness, then there's nothing that you cannot justify. There's nothing you can't survive,
because there's nothing that you will not do." Such as show up at
a pizza parlor with gun ablaze, ready to free the enslaved children
from Hillary Clinton's child sex-slave ring, as one North Carolina man did.[20] Or go on a shooting rampage and kill six innocent
people, as one incel blogger did after posting about being driven
to it by the "mental damage/stress from being isolated from meaningful human contact for too long."[21]

Reading in my cozy armchair with a lap cat and a glass of
wine, I put Barkun's dark red tome down for a minute, use my
finger to trace the triangle outline of the Illuminati symbol on it,
and shudder.

One hopes that we aren't too far down the rabbit hole quite yet and that there is still time to change course. But I would be lying if I said I weren't very much disquieted.

Before we begin to consider solutions to some of these problems, we have one more peril of our hivemind in the social media age to consider: are our smartphones ruining our mental health, and are they actually engineered to do so? In the next chapter, we'll visit Las Vegas, land of excess and compulsion, to consider research arguing that our smartphones are making us more depressed, more dependent, more distracted, and more divided.

Chapter Seven

Hacked

Las Vegas, Nevada

The plane lands with a teeth-clattering clamor, an abrupter transition than usual, and a few of my fellow passengers exclaim at the shock of it. It is midweek and I'm coming to Las Vegas not for show tunes and slot machines but to give a talk about emotions and teaching for Touro University. Over the course of the flight it was increasingly obvious that a number of my copassengers were arriving for more hedonistic motivations. When the flight attendant came around for a drink order, the gentleman next to me said, "Three gin and tonics, please." The row behind me began the flight as strangers but by the end were increasingly sloppy, buying each other rounds and laughing uproariously.

I thus get off the flight wearier than I might otherwise have been. The very first thing my eyes land on when I exit the jet-bridge is a row of slot machines, disconcertingly whirring and buzzing and flashing right next to the monitors listing arrivals and departures. The carpet is grimy, and everywhere I look there are digital billboards and animated videos and row upon row of gambling devices. People either jostle and shout, many like my flight mates already inebriated, or else they sit with hunched shoulders at the slot machines, their faces slack and defeated.

Welcome to Las Vegas.*

The seeming relentless draw of the flashing lights and the slumped posture of the slot machine occupants make me wonder about my own techno-optimism—though really, I like to think of it more as techno-agnosticism. Is my positive attitude its own set of blinders? What if all of the techno-alarmists are right, and the alluring screens in our pockets will be our destruction?

At the same time, for every person in Las Vegas glued to the screens and levers, there is someone like me, utterly disinterested. For every person who sacrifices their marriage and life savings to the god of the slot machine, there is a person who can gamble once on a lark and never again.

A common error in logic is called "technological determinism." When you read considerations of how technology may be affecting teenagers or parents or people at large, the underlying assumption is that the effect resides in the technology itself, that it will have unilaterally negative or positive effects. Smartphones are addictive. Frequent selfies lead to narcissism. Fitbits will launch a revolution in exercise among the active and sedentary alike.

This is not how human beings work.

Human beings are infinitely complex and incredibly varied. Selfies may possess the capacity to increase narcissism in people whose sole pleasure in life is their appearance, but for others they may operate as radical acts of self-acceptance in the face of body-shaming and restrictive beauty standards that are overwhelmingly white, European, and thin. For some adolescents, social media may increase their anxiety and depression as they watch all of their friends smiling it up at parties they weren't invited to and snuggling up to the people they have secret crushes on—but for other adolescents, social media may be a blessed lifeline of a

---

* To residents of Las Vegas: Sorry for this depiction! All of my Lyft drivers that week expressed great disdain for "the strip," and what I saw of Las Vegas once we got beyond that was beautiful.

connection to people who share their hidden sexual orientation or gender identity. The impact of technology on your well-being will likely vary based on who you were when you adopted the technology, your likes and dislikes, your other outlets and behaviors, and your social context. It probably also matters how you frame the technology and your relationship to it—the appraisals you make.

For all of these reasons, the question I'd like to pursue in this chapter is not whether social media is inherently traumatizing, depressing, addicting, or polarizing. Instead, the question that I think we ought to be studying, contemplating, and arguing is, *For whom among us* might social media be potentially traumatizing, depressing, addicting, or polarizing.? Who is vulnerable? And how can we protect them?

THE VULNERABLE AMONG US

My research in graduate school centered on a somewhat related question, which was the etiology of posttraumatic stress disorder (PTSD). Why are some people able to suffer unspeakable events in their lives and bounce back from those events relatively quickly, while others are lost in the thicket of nightmares, hyper-reactivity to threat, and constant reminders of the trauma that represent a more pathological response? I studied with neuroscientist Lisa M. Shin, whose research program questioned whether people who did and didn't develop posttraumatic stress disorder after their traumas differed in their brain function while they performed tasks that involved emotion, memory, and attention.[1]

Most scientific work on PTSD evaluates people who have been through personal traumas in the context of their daily lives. Veterans experiencing wartime atrocities, people assaulted by strangers (or worse, and sadly more commonly, people they trusted), those caught unaware by natural disasters and other crises. For instance, one study Lisa and I conducted included parents whose children had been severely burned under their watch, and another, people with a recent limb amputation.[2] These are the sort of extreme events that lead to PTSD in vulnerable people.

One month into my graduate work, two planes struck the World Trade Towers in New York City. Along with many Americans, I watched the event unfold in real time on the news, turning on the television after the first plane hit and then watching as the second followed, as the buildings began to burn, as human beings on the higher levels of the towers began tumbling into unprotected air, as the skyscrapers collapsed out of the sky. In the days and weeks that followed, news coverage was around the clock. Cable anchors and their fleet of experts on terrorism, politics, and international relations speculated about what had happened and what might happen in the future. The reels of the collapsing towers ran on constant repeat.

Not long after, research examining people's experiences of this national trauma began appearing in the psychological literature. I took a deep dive into this work, evaluating whether people could be traumatized not only by events that they personally experienced in real life, such as amputations and assaults, but also those that they experienced secondhand, such as through news coverage. Could people be traumatized by media footage of 9/11? Had some of us living in the United States at the time been collectively traumatized at a digital remove, by these images and clips being so ever-present in the cultural hivemind?

The data at the time didn't seem to support a model of PTSD that allowed for trauma at a televised remove. People were profoundly upset by the events surrounding 9/11 and the resulting news coverage, and some people were much more upset than others. Some research studies did indicate associations between greater exposure to televised footage and greater levels of distress.

But typically these people didn't meet the diagnostic criteria for the full-blown version of PTSD, with all of the attendant nightmares and panic attacks and recurrent memories. It seemed that perhaps a higher level of exposure, a lived immediacy in the event, was required.

Social technology has introduced a new source of potentially traumatizing digital footage: cell phone camera videos of violent or explicit imagery uploaded to social media. With disturbing regularity, people upload content to social media platforms that is violent, racist, sexually explicit, or generally horrifying. In just the past few years, Facebook has had to grapple with screening content for videos of actual murders, beatings, suicides, violence against animals, and gang rape. Thousands of people are currently employed by Facebook (or companies it hires) to manually review content reported as objectionable by other users, and these workers often have only a few seconds to decide if the content should be removed or not before flipping to the next. Many quickly quit,[3] the flow of horrifying images washing over them in an unending stream too much to bear.

While these screeners hopefully shield the worst of the images for us, they certainly don't catch them all, or catch them quickly enough. Famed YouTube vlogger (video blogger) Logan Paul recently apologized after entering Japan's Aokigahara "Sea of Trees" forest, which is known to be a common site for suicide. Entering the forest for clicks was itself a culturally insensitive thing to do, but Paul went one step further, publishing a video that included a corpse hanging from a tree to his audience of millions, including many quite young viewers who followed him for stunts and comedy.[4]

The public at large has been exposed to graphic, real-life videos of black men dying at the hands of law enforcement. These videos, often bloody and with heartrending details—like a four-year-old girl crying and begging her mother to stop yelling at the police because she doesn't want her mother to also get "shooted"[5]—have been much more widely viewed than the ones that social media platforms struggle to identify and wipe away as quickly as possible.

How does this availability of disturbing images and content impact us? Speculative fiction writer Margaret Atwood imagined the possible effects of such videos in her haunting futuristic trilogy *Oryx and Crake*. The protagonist, Jimmy, and his best friend, Crake, watch endless parades of violent and sexual videos online for leisure, and the exposure dissociates them from human empathy:

> So they'd roll a few joints and smoke them while watching the executions and the porn—the body parts moving around on the screen in slow motion, an underwater ballet of flesh and blood under stress, hard and soft joining and separating, groans and screams, close-ups of clenched eyes and clenched teeth, spurts of this or that. If you switched back and forth fast, it all came to look like the same event.

Could we be affected similarly? I find myself wondering whether these newer, close-up, more graphic videos of the sorts that litter Facebook and Twitter at times and which were the generative fuel for the Black Lives Matter movement could hold greater potential for "virtual trauma" than the likes of the old, distant videos of the towers falling. They are close-up, vivid snapshots of real-life violence and threat shared on social media. They also seem to depict things that could happen in one's life at any time—rather than the surreal, infrequent nature of events like 9/11.

It is in this context that I was greatly moved by a talk by Smith College professor Nnamdi Pole at a convention of research psychologists. Nnamdi's talk focused on the link between traumatic experiences in police officers and their risk for using inappropriate force in subsequent encounters. The hivemind narrative surrounding law enforcement reform is yet another example of our penchant for false binaries: that you can *either* be grateful for the good that so many police officers do *or* you can be horrified by the racial inequities present in every level of our criminal justice system. In contrast, Nnamdi's talk exemplified compassion for all of the communities involved, which I found compelling.

Nnamdi is a clinical psychologist, which means that in addition to academic research and teaching he also performs psychotherapy. His research focuses on both trauma and biobehavioral synchrony between therapists and clients during the process of therapy. This double intersection of our interests was too much to resist, and so I contacted him for an interview.

Happily, he agreed.

One icy morning in midwinter I head out to meet Nnamdi at Mosaic, a Mediterranean café in Northampton, Massachusetts. The sky is dark and heavy and the trees on either side of the highway droop with their burden of ice, giving my route the feel of an enchanted frosty tunnel. My teeth are too clenched for me to fully appreciate the scenery, though, since I assume that the same ice that glitters on the trees is spread thinly across the pavement I'm driving on.

It is a relief to reach the quiet downtown and enter the warmth of the small café and Nnamdi's welcome company. In addition to the requisite coffee to dial back the headache radiating upward from my jaw, I order a crepe stuffed with goat cheese, red peppers, and wild mushrooms. Nnamdi opts for a large heaping of steaming tangier chicken stew. We dig in to the comforting food and eagerly chat and discover several unexpected intersections of our social and academic networks.

I tell Nnamdi about my past investigations into so-called virtual trauma after 9/11 and ask whether contemporary smartphone videos like the ones that plague Facebook and the ones that launched the Black Lives Matter movement are more likely to elicit posttraumatic symptoms.

"Before I answer that question," Nnamdi says, "what did you conclude based on your research review?"

I share that I didn't find convincing evidence that PTSD was a common outcome of watching too much footage of the towers collapsing.

Nnamdi nods. He feels that PTSD is a specific psychiatric condition that results from an event that is deeply personal, highly unexpected, and disturbing, where the memory of the event never seems to be effectively woven into the rest of your experiences. Where, as he puts it, "remembering is reliving, and the line between the present and the past is very hazy."

Nnamdi is less concerned than some people about the potentially traumatizing effect of digital videos on social media. As a trauma researcher and clinician, he routinely listens to people's stories about the very worst days in their lives and feels that videos would have a hard time measuring up—no matter how graphic. He also feels that our entertainment is so very violent that we probably have developed a pretty strong desensitization to its effects. Given that images of this type are airing on nightly news and mainstream television programming, he isn't even sure it would be possible to regulate them.

"Oh," I say, thinking of the videos of police brutality specifically, "my question isn't so much about regulation per se, but rather about the potential traumatizing effects of viewing the videos on the community."

"Which community?" Nnamdi asks, tilting his head. "Because we have so many relevant communities. There is the law enforcement community, the black community, the urban community…."

I clarify that for this specific question, I meant the black community. I recall a recent weekend when a friend, a black woman, stayed over at my house after one of my Halloween parties. The next morning, I was puttering around, doing dishes or some such, when out of my peripheral vision I saw her posture stiffen and her face go suddenly tight. I followed her line of gaze and saw that a police cruiser was parked outside my neighbor's house. Her reaction was so automatic and so consistent with the sort of hypervigilant stance I would associate with PTSD that I was shocked and dismayed.

Nnamdi nods again. He feels that these sorts of reactions have more in common with the impact of hate crimes than clinically defined traumas per se. Hate crime legislation is motivated by the knowledge that when people feel targeted on the basis of their belonging to a certain social category, their mental well-being can be adversely affected. As we know well by this point in this book, we all have multiple, layered identities that tag us as belonging to different overlapping social groups—our gender, ethnicity, political affiliation, alma maters, sports teams, generation. Hate crimes, especially those against groups who have visible markers like race, result in a feeling of threat and vulnerability based solely on one's social grouping.

Nnamdi says, "Though when you ask me about the potential for trauma based on social media images, I guess I default to thinking about the effects on healthy, well-functioning people with mature defenses rather than the more vulnerable—the young, the poorly functioning, the already traumatized. Do you listen to NPR?"

I confess that I don't.

Nnamdi tells me that just that morning they aired a piece on the influenza outbreak, which in 2018 was a particularly widespread and deadly one. Part of the conversation was centered on things everyone ought to be doing, in terms of getting a flu shot and the like. A subdiscussion was focused on the more vulnerable:

the old, the young, people with HIV or some other sort of vulnerability. Thinking about flu risk in these populations becomes another thing entirely.

"So," Nnamdi says, "how do we create a set of media that doesn't do harm to people who are highly vulnerable for other reasons?"

Nnamdi hasn't done much research or clinical work on young people and social media, but he has two related thoughts on the topic of vulnerability. First, he wonders what transferring everything online might do for real-life social support, which as we know from previous sections in this book is critically important for well-being. He also wonders about the development of social skills that are so important for real-life interactions, and whether children are learning these correctly if most of their interactions are occurring mediated through technology rather than face-to-face.

Nnamdi sees this dynamic less in his clinical office and more in his classroom, where two types of contentious classroom dynamics seem to be repeatedly emerging more and more—one being that students feel too vulnerable to tackle certain difficult topics and another that they resist certain types of classroom assignments, often those that involve public speaking or other forms of taking risks in front of a group. He seems to see a common theme in which the way students relate to one another and to authority is changing for the worse as the years go on.

"Maybe some of this is what forty-something people always say about twenty-something people," he admits. "But I speculate that there is real value to having face-to-face interactions with people, that you learn skills about how to dial back from the strength of the way you say things that could potentially hurt other people. You see this in the animal kingdom—like with puppies who haven't been adequately socialized with other puppies, they have to relearn to control their bite."

Nnamdi agrees that social media has made it even easier to find communities of like-minded others and points out that in some cases this extreme homophily can make it startling to encounter contrasting opinions—even on a seemingly benign topic. "I think that really amps up the salience of your own identity, which may make it difficult to have empathy for people who are different than you."

Thinking of all of the research we reviewed in chapter 4 suggesting that social media can build us up as well as take us down, I ask whether social media couldn't also possess the power to bring us closer together.

Nnamdi shrugs and confesses that he doesn't actually engage much in social media and so is not the best judge. He tells me that he attended the recent *Star Wars* movie, feeling particularly nostalgic for a time when he was a seven-year-old boy seeing the original trilogy in a theater—safe and able to escape into this fictional universe of Ewoks and light sabers. But then for whatever reason he dipped his toes into social media and witnessed the fury of some fans that many of the lead heroes were people of color and white women, feeling that the filmmakers had catered to what they saw as "PC culture" enacted by "social justice warriors." (And those were the nice folks.)

Nnamdi muses for a moment. I follow his gaze to the window, where the melting ice is leaving long trails on the glass.

"Even there, now." he says. "Even in our fantasies, we're divided."

I decide to take up Nnamdi's challenge to think about who might be more vulnerable to the negative effects of social technology and how to create a set of media that helps rather than harms them. Specifically, whether some people are at greater risk of increased depression, addiction, and distraction than others.

VULNERABLE TO DEPRESSION AND ANXIETY

In 2017 psychologist Jean Twenge published a book called *iGen: Why Today's Super-Connected Kids Are Growing Up Less Rebellious,*

*More Tolerant, Less Happy—and Completely Unprepared for Adulthood—
and What That Means for the Rest of Us*. Twenge is an active, productive researcher of generational differences and author of several
popular books on the topic. Around the time of the book's publication, she also wrote a piece in the *Atlantic* called "Have Smartphones Destroyed a Generation?"[6]

The arguments in the piece were not less dramatic than the
title.

"Rates of teen depression and suicide have skyrocketed since
2011," Twenge writes. "It is not an exaggeration to describe iGen
as being on the brink of the worst mental-health crisis in decades.
Much of this deterioration can be traced to their phones.... The
twin rise of the smartphone and social media has caused an earthquake of a magnitude we've not seen in a very long time, if ever."

She acknowledges that while these indicators of mental health
have risen in this latest generation, on nearly every other account
they're faring *better* than earlier generations, with significant
decreases (and delays) in early sexual activity, teen pregnancy, and
alcohol use. But she points out that these trends seem to be tied
to teens spending less time together in person, and more time
together alone in their rooms with their phones on—it is hard to
get into a car accident when you're spread out on your bed flipping through Snapchat.

Twenge has been doing research on generational differences in
the United States since the beginning of her research career. Historically, most generational shifts she saw were subtle and slow,
and peering at the data on her computer was looking at lots of
gradual, small peaks and valleys. But she claims that starting in
2012, which she marks as the year that smartphone ownership
passed 50 percent, these slow slopes became "steep mountains and
sheer cliffs"—the slopes being higher rates of depression, anxiety,
and loneliness in young people.

Using giant national data sets, in numerous studies Twenge

found that the more teens use their smartphones, the worse they are feeling, the more they are suffering. She also reviewed experimental studies in which people who are asked to refrain from using Facebook for a week report elevations in happiness compared to people assigned to business as usual.

Twenge's essay went viral, dominating all of my social media networks. Everyone and their grandmother clicked the "share" button, crowing, "I knew it!"

As you probably know by now, my immediate reaction was that nothing is that simple. In my mind, claiming unilateral effects of a technology on an entire generation is unlikely to hold up to scrutiny. I posted a rebuttal call to caution called "No, Smartphones Have Not Destroyed a Generation" to my *Psychology Today* blog. I had several concerns about Twenge's interpretation of her data yielding a claim that we were facing a crisis of untold magnitude.

Let's consider just a few of these before asking the more interesting question of whether the effects might hold true for a vulnerable subset of us.

For one, as we saw in chapter 4, there is extensive research showing that social media can build us up rather than take us down, and this research is ignored. Second, especially with large data sets like the ones Twenge was working with, you can find significant correlations between variables that are probably not meaningfully related in actual life. For instance, other strong correlations you can find in publicly available data include correlations between the number of people drowning by falling into a swimming pool and the number of films Nicolas Cage appears in, or the per capita consumption of cheese and the number of people who die being tangled in their bedsheets.[7] Obviously, Nic Cage isn't going around shoving people into swimming pools during years he has a lot of movies to promote, and these correlations are spurious.

Out of the University of Oxford, researchers Amy Orben and Andrew Przybylski have taken the lead on critiquing Twenge's analyses,[8] downloading her data and running their own stats, and found that some of the effects are tiny. For example, the degree of explanatory power of smartphones to predict depression levels is of similar magnitude as the number of potatoes people reported eating and whether or not they wear eyeglasses. Even more worrisome, some of the findings don't replicate from one year to the next (e.g., from 2016 to 2017) and seem to be vulnerable to flexibility in experimenter decisions about which variables to include. Different decisions using the same data sets can find a positive effect, a negative effect, or no effect at all.

But ultimately, the question of the relationships between smartphone use and adolescent well-being is too blunt a question. The dependent measure of "hours on a screen per day" is so broad as to be almost meaningless. Screen time could mean texting friends, playing Candy Crush, using Duolingo to learn a new language, lurking jealously on your ex's Instagram, discovering new music, reading about neuroscience on Twitter, or rifling through endless filters for your selfies. Some of these activities might contribute negatively to well-being, others positively.

So what makes up vulnerability? What characteristics, volumes of use, types of activities might put some people at greater risk than others?

In part, we already answered this question back in chapter 4, when we saw that some activities on social media are linked to better outcomes (e.g., personalized sharing among real-life friends) and some are linked to poor outcomes of the type Twenge is discussing (e.g., lurking on the profiles of your socially connected friends who don't invite you to girls' night with them). We surveyed the many ways that social media can build us up and take us down and concluded: *enhance, don't eclipse.*

Intriguingly, Przybylski has also found that those who barely use social media and smartphones *and* those who use them the most are both faring worse than those who use them a moderate amount. He uses a Goldilocks metaphor to explain his finding—too little and too much are both linked to unhealthy outcomes, but there is a just-right amount in the middle associated with the best outcomes.[9]

In a wonderful example of the power of social media to better our world, Twenge and social psychologist Jonathan Haidt recently posted an annotated bibliography of research studies on teens, social media, and mental health, and issued an open invitation to researchers to contribute references and counterarguments.[10] It didn't result in everyone agreeing, but the weight of the data do seem to suggest that very heavy volume of use could be a risk factor, and that teen girls may be particularly vulnerable.

Twenge herself has delved into contextual influences and found them to be important, with social media use that interferes with sleep or replaces face-to-face interaction—rather than potentially augmenting it, as it might with friends making plans and sharing photos from time together—being particularly worrisome.[11] Multiple personality factors also seem to be associated with greater vulnerability, including people who are prone to feeling "Fear of Missing Out" (FoMO),[12] who are more prone to making social comparisons,[13] who are bothered by being tagged in unflattering pictures,[14] and who are less likely to post pictures of themselves with others.[15]

There are also a handful of actual experimental studies that assign people to reduce or cut out their social media usage, and while these studies are not perfect either (the participants were quite aware of the manipulation and probably the experimenters' expectation that they would benefit), these practices seem to lead to happier people.[16]

These are early days in our scientific inquiry on this topic, but social media replacing existing face-to-face time or supplanting healthy activities such as sleep or exercise seems to be the most problematic. People who are especially prone to negative social comparison or self-evaluation seem to suffer more. But we need more research—careful research that takes into account contextual factors like how often one uses social media, whether one is using it to enhance social connectedness, whether one has other vulnerabilities, and the size of the effects.

VULNERABLE TO ADDICTION

Perhaps even more common than the hivemind narrative that our phones are making us depressed is the hivemind narrative that we are addicted to our phones. Recently someone I follow on Twitter posted a thread of artwork depicting our reliance on our phones. In one, a disembodied hand held a smartphone and tentacles from the device had embedded themselves in the person's arm, worming their way into the skin. In another, a man reeled, a smartphone gripping his face in classic *Alien* fashion. A third had a person pinned to his phone like a dead butterfly, his four limbs spread-eagle and latched in place by the icons of the major social media platforms.

Many accounts of technology addiction rely on a neuroscientific model that goes like this: Pleasure results in a spike in the neurotransmitter dopamine. Common drugs of abuse also result in a release of dopamine in the so-called pleasure circuit in the brain, and the more directly the drug affects this circuit, the more addictive they are. People seem to find social technology rewarding and return to it again and again. Therefore, these behaviors must involve dopamine, and since they involve dopamine, they must be addictive.

But there is little to no experimental evidence that seeing a text notification or launching a video game quest to save the princess yields increases in dopamine release. Moreover, an account of dopamine as a "pleasure chemical" is so oversimplified as to be basically false. You see all over the popular press the idea that this or that behavior gives you a "squirt of dopamine" or that you feel a "rush like that of cocaine." But dopamine is a complicated neurotransmitter involved in numerous behaviors, from learning movement to, yes, tracking rewards—but even there, dopamine is as involved in near misses as it is in sure hits, and so it is more involved in tracking predictions and outcomes than in tracking pleasure.

I also believe that the logic for using the metaphor of addiction is manipulatively circular—I am going to slap this label on something, and the label strikes a nerve, calls up some of our worst fears, and then I'm going to use the fact that it has this label *that I chose* to drum up alarm. Appraisals at work again.

At the Center on Media and Child Health in Boston, Massachusetts, "mediatrician" Dr. Michael Rich and his colleagues have made an explicit move away from calling unhealthy media habits "addiction" at all, instead referring to them as Problematic Interactive Media Use, or PIMU for short. I like this not just for its move away from the dubious addiction model but because it reflects that almost any behavior can become problematic when taken to extremes—exercising, shopping, collecting stray cats.

For this particular vulnerability, I think our attention should be most focused on the fact that the social media giants are actively working against us in our efforts to determine healthiest media practices and to protect the vulnerable. As professor of media studies Siva Vaidhyanathan sums up succinctly, "Like casinos, slot machines, and potato chips, Facebook is designed to keep you immersed, to disorient you just enough so you lose track of the duration and depth of your immersion in the experience, and to reward you just enough that you often return, even when you have more edifying, rewarding, or pleasurable options for your time and effort within your reach."[17]

In his book *Irresistible: The Rise of Addictive Technologies and the Business of Keeping Us Hooked*, Adam Alter reviews how social tech companies are specifically tapping into psychological research on goals, feedback, progress, escalation, cliff-hangers, and social interaction to draw us in again and again, more and more. This practice of tapping into psychological principles to control consumer behavior is again nothing new—casinos have done so for a lot longer and with more pernicious societal results than Candy Crush has—but we don't carry casinos in our pockets, so the potential for life invasiveness is a lot higher with these mobile apps. Alter provides a handy guide to using psychological principles in defense against these companies. Writing that "the answer is not to medicalize these moderate forms of addiction, but to alter the structure of how we live, both at a societal level and more narrowly, as we construct our day-to-day lives," he argues not for tech abstinence but rather for crafting intentional tech habits that prioritize our larger goals and values.

We'll review many of these possible habits in the conclusion of the book.

VULNERABLE TO DISTRACTION

The final criticism of smartphones and social media to which I'd like to attend with our vulnerability lens is that they have permanently destroyed our ability to pay attention—that the constant buzzing and notifications and refreshing are altering how we process the world. Worse, that our children with their still-forming brains will never learn how to pay attention in the first place.

Social psychologist Larry Rosen and neuroscientist Adam Gazzaley have coauthored a handy overview of this body of work called *The Distracted Mind: Ancient Brains in a High-Tech World*. In the book, Gazzaley and Rosen argue that distraction was not invented by mobile phones but rather by a "fundamental vulnerability of our brain." We have evolved multiple systems for focusing attention on our goal-directed behavior (e.g., studying your notes, working on your book chapter) while also distributing attention to the environment in case survival-related or goal-related events arise that require our attention (e.g., the saber-toothed tiger about to jump at your throat, the imminent downpour). These competing systems mean we're bred to be vulnerable to multiple sorts of distractions both internal, like daydreaming, and external, like receiving a text.

The authors develop a theory based on the idea that we forage for information much like other animals forage for food. "We engage in interference-inducing behaviors because, from an evolutionary perspective, we are merely acting in an optimal manner to satisfy our innate drive to seek *information*." Much like a creature snuffling through the grass looking for tasty treats, we must evaluate and balance the potential risks and benefits of staying in our current spot versus venturing out and seeing if we can find a new, untapped source of tasty richness. So, too, Gazzaley and Rosen argue, do we flip from Instagram to Snapchat to Twitter.

The problem with all of this information foraging, in these days of mobile phones and the internet, is that we pay a mental cost when we switch information streams or tasks that we're working on. Doing two things at once spreads our available stores of attention and working memory too thinly and disadvantages performance. Here the answer of who might be more vulnerable is easily provided by the authors: these costs are redoubled for people marked by cognitive vulnerability of different sorts—people with attention-deficit problems, the young and the old, and those with dementia.

Echoing Alter, Gazzaley and Rosen provide evidence that these apps and platforms and programs have been designed, often intentionally, to maximize the extent to which they will encourage you to check, check, and check again, to distract yourself from your goal-directed behavior. Smartphones and social media have made these "information patches" increasingly accessible and increasingly alluring.

Gazzaley and Rosen don't argue that we should waste a lot of energy fretting about going on long digital detoxes or buying our teenagers flip phones. Rather, we must adapt, as we have done to so many technologies and revolutions in the past, and as we are so very skilled as human beings at doing. We cannot expect to instinctively stumble into the proper balance of usage for every revolutionary development. We must use the more advanced, metacognitive (thinking about thinking, intentional control) parts of our brain to regulate the hotter, more emotional, more stimulus-drawn parts of our brain. I love this approach, and as you'll see in a few chapters it has a lot in common with what I think is one antidote to the uglier sides of our collective natures.

Now that we've considered the triad of possible negative effects of social media on well-being (depression, addiction, distraction), I'd like to introduce two twists.

ARE THE MOST VULNERABLE ACTUALLY THE LEAST VULNERABLE?

First, ironically, those we think of as vulnerable in day-to-day life, such as people who are painfully introverted or depressed or socially anxious, may be the *least* vulnerable to the pernicious possible effects of social media. These platforms allow them an outlet to express their feelings, to interact socially, and to reach out for help when needed, even if they find initiating social interactions difficult in real life—it lowers the "cost of admission" to social interaction. Gazzaley and Rosen review research demonstrating that people who have more Facebook friends experience less depression, and that increased use of the internet for social reasons predicts less depression, less compulsive internet use, and more satisfaction with social support. People with depression sometimes report that social media allow an easier way to reach out for help if they are feeling down or at risk to themselves, and in fact, research psychologists are exploring ways that we can use online social networking to provide support to people suffering from mental health symptoms.[18]

It isn't just those who are psychologically vulnerable who might benefit from social media. Other research suggests that people with hearing impairments, elderly people with movement restrictions, patients with breast cancer, and neurodivergent people may all benefit from taking sociality online.[19]

These early studies hold promise, but we need more data before making firm conclusions.

Our second twist is a way that we might *all* be vulnerable.

VULNERABLE TO FEAR: ALL OF US?

I was recently at a big outdoor party at my sister-in-law's house, chatting with one of her good friends. The friend was asking about this book and my progress, and when I described the subject matter, she flung out her hand and gripped my arm tight.

"Oh, Sarah," she said. "Can you send me an early copy?" She told me her daughter is at a transitional age—she doesn't yet have a smartphone or an Instagram account but is peering over into that cavernous transition. "I am just *so* terrified," the friend continued, and the quake in her voice and the intensity of her grip on my arm did not belie her words. The dominant hivemind narrative surrounding social technology is one of fear, and it is whipping my sister-in-law's friend and all of us into a froth of terror.

In my introductory psychology class, I present my students with a 2010 article by British psychologist Vaughan Bell called "Don't Touch That Dial!: A History of Media Technology Scares, from the Printing Press to Facebook."[20] Bell is a researcher in the field of social cognition and psychosis, but he is probably most widely known for his work on a blog called *Mind Hacks* and his Twitter presence, as he is one of the most followed and most respected psychology voices on social media.

In "Don't Touch That Dial!" Bell presents evidence that moral panics about technology have been part of the human experience for about as long as there has been technology. He starts with Socrates, who was reportedly alarmed at the spread of writing. If you can write information down, what motivation do you have to remember it? Couldn't it be that if we stopped relying on our memories, our memory stores would crumble, our capacity to commit knowledge to our brains to recollect it at a future time fade away? Another transition was when people started getting their news from print rather than the town crier. People isolated, silent in their houses, the decay of social connections! The fabric of our society has been threatened with every new medium of sharing information—from the printing press to the radio to the television to the personal computer, and of course then to the internet and our present age of social media and smartphones.

But Bell points out that all of these moral panics have in common three appraisals: (1) that because the technology is new, the concern is also new, (2) that these technologies are rubbish compared to the technology we had before the new ones came on the scene, and (3) that these developments promise terrible danger to our minds, social fabric, and the well-being of our youngsters. Previous Facebook executive Athena Chavarria, as quoted in the *New York Times*: "I am convinced the devil lives in our phones and is wreaking havoc on our children."[21]

The devil himself.

Other than perhaps fear for one's own life, fear for our children is the most instinctual fear we have.

In her novel *A Little Life* Hanya Yanagihara writes,

You have never known fear until you have a child.... Every day, your first thought is not "I love him" but "How is he?" The world, overnight, rearranges itself into an obstacle course of terrors. I would hold him in my arms and wait to cross the street and would think how absurd it was that my child, that any child, could expect to survive this life. It seemed as improbable as the survival of one of those late-spring butterflies—you know, those little white ones—I sometimes saw wobbling through the air, always just millimeters away from smacking itself against a windshield.

If we appraise social technologies as inherently dangerous, the result is going to be fear and anxiety, and this fear and anxiety will spread through the process of emotional contagion. But we should always be wary of fear.

Renowned philosopher Martha Nussbaum wrote *The Monarchy of Fear: A Philosopher Looks at Our Political Crisis* on just this subject: our preoccupation with fear and its potential ramifications. She believes that we have succumbed totally to fear—not just about technology and its effects but also about the economy, climate change, the current degree of political polarization, the rise of populism, and so on. These topics do warrant immediate attention and concern, but Nussbaum's point is that fear impedes making any progress on these issues. Fear leads to an inward focus and an embrace of sameness and comfort. We cling to our ingroups and shun outgroups and narrow our behavior and the options we consider—which is the opposite of what we should be doing. The solutions to the complex problems we face are likely outward and require creativity and collaboration across different perspectives. Embracing fear in the face of challenge leads us to a shutting down of options when what we need is open possibilities and action.

What's more, fear can easily be manipulated and turned into a weapon of distraction and diversion. All the way back to Aristotle, we have been aware of the power of political leaders to directly manipulate the populace by provoking fear, usually by activating the appraisal that there is an uncontrolled threat to the group that needs to be addressed, and this fear usually leads to support for more restrictive policies. Witness the passing of the USA Patriot Act ("Uniting and Strengthening America by Providing Appropriate Tools Required to Intercept and Obstruct Terrorism Act of 2001") mere weeks after 9/11. In addition to expanding antiterrorism intelligence efforts, the act allowed the federal government previously unheard-of freedom to spy on its own citizens.

Fear also encourages self-focus, a narcissistic narrowing of attention away from the collective and toward the individual self. Nussbaum argues that fear marks much of infancy, when the unknown is everywhere and separation from caregivers spells death. Maturation into adulthood involves learning to inhibit fear, to stop worrying about enemies above, below, within, and without, to embrace the full spectrum of other emotions, and to consider the perspectives of others different from us.

We'll consider some alternatives to fear in the next chapter, in the shadow of the mountains of Salt Lake City.

PROTECTING THE VULNERABLE

Back at the horrifying airport on my way to home, I field a phone call from my Irish twin, Dan. He scoffs at the idea of me being in Las Vegas for the first time and not gambling even once. I've gotten to midlife without ever having used a slot machine because, as a defensive pessimist, I have no belief that I might actually win something. Gambling to me feels the same as lighting money on fire and watching it burn. Just noisier. But Dan strong-arms me into promising to try it. One spin of the wheel, one dance with Lady Luck. For him. I grumble but hang up and approach the whirring, buzzing machines warily.

A *Wheel of Fortune* machine in front of me, I feel a bit like I do when I open Snapchat. I press a few buttons and nothing happens.

I take out my credit card and put it into an available slot, but the machine doesn't acknowledge it.

I try talking to it like Scotty in the *Star Trek* movie with the humpback whales: "Hello, Computer?" Nothing.

I grab the attention of a local technician and she rolls her eyes at me: "Cash only, honey."

Mentally cursing out my brother, I place a ten-dollar bill in the same slot that I tried the credit card in and gasp as it is suddenly sucked away. I frown at the machine. What next? I find a button to press and the three slots whiz and buzz and spin and land on little shapes—a glowing bar, triple sevens on fire, a gold five—that don't match at all. There seems to be no indication of how many spins I get for my ten dollars, so I shrug and randomly press the button a few more times until the machine stops responding.

And that's a wrap.

I just don't get the draw.

But the entire experience drives home for me the theme of this chapter. Namely, that my personal relationship to technology may give me a biased view of the interactions between technology and mental health. That perhaps whatever mixture of genetics and environment and personality and worldview combine to make the motivations behind gambling opaque to me also make the addictive lure of constant checking or the fear of missing out opaque to me. That because of this viewpoint, to me my smartphone seems not like a burden or a crutch but a marvelous tool.

I reflect on Nnamdi's idea that we need to consider the impact of social technology on the most vulnerable among us, not the most resilient among us. I appreciate this viewpoint. As we saw in this chapter, much like some people are more vulnerable to the lures of gambling or the sway of peer pressure or obedience to authority, so, too, could some people be particularly vulnerable to negative impacts of technology on well-being.

I'm also quite in favor of moderation, self-control, and healthy limits, both as an individual and as a parent. My tween daughter will tell you that she's the only middle-schooler in the world who isn't allowed on YouTube. Teens and adults especially prone to fear of missing out, social comparison, or difficulty regulating their behavior in general may need especial support in setting healthy limits with technology. As we discussed in the Preface, I'm also quite supportive of much greater regulation of industry.

What I *am* against is moral panics, especially those that may have more impact on well-being than the object of the moral panic. Especially when the data supporting said moral panic are so very inconclusive. I also oppose appraisals that cast us as helpless victims dragged under a wave of notifications rather than active, autonomous beings who can regulate our own usage. I object to solutions that force teens out of the social media ecosphere where their peers are doing much of their social networking and identity development, and which shelter them out of developing the digital-literacy skills they will need later in life.

I suspect that much like our worst fears about the written word and newspapers and personal computers did not materialize, neither will we all become slaves to our devices or end up with attention spans shorter than a goldfish or be unwillingly drafted into a second civil war.

Good news: in the next few chapters we're going to talk with people who have a positive view of the landscape of social technology and the path we're on together as human beings.

For spring, she is dawning.

SPRING

Chapter Eight

Walking Amygdalas

Salt Lake City, Utah

A silver Nissan pulls up to my hotel in downtown Salt Lake City. I climb in and greet my Lyft driver, Trevor.★ An early spring snowstorm rages back home, but here in Utah the sun is shining and the air is warm, if a bit dry for my tastes. Inevitably, Trevor and I chat about the weather, and I tell him about the storm back in Boston. He amuses me by saying, "Oh, you're from Boston? It must be so confusing to have everyone be so nice to you here!" I smile and laugh to combat the unfriendly Beantowner stereotype but also admit that I do appreciate a certain degree of curmudgeonly silence on elevators.

We pass a few moments in quiet while I gaze in awe at the snow-covered mountain peaks that surround the city. Salt Lake City is technically a valley in these mountain ranges—the coordinator for the event that brought me to the city said that visitors sometimes experience mild altitude sickness and get dehydrated, and so to rest well and drink lots of liquids. It is amazing to me that anyone could habituate to the gorgeousness of the scenery. One could almost believe that the mountains are not real, that they are instead some sort of projected movie backdrop.

★ Not his real name.

Then, for reasons unknown to me, Trevor breaks the silence by launching into an ominous story about Mormons frantically photocopying records to bury in deep, secret tunnels under the towering mountain peaks that surround the city. The story goes like this: He once picked up a job delivering copy machines. Prior to taking the job, he didn't even know they made copiers as big as the ones he was delivering to one of the Mormon temples in the city—they were monstrous, hulking beasts of equipment. He had to go through several layers of security clearances to work the job, and at each step he was given information only on a need-to-know basis. When it came time to deliver the copiers, he entered at the ground floor and then took a series of elevators down, down, down—well below ground level—and finally wheeled the machine off to another man, presumably with higher security clearance, who took it off to yet another elevator, which led to an even *deeper* subterranean level.

"I've heard," he says, gesturing to the scenery I'd just been admiring, "that they're frantically copying everything they have and then hiding the copies in secret caverns in the mountains." He tells me more, about Mitt Romney and his suspicious ways, about secret wars between the Church of Jesus Christ of Latter-day Saints and the US government that don't make it into the history books, about secrecy and distrust and dastardly doings deep underground. It strikes me as both a bit conspiracist and anti-Mormon, so I let the conversation lapse without much encouragement. We arrive at our coffeehouse destination and I wish him well.

Publik Coffeehouse has big, floor-to-ceiling windows, black metal stools, and reportedly amazing coffee. I'm meeting journalist and tech expert Anne Collier here. A Boston native, she moved to Salt Lake City, and in contrast to Trevor's opening story, she found it a welcoming, modern place far removed from its stereotypes. I'm lucky to have caught Anne in town, as she travels globally, speaking, serving on task forces, and attending summits. In fact, she was joining me today having just flown in from SXSW EDU, the hipster of academic conferences for educators. At the conference she had run a role-playing panel for high school administrators on how to deal with challenges like Instagram bullying and nonconsensual sexting.

I set myself up in a long, elevated wooden booth and get some of Publick's famed coffee, which is indeed strong and delicious. A few minutes later Anne rushes in with a burst of energy, the swoop of her short blond hair a bit in her eyes, dressed comfortably in a zip-up jacket. Though neither of us is a millennial, we both order avocado toasts, generous servings with cracked sea salt and fresh pepper and a solid drizzle of olive oil.

Anne began her career as a journalist and has been observing, writing about, and advising on technology for decades. She writes, blogs, and speaks about online health and safety, but she does so with one foot in the academic research world and one foot in the world of industry. A unique trifecta of expertise—clear communication, research literacy, and knowledge of social media platforms—has made her a coveted voice in matters media. She has served on three national task forces examining the data on youth digital safety, including cochairing the Obama administration's Online Safety and Technology Working Group. At the same time, she also serves on the safety advisory boards of Facebook, Snapchat, Twitter, and Kik. She also works closely with Google on family technology.

Anne and I discuss the topic that first brought us onto each other's digital radar, that of the uproar regarding youth, anxiety, and social technology. Having spent so much time watching the rise and fall of new technologies, she is unusually conversant with how panics also rise and fall. She points to a previous peak around 2006, when the biggest worry was online predators, a fear exacerbated and encouraged by the popular show called *To Catch a Predator.* Premiering in 2004, this programming gem tapped into a perfect storm of fears about both hidden child molesters (enemies within) and new social technologies. In our current panic, people seem to focus less on what may happen to children when they're online and more on whether being online itself is a problem, whether being glued to one's smartphone raises risks of addiction or depression or fear of not measuring up.

Over a decade ago I headed to the theaters to see *Bowling for Columbine*, Michael Moore's documentary film on gun violence. I expected to leave the theater thinking that the sole culprits were gun culture and the NRA. But while Moore certainly takes aim at those groups, he also targets the American media's obsession with fearmongering, with our nightly news dump of killer snakes and carcinogenic soap ingredients and terror plots on every corner. According to the twenty-four-hour news cycle, the world is overrun with enemies within, outside, above, and below, a collection of ghost stories designed to make us tune in for the next installment of our nightly ghost stories. Constantly dwelling on such stories of danger and persecution is likely to drive up anxiety, polarization, and the perception that everyone needs a gun under the pillow for protection.

I tell Anne that one of the strangest aspects of researching and writing this book has been encountering the seemingly universal assumption that there are two possible reactions to smartphones and social media: either blind panic or uncritical adulation. I once appeared on an Ontario-based radio show to talk about my blog post on smartphones not destroying a generation. While the assistant was prepping me, she discovered that my own ten-year-old didn't have a smartphone yet. She fretted. I explained that my position wasn't that Twenge and others were wrong to be concerned about teen mental health, but rather that the evidence she pointed to had flaws and that it ignored hugely important contextual factors, such as what teens are using the phones to what other supports they have, and how socially embedded they are. I thought it was important to remind listeners that, as with almost everything else in life, moderation would likely be the healthiest approach. Panicked, the radio assistant exclaimed: "Well, you can't say *that!*"

After the blog post, I received a fair bit of hate mail for this moderate position—that smartphones and social media are neither inherently dangerous nor wonderful, that the choice facing parents doesn't have to be between massive regulation or laissez-faire anything-goes—which is just bizarre to me. I've written about sex and race and took internet ire surrounding these topics for granted, but saying that we should approach social tech with moderation didn't seem like an especially provocative position to me.

"We love binaries," Anne reflects, when I tell her about the kerfuffle. "We want there to be right and wrong, black and white, good guys and bad guys."

Anne thinks that part of this insistence on binary viewpoints is due to the overwhelming nature of change plaguing our society. Things have always changed, obviously, but the rate of change—technological, economic, climate—has accelerated. This might be why we're in such a panic upswing, and as we discussed before, we always fear particularly for our children.

A large national survey found that 93 percent of parents worried that a stranger would harmfully contact their children online, whereas only 1 percent had ever experienced this happening.[1] Like many of our other fears, our screen fears are out of step with reality. Director of the Crimes Against Children Research Center David Finkelhor coined the term *juvenoia*, which he referred to as the exaggerated fear of the influence of social change on young people, including technology.[2] Writing about internet fears in particular, he emphasizes that there are real risks online, but the problem is that the hivemind fixates on these risks as above and beyond those one might encounter in other life environments, with no real evidence that this is the case.

"There is just *so much* fear right now," Anne says, shaking her head in dismay. "We're like walking amygdalas."

This metaphor appeals to me.★ Much like those almond-shaped nuggets of brain tissue deep in our temporal lobes, we seem to be on constant alert for potential threats in our environment. Fear evolved to help us react to aspects of our environments that hold biological relevance for our survival and reproduction (using a circuit involving the amygdala)—not to be on constant blaring alarm mode, all of the time.

It reminds me of neuroendocrinologist Robert Sapolsky's life-work on stress:[3] Our fight-or-flight response evolved to respond to acute, present dangers. When your brain detects that you are being chased by a tiger, it activates a wing of your nervous system that speeds up your heart, accelerates your breathing, gives you a shot of adrenaline, and releases glucose to your large muscles, all of which help you to flee to safety. In modern Western lifestyles, we aren't stressed by these sorts of events very often. Instead, we are routinely, chronically, and unrelentingly activating our fight-or-flight response to stressors such as deadlines, taxes, saving for college, and worrying about whether our children are as smart and kind and talented as our neighbors' children. Chronically activating this emergency response wears down almost every biological system in our body, which translates into an array of stress-related maladies and diseases. We used to activate this stress response to flee tigers, and we used to die young from being mauled by tigers. Now we use this stress response chronically to respond to psychological stressors, and we die young from stress-related diseases (e.g., heart attacks, strokes, some cancers). And of

---

★ Since we all have amygdalas and do walk them around, I suppose this is both literally true and a good metaphor for our cultural hypervigilance.

course, rising higher on the list of chronic stressors is stress about screens—are we addicted, are we distracted, will our children grow up incapable of empathy or critical thinking or sustained attention?

Today's youth can't help but feel our fear and be affected by this vat of anxiety we're simmering in, for all of the reasons of emotional contagion and neural synchrony we reviewed earlier in the book. Our panic becomes their panic, what writer John Warner calls "trickle-down anxiety."

In the UK in 2013, professors Sonia Livingstone and Julian Sefton-Green followed a class of year nine students (US equivalent would be eighth graders) for a year, talking to them and observing them in school, in their homes, and in their digital spaces, and published the results in a book called *The Class: Living and Learning in the Digital Age*. These students do admit to a growing unease, an uncertainty about their place in the world. But based on both their research and their conversations with and observations of these young people living their lives, Livingstone and Sefton-Green don't attribute this anxiety to their smartphones. Rather, their data point to other contributors: greater levels of dependency on parents, a lack of meaningful work outside the home, weighty pressures from schoolwork, reduced involvement in religious and civic communities, and even decreased helping roles in the household.

Cultural analyses suggest this generation can't expect a better life than their parents. They are also watching their parents working multiple jobs to make ends meet while striving to match society's increasingly neoliberal demands to lead perfectly fit, perfectly fulfilled, Pinterest-worthy lives. Livingstone and Sefton-Green write, "We wonder, then, if young people's worries about the future are founded in genuinely unsettling social changes or are, instead, a reflection of the anxious discourses that surround them." Our youth rely on us to have answers when they are flailing, and they'll certainly flail on social media as much as they do in other avenues of life—if we are *also* flailing, they're going to be without an anchor.

Anne says that a lot of what happens with parents and educators when it comes to social media is that they throw up their hands and feel like they don't have the tools to help their youth, when really the digital is just a new realm that requires many of the same old tools as navigating any other social space. She runs a social media helpline called ICanHelp.Com for schools looking for guidance interfacing with the online social media platforms. For example, a recent case involved an anonymous Snapchat profile that was attempting to solicit nudes from many young women in the same high school. Anne was able to contact Snapchat, and the account was disabled within hours. But a lot more of what Anne and others do at the helpline is remind high school administrators that they have been dealing with gossip and harassment and cliques as long as there have been high schools, and those skills are still quite relevant in the digital realm: talking to students, interfacing with them, following through with consequences, and doing psychoeducation with both parents and students are all skills that are still relevant even though the challenges have moved online.

She shares the story that some very painful gossip about one of her sons was posted online and spread like wildfire. It ended in a friendship dissolved and an anguished sixty or so hours. But then it was over, and he had weathered the experience and was stronger for it. It is not as if gossip or harassment were invented by social media. Even the anonymity isn't completely new.

"Slam books!" Anne and I both say at the same time.

Back in our days, teens would create little booklets where students could anonymously roast their schoolmates. In the hugely popular 2004 movie *Mean Girls*, they call such a notebook their "burn book."

Anne also worries that policing youth technology too heavily prevents children from learning their own self-regulatory skills. If their relationship with digital media is controlled entirely externally, how will they ever learn to navigate those limits themselves? She shares a story of her then eleven-year-old son being desperate for an Xbox 360 on which to play Halo. After he received it, he played the game for endless hours...and hours...and hours, and Anne grew concerned. She wondered whether she ought not step in, contradict her own advice, and externally regulate him. She resisted; not long after, he grew tired of the game. A natural athlete, he missed his time outside and self-regulated, presumably learning some lessons about excess and regulation and prioritization along the way. I reflect on one February school vacation when all I did the entire week was play Bionic Commando on my Nintendo in my pajamas, and smile nostalgically.

Anne reflects that when a moral panic about technology spreads, the response is usually guilt—we worry that we aren't protecting our children well enough. The constantly shifting tides of technology are hard to keep up with, and that can leave users and parents feeling ill at ease. But it is often the parents who are more mystified by the new technologies and more likely to assume that they are pernicious. Young people are born into this world of digital technologies and don't need to adapt in the same way. Rather than focus our response on the aspects of the changing technologies that we fear—instead of using our time and bandwidth to wring our hands over the damage technology can do—what if instead we were to roll up our sleeves and figure it out together? It might have the dual reward of alleviating our concerns and also giving us a way to connect to youth on their own terms.

IT'S COMPLICATED

In her fantastic book *It's Complicated: The Social Life of Networked Teens*, danah boyd explores this very issue. Boyd is a researcher at Microsoft and founder of Data & Society, a research institute focused on the intersections of social and cultural issues and technology. *It's Complicated* is the culmination of more than a decade of boyd's conversations with young people about their relationships with technology and how they use it. While some of the tech has inevitably already dated itself—there are many MySpace stories—the lessons hold lasting appeal.

The book opens at a football game in Nashville, where boyd noticed that indeed, everyone seemed to be on a smartphone. But it was the *parents* who were glued to their phones in ways that were isolating, silently scrolling even with their spouses and neighbors at their elbows, available for face-to-face socialization. The young people were instead using their phones as "glorified camera plus coordination devices," taking and posting photos, texting one another about where to meet up, showing one another goofy cat videos, and generally using their phones as a tool to interact rather than a device to isolate.

Boyd talked afterward with one teen girl at the game who opened up her Facebook page and showed it to her. While the teen hadn't used Facebook at the event, afterward she uploaded pictures, tagged her friends, and then interacted in long conversations in the comment sections, which were full of references to conversations that took place at the game. She used the social media site to continue the conversation, to extend the social setting, rather than as a distraction at the game itself.

In this way, adolescents use social media (including texting and other forms of direct messaging) as a form of *public*, which boyd defines as a social space or community that can be concrete, imaginary, or a blend of the two. We all belong to multiple publics, each with its own spaces (physical and virtual) for interaction: churches, political parties, alumni groups, work teams. Boyd writes, "Publics provide a space and a community for people to gather, connect, and help construct society as we understand it." With multiple advancements in technology, internet, and social media, these publics have moved online and become increasingly networked.

We have shrunk the social landscapes of our young people, boyd claims, through greater rules, fear of strangers, endless extracurricular activities, and intolerance of public spaces for loitering. We've shrunk our youth's publics, and they're responded by moving them online. Teens desperately want to be with their friends. Specifically, they want to be with their friends in the absence of adult supervision, in publics of their choosing, and on their own terms. We cannot understand the widespread success of social media among teens without considering the context of this ever-dwindling social landscape available to them.

When I was a preteen, I would roam freely within a several-mile perimeter of my house from breakfast till dinner, lolling about with friends in publics made up of various treehouses, outside the local store with the cheap candy bars, and in the woods surrounding our local reservoir. My preteen daughter, in contrast, goes only to organized, parent-supervised playdates and a never-ending carousel of lessons and activities. Even if I wanted to let her wander, there would be no one for her to wander with—her friends think I'm a rebel parent because I let her go to the library alone, across the street and down a few buildings. In *The Coddling of the American Mind: How Good Intentions And Bad Ideas Are Setting Up a Generation for Failure*, Greg Lukianoff and Jonathan Haidt call this overprotective parenting style "safetyism" and argue that it is disempowering our youth, perhaps a major contributor to the elevations in depression and anxiety we've been discussing.

Teens are not flocking to social media because they're being hypnotized by whizbang techno devices, they're compelled by their own innate sociality and growing desire to control and navigate their own social space. "Social media—far from being the seductive Trojan horse—is a release valve," boyd writes, "allowing youth to reclaim meaningful sociality as a tool for managing the pressures and limitations around them." In interviews with teens, boyd heard again and again that they'd much rather gather face-to-face, but that opportunities for such gatherings are limited. Limited, again, by parental fears and overstructured lives.

For teens, social media also provides an exciting new venue for self-presentation and representation. Much as teens decorate their lockers and bedroom walls with mementos and posters of their likes, dislikes, and group identities (athletics, musical tastes, other activities), timelines, tweets, and posting pictures of their lives online follows the same pattern, a form of self-expression and a place to test out their different identities. Adolescence is a time to try on new selves like hats and test them out, and teens want to do so out of the prying eyes of scolding adults. A lot of what teens are doing with one another online is representative of things that teens have always done.

But of course, one of the major differences is that many of these behaviors have become public, permanent, and available to multiple audiences. Digital media often has invisible audiences, which makes things even more difficult. The inside of one's own locker or bedroom is visible only to a few people, and they shift along with the developing identity of the teen, past iterations lost to the sands of time. The content of one's Twitter feed is available to anyone with an internet connection—college admissions officers, potential employers, past and future dating partners—and can become part of the permanent record. All of these interest groups mashed together on digital platforms can lead to what boyd dubbed "context collapse," when a post or message intended for one audience with the poster's own shared history and set of understandings is shared with a wider audience, who do not have the correct context to interpret the post.

And of course, some teens do have problems regulating their use of social media, gaming, and other screens, demonstrating the problematic interactive media use we discussed in an earlier chapter. Boyd feels that problematic engagement is usually a symptom reflective of underlying depression, anxiety, or other maladjustment. People who struggle with impulse control may well have trouble regulating their screen use, and they deserve our attention. "But instead of prompting a productive conversation," boyd writes, "addiction rhetoric positions new technologies as devilish and teenagers as constitutionally incapable of having agency in response to the temptations that surround them."

Anne says that she loves USC media professor Henry Jenkins's advice for parents: instead of looking over your children's shoulders, have their backs. She recommends: "Sit down with your kids and ask—I've heard a lot about this thing called streaking—what is that, does it make you nervous, does it annoy you?" Good parenting in the age of social media bears a remarkable resemblance to good parenting through the ages, just as good living with technology bears a remarkable resemblance to good living through the ages— moderation and conscious, thoughtful decision making. The good habits we develop throughout life when it comes to work-life balance, diet, spending, and substance use apply to technology as well.

DIGITAL CITIZENS

In addition to being coauthor of *The Class*, Sonia Livingstone is a social psychology professor at the London School of Economics and Political Science and author of twenty books on kids and media. She is one of the leading thinkers about our rights as digital citizens. She is also one of the lead researchers in the then EU Kids Online and now Global Kids Online, an international research project whose mission is to create a global network of researchers to build and report unbiased, empirical evidence on children's digital media use and well-being.

Just one of the many reports and papers to come out of this project is one called *In Their Own Words: What Bothers Children*

Online?,[4] a collation of conversations with young people ages nine to sixteen in twenty-five different countries. The researchers sat down and talked with these young people about their experiences online. According to Anne, the take-home message was that the current public policy agenda was nearly entirely based on adult concerns and fears, not on the concerns, interests, and experiences of young people around the world. What they're really worried about is the future and how they fit in with their social peers.

We need to spend good thought, time, effort, and funds on increasing digital literacies. We absolutely need methods of sorting good information from bad, for cultivating skepticism without losing our faith in facts and truth. And young people are as much in need of social and emotional literacy work as they ever have been, particularly now that many of their social engagements are being conducted without face-to-face, moment-by-moment feedback. But young people provide ample evidence that they have the capacity to protect themselves and each other in these new climates and are even trying to protect their parents. "Children are stakeholders in their own well-being and that of their peers and their communities, online and offline," Anne says, "not just potential victims as we have represented them for so long in internet safety."

"We like to think these problems are technological, because that seems somehow easier to solve," she continues, "but these aren't technology problems. They are *humanity* problems." Problems like how to stay literate in a world that is constantly changing, how to build social connections that engage on a deep versus a superficial level, how to network, how to balance ambition for the future with being in the present moment, how to dismantle social inequalities, how to allow our children to have autonomy while protecting them from real threats that exist in the world. And we need all hands on deck—activists, academics, people in media, people in industry, and the next generations that are going to carry on the mission.

Young people are using social media to develop powerful new ways of connecting with one another and create meaning. Critically, many of these young people are not only extensively civically engaged, but they also are using the tools of social media to rally supporters, fund-raise, and organize collective action across the globe, leading to an unprecedented level of group action. The Parkland students garnered global attention after their school in Florida was the site of a horrific school shooting. They translated the power of their story and the tools of social media to invigorate gun control efforts, to shame adults out of their helpless passivity surrounding the issue.

As another example, Anne notes that she recently attended a Facebook summit panel of young women from all over the globe working on a new initiative they pioneered called #freeperiods. Headliner Amika George from the United Kingdom read that many girls at low income schools could not afford menstrual products and so were either skipping school altogether or using hacked-together solutions such as socks taped to their underwear or stolen rolls of toilet paper lodged between their legs. Amika and others used social media to join forces across the globe, organizing panels, peaceful protests, petitions, and active social media campaigns.[5] The campaign reached Parliament, whose members are actively considering policy changes to address the issue.

"And these are young people under twenty years old!" Anne exclaims. "They're changing their world. Our world."

I can't think of a better place to end the interview than there, so I flip off the audio recording, and Anne and I relax into some ordinary chitchat before she darts off to her next engagement.

I stay, moving to a long bench near the bright windows where I can plug in my laptop. I open up the family Slack channel I share with my mother and two brothers and drop in an update about how the interview went and also the funny coincidence that my Lyft driver was an apparent conspiracy theorist.

At the sound of some laughter I look up. Next to me are two friends in their late twenties, one with a sixish-month-old infant in her lap. They are laughing and chatting. One pulls out her smartphone and shows a few pictures to her friend. Next they use the camera app to snap a picture of the friend snuggling the baby on her lap. The friend with the phone then places it to the side on the table next to me, its screen still bright with the snapshot of her happy face and the beaming youngster. She and her friend dissolve into animated conversation, exchanging updates and gossip and the minutiae of daily living.

I smile and think how both Anne and danah boyd would enjoy this visual underscoring of their points, that the draw of social media and smartphones is not the technology but the sociality. We would expect nothing less from our bee-like selves.

My laptop dings and I flip back to Slack, where my brother has posted some links. Apparently, the Mormon church really is photocopying all of their records for storage offsite, but there isn't anything nefarious about it—they just want to keep their sacred records safely distributed across multiple locations.

Sometimes, our fears quite outpace the actual danger. Sometimes, what we really should fear is fear itself.

The vast move of our social lives online is not without consequences and challenges. But in sharp contrast to the popular headline perspectives from the last chapter, Anne and dana boyd and Sonia Livingstone and other experts who have sat down with our young people and had long, open, data-driven conversations with them have a refreshing alternative position to consider.

What if we stopped trying to go backward in time and instead accepted our current challenges and faced them head-on and with a positive mind-set? What if we sat down with our youth and asked for their perspective?

I find the idea both exhilarating and refreshing.

Chapter Nine

Antidote

Tokyo, Japan

Brains are curiously inconsistent machines. At times, they are stunning in their ingenuity, at others surprisingly inept. The morning of March 11, 2011, I was working on a computer, tweaking a psychology experiment. I was focusing hard on the task but thanks to our digital age also had a diffuse awareness of the larger world. In my mental background, I was aware that my social media platforms had begun pinging with alarming reports of a massive earthquake and tsunami in Japan. I felt the deep but muted tug of dismay that accompanies hearing about bad news happening at a distance.

Still immersed in the experiment, I opened my email and crafted a message to Erin Fitzgerald, an undergraduate in my lab conducting the experiment for her senior honors thesis. The experiment was designed to assess cross-cultural differences in the experience of emotion. Erin had sent me an enthusiastic "Dare I say it—are we safe to start?" message the day before. I wanted to be sure the experiment worked flawlessly before launch, since she would be conducting the research on her own half a globe away while studying abroad. I wouldn't be present to do any last-minute troubleshooting should anything go wrong. I hit send on the email and at that very moment all of these threads of information coalesced into realization and I cried out, loud enough to startle my dog.

Erin was in Japan.

Thankfully, I didn't have to wait long before Erin messaged me that she was physically safe. All her belongings had been destroyed when her apartment crashed to the ground during the earthquake, but as you might imagine, this loss was a smaller blow than the psychological impact.

Our original intention was to study cross-cultural differences between American and Japanese students in how they regulated their emotions. Emotion regulation is the process by which people influence or change how they feel in reaction to emotionally provocative stimuli like pictures or video (in the lab) and arguments or bad news (in real life). We were interested in cross-cultural differences in one particular strategy people use to regulate their emotions, called cognitive reappraisal.

As we have discussed throughout the book, an appraisal is an interpretation of the meaning or significance of an event—in other words, the story you tell yourself about something that happened. If you interview for a job and do not get it, there are multiple appraisals you could apply to the event. Perhaps you might assume that there was a better-qualified candidate, someone whose past work experience was more relevant or more extensive than your own. An alternative appraisal you might apply is that you totally flubbed the interview, that the team thought your ideas were terrible, and that you may never get a job ever again. It isn't hard to see which set of appraisals might lead to a more positive emotional state and which to a more negative one.

These appraisals are fairly automatic and reflexive. Things happen in the world, our brains do their automatic meaning-making, and we feel the impact of the narrative. What cognitive reappraisal does is take your original, reflexive appraisals and intentionally shifts them to a more productive set of interpretations. Back to the job rejection example: you get the rejection email and your brain plays you the "you're terrible and everyone hates

174

you" narrative. If you were to engage in cognitive reappraisal, you would assess your original appraisal and then much like a parent might for a child, kindly nudge the alternative explanation of the more qualified candidate.

You might do so by engaging in a little self-talk, as if one part of your brain were talking to another part of your brain, like two selves engaged in a little dialogue: "Look, I know you are assuming that this rejection means you are terrible and everyone hates you. But an equal or even more likely possibility is that the job went to someone who has done exactly this work before, or to the boss's niece, or they had an all-male team and were looking to diversify viewpoints a bit. It doesn't necessarily say anything about you as a person." In fact, much of cognitive behavioral therapy (CBT), the most effective form of psychotherapy we have, gives people "homework" in which they are challenged to engage in these sorts of reappraisals.

This two-parts-of-the-brain scenario isn't just a metaphor. Extensive research demonstrates that when you put people in a neuroimaging scanner and evoke emotion, brain regions deep below the cerebral cortex activate as the person feels the emotional impact. When you then ask them to engage in cognitive reappraisal, more prefrontal cortical areas come online and seemingly down-regulate the activity in the emotional areas.[1]

Emotion regulation research in general and the examination of cognitive reappraisal specifically has been a huge collective endeavor in emotion science. This research has benefited from both the initial spark and the calm ongoing stewardship of Stanford psychologist James Gross.[2] Gross and many others have published quite a lot of work indicating that cognitive reappraisal is one of the most effective emotion regulation techniques (i.e., best at calming the emotional reactivity that occurs when someone experiences negative emotion), as well as one linked with some of the best psychological outcomes (i.e., people who use it well and regularly have the highest levels of well-being and lowest levels of depressive symptoms).

But at the time that Erin and I were putting together our experiment, almost all of this research had been performed on Western samples, and mostly on American undergraduates at selective universities. There were one or two evaluations that spoke to culture, but even those tended to compare Asian American or Asian international students studying in the United States with American students. Erin and I had intended on collecting a sample of Japanese participants living in Tokyo and comparing them to students at Assumption College in America to see whether there were cultural differences in these associations between reappraisal and good outcomes. Erin had brought a laptop with the experimental software to Tokyo.

The laptop, and our original plans, were now so much rubble.

We scrambled to retool and get ethics approval for a new version of our experiment. Since Erin had a connection to the embassy in Tokyo, our new experiment focused on people either working in or associated with the embassy during the triple disaster (earthquake, tsunami, nuclear emergency). Our participants told us harrowing stories of their experiences*—one woman was at work, and when she realized how large the disaster was shaping up to be, she called her nanny and asked her to get her two children to the street from the tenth floor. The nanny couldn't handle both children on the rumbling, tilting staircase and had to choose between a seven-month-old baby and a toddler. Others told us of stumbling around downtown Tokyo watching giant skyscrapers sway like leaves of grass in the wind, others of being trapped in small windowless rooms not knowing if they might escape.

We didn't find evidence of cross-cultural differences, but we did find that the better you were able to implement reappraisal on

---

* Participants in this research study gave informed consent for their stories to be used in reports of the research.

the experimental task (e.g., reduce your negative reaction to an image of a crying woman sitting on a pile of destroyed buildings by focusing on positive reappraisals), the fewer your symptoms of depression and posttraumatic stress in the wake of the disasters.[3]

As the pictures were all related to the disasters and thus reminders of this potentially traumatic experience, we believe that this statistical relationship on the computerized task reflected how our participants were dealing with their negative emotions in the real world. That is, people who were better at down-regulating negative emotion to pictures on the computer task may in their daily lives have been better at down-regulating their negative emotions when they flipped on the news and it was full of dire reports about the nuclear plant meltdown, when they went to the grocery store and found it lacking eggs and bread and milk, or when their relatives in the States kept calling asking when they were going to evacuate.

People who were better at doing this sort of regulation on the task reported having fewer nightmares about the disaster, lower startle response, not as many feelings of despair and impending doom. Our small study joined legions of others echoing this basic finding—cognitive reappraisal, new stories for negative events—are associated with positive outcomes.

Given the impressive weight of all of this research, reappraisal might be a good candidate to target some of our problems of tribalism and polarization. Happily, I know some folks who are investigating just this possibility.

Let's take reappraisal for a test-drive.

TEST-DRIVE: INSIDE MY COMFORT ZONE

Keith Maddox opens the cocktail menu and groans.

Keith and I are in Davis Square, a bustling little town common near Boston, lined with cobblestone streets and studded with independent movie theaters and used bookstores. We checked out the coffeeshops, but they were all crowded and playing loud music, so instead we tucked into a local restaurant called The Foundry. It is a place of quiet, soothing darkness and tall red leather seats.

It is also, apparently, a place where the menu is displeasing Keith.

I ask what the problem is, and he points to an item called Kitten Mittens.

"I really want this delicious-looking bourbon drink...but why did they have to give it such a silly name?"

Keith is not my only male friend who has a slight hang-up about ordering drinks that look or sound like stereotypical "girly" drinks. He is, however, the only friend with this hang-up who *spends his life studying how to combat stereotypes*. But I know my role here. I rib Keith about buying into strict gender roles and being controlled by The Man, which puts him in the tough position of having to choose between two different threats to his autonomy. Which actually isn't a tough position at all, because it allows him to do what he really wants to do, which is order the damn Kitten Mittens.

These are the services we provide for our friends.

In addition to drinking some Kitten Mittens and sharing an appetizer of green curried mussels with fries, we're here to talk about some of Keith's recent research with his and my mutual friend and fellow psychologist Heather Urry.

Keith is a social psychologist who researches a specific type of racial bias called phenotypicality bias.[4] He finds that racial bias is not a unilateral construct applied equally to all people belonging to a given racial group. Rather, an undue share of the burden is shouldered by members of the group who exhibit physical traits closer to the prototypical member of a given race—for instance, greater levels of bias against black people who have darker versus lighter skin or fuller versus thinner lips.

Due to his generous, extraverted manner, Keith is also one of the best known and best liked people in our field. It once took Herculean effort and over an hour for my friend Jeff and me to drag Keith out of a conference cocktail hour in time to make our dinner reservations because seemingly every last person in the place wanted a few minutes with him. Then, once we thought we had him safely stashed between us in the backseat of our Uber, we heard "KEITH!" from the sidewalk...and Keith ended up nearly in my lap, hanging out of the window to talk to yet another long-lost friend.

Heather was my postdoctoral mentor and so, like me, specializes in the study of emotion regulation. Her particular focus is teasing out which strategies work for which people in which contexts—for example, whether some people experience emotional benefits in changing their focus of attention whereas others benefit more from changing their interpretation of the situation.[5] Her quiet, reflective demeanor contrasts with Keith's more convivial one, but they both share a down-to-earth optimism and a playful sense of humor that undergird their strong friendship.

Heather and Keith had recently realized that combining their research programs might suggest a solution to some of our problems interacting with people from outgroups. Since they both work at Tufts University, it was easy enough to set up a collaboration. Their work evaluated whether giving participants some reappraisal-like tools to manage anxiety would make people feel more comfortable talking to cross-race partners about issues regarding racial discrimination.[6]

Their research was headed up by Jenny Schultz, a graduate student in Keith's lab, and conducted with fellow researcher Sarah Gaither. In devising the experiment, their logic was this: research has shown that talking with someone of a different race often results in heightened anxiety, revealed by both internal (self-report, physiologic responding) and external (behavior, nonverbal cues) measurements. They thought that this anxiety might lead people of all races to avoid such interactions in real life, or if they were unable to avoid them, yield the kind of discomforted non-verbal signals that would communicate that the interaction was not going well, thus setting it up for failure.

The participants who received the intervention were told: "Sometimes people feel anxious about interacting with a person from another race. To reduce this anxiety, they might choose to avoid situations in which a cross-race interaction is likely because avoiding that situation reduces your anxiety. However, research suggests that choosing to put yourself in situations in which you interact with a person from another race actually helps to reduce future feelings of anxiety." The participants (who were all white) were then told that they were going to be assigned to discuss racial discrimination, and that they could choose a black or a white conversation partner.

"One of the things that got me motivated and interested in this topic," Keith says, waving a french fry for emphasis, "is the idea of creating allies." Often the burden of challenging societal inequalities falls to the targeted group. The majority group plays a much larger role in the perpetuation of bias, and so if they aren't part of the solution, any solution you come up with isn't going to be effective in the larger scheme of things. "And in a way that is hard because it does sometimes feel like 'Oh, poor white people, let's make them feel comfortable,'" Keith says. But he feels that when people aren't comfortable, they aren't going to engage. They'll avoid and they'll pull away, and no progress will be made. He feels that it is important to get people to come to the table to discuss difficult topics such as racial discrimination.

What Heather and Keith's research participants get once they come to the table isn't watered down. In the study, the research participants go on to discuss racial discrimination—a difficult topic to discuss in any circumstance, but particularly so in a cross-race context. Keith shares that something he hears a lot from black communities is that they are exhausted from constantly battling racial bias and trying to educate well-meaning white friends and relatives about what it is like to navigate the world as a person of color, and that they want to put down this latter burden and let it be picked up by white allies. This is a sentiment I've seen expressed all over my social media: the exhaustion of continually bearing the weight of enduring discrimination while also having to convince other people that said discrimination is not all in your head.

As a black man, Keith knows well how painful and tiring this dual weight can be, but feels that as a professional educator it is part of his job: "I feel like there are different identities and roles that we play in society that are going to make us more or less likely to take that hit in order to get majority groups to engage." He hopes that this research could help in this effort.

I ask if their research hypotheses panned out, whether the participants were more likely to choose a cross-race partner when they received the anxiety-reducing intervention.

The intervention did work—in a way. People who received the anxiety-reducing intervention were significantly more likely to choose to speak to someone of a different race rather than their own race. People who chose to interact with the black partner, regardless of whether they got the intervention or not, also showed fewer signs of nonverbal anxiety compared to those who chose to interact with a white partner.

Yet another way that reappraisal can shape a more hopeful world.

EMBRACING DIFFERENCE

Discussing this research study calls to mind one of the central tensions in all of the ideas we have considered in this book. Namely, our evolved drive toward forming ingroups of meaning and solidarity isn't going anywhere, and we shouldn't want it to. Our richest human experiences are sourced from these connections with families and religions and ethnic histories. But yet, these same inclinations to ingroup bonding may set up cross-group divisions and even dehumanization. Might we not have a choice in the matter? Can we appraise our ingroup as one threshold of inclusion, people perhaps closer to our self-identity, while still including outgroups within a wider threshold of fellow human beings?

I ask Keith what he would think about a version of his study in which instead of activating people's ideas of racial identity, participants were reminded of their shared identities, for instance of all being Tufts University students.

Keith nods, but not enthusiastically. He says, "I think that what is going to happen is that you are going to say something awkward that will immediately jar people back into their subordinate categories. You can say, 'We're all Tufts students,' but then as soon as you start talking you are going to think, Okay, but our experiences really aren't the same. My Tufts degree means something different than your Tufts degree, and my experiences on campus are entirely different from your experiences. And then that reaction is going to show in your nonverbal cues and the other person is going to think, Oh god, that's not what I meant by that, now he thinks I'm racist or insensitive or whatever—and *that* is going to show. And then we're back to square one."

Keith feels that in a magical mistake-free interaction, priming these superordinate identities might work well. But our perspectives are so different that mistakes are nearly inevitable. You are eventually going to say something that betrays a lack of understanding of the other person's perspective, and then the threat is back. Group interventions emphasizing a superordinate "we" category between different groups seem to reduce some of the negative feelings without impacting real change, and moreover any real change seems to require a degree of conflict. Keith believes it is better to address the threat of different experiences and the emotions that come with it head-on and give people some skills to deal with it when it happens.

Investigating these differences in experience and viewpoints, probing them, is probably a big part of getting close to someone. The general principle of getting close to someone by exploring their inner worlds echoes Pierre Bayard's thoughts on getting to know people's inner libraries and also how we fall in love. These ideas put the greater weight on understanding and appreciating similarities: I wonder aloud how people may differ in how curious they are about exploring *dissimilarities*, and also how they may differ in their reactions to dissimilarities, once discovered.

"I think for a lot of people, closeness is akin to sameness," I say, "but I love it when people disagree with me, because then we get to tussle. For me, intimacy is having gotten into it, dug deep— regardless of whether we agree."

In contrast to me, Keith thinks he feels threatened when close friends express divergent opinions. "I mean," Keith says, "I've come to terms with our differences when it comes to Nathan Fillion…"

"Are you, Keith?" I tease. "Are you really?"

Keith and I both love the actor Nathan Fillion, but my love is restricted mostly to his portrayal of Captain Mal Reynolds in Joss Whedon's sci-fi Western soap opera *Firefly*, all swashbuckling leather pants and confident swagger and outer tough guy with inner heart of gold. Keith has a continuing affection for his role in the police procedural *Castle*, whereas I'm not a fan of police procedurals and also felt that Fillion was phoning in only a minor fraction of his charismatic wattage.

"Yes, Fillion-level disagreement is okay. But," Keith points out, "if I discover that a close friend or someone who is becoming a close friend has a strongly divergent view about something closer to my most core values—like Black Lives Matter, for instance—then that is going to present a bigger problem. Unless you can some-how get me to understand why you might feel that black lives *don't* actually matter, which..."

Keith shakes his head, takes a moment. I can guess he's both grappling with a surge of emotions and attempting to leverage his knowledge of psychological principles like reappraisal to his own thoughts and feelings. Which is difficult no matter what the topic, but one provoking such raw feelings is a challenge even for those well versed in the techniques.

He says at last, "No—I know that there are people who believe that black lives do matter but just don't think that racial bias and police brutality are as much of a problem in the world as I do. But even then, even if I can get myself to that viewpoint, I think that that difference would keep us from getting close, you know?"

In this new world, disagreements on matters political seem to be in their own category, to be more raw and visceral—even for those issues that don't directly impact one's communities. When the issues are political and also impact people in one's inner moral circles, I have trouble imagining surmounting that challenge and becoming close friends. Research supports this hunch, demon-strating that increasingly in America, Republicans and Democrats don't just dislike but instead report actually *loathing* each other, not so much based on policy positions but on social identity.[7]

What drives this increased political polarization is a multifac-eted problem. One line of work that sheds light on the issue is that our politics have become moralized, and when issues of morality are at play, people dig in their heels. The leader of this charge is Jonathan Haidt, who sums up his perspective in his book *The Righteous Mind: Why Good People Are Divided by Politics and Reli-gion*. We discussed Haidt's work at length back in chapter 1, his ideas about human beings being 90 percent chimp and 10 per-cent bee. But his intellectual home, the real focus of his research, is in moral psychology. In his book he argues that liberals and conservatives are living in different moral matrices. Like the movie *The Matrix*, we have swallowed either the red pill or the blue pill, and according to our decision we live in entirely different universes, with different principles, facts, values, and perceived existential threats.

He argues that the reason for these contrasting realities is that conservatives and liberals have different foundations of their morality. Pretty much everyone, conservative and liberal and everywhere in between, agrees that three important moral values are harm/care, fairness, and liberty—that it is wrong to harm others and right to care for them, and everyone should be treated fairly, and that we should be free.

But then conservatives have a few extra layers to their moral value system that liberals don't code as having to do with morality at all. One is authority, submitting to external rules and people in charge—conservatives have a great respect for authority, whereas in contrast Haidt notes the famous liberal bumper sticker "Question Authority." Another is purity, which relates to conservative viewpoints on sexuality and reproduction. And the third is loyalty, which one can see in the common observation that conservatives seem to be able to put aside differences and get behind one another, whereas the left is constantly nitpicking and splicing, and also in the liberal tendency to shy away from strong displays of patriotism because it feels like nationalism. In terms of personality, conservatives and liberals also tend to differ most strongly on the personality trait called openness to experience, which is the degree to which you desire traditional experiences and comfort zones versus new experiences and boundary pushing.

Put all of this together and you have one group of people who prefer tradition, respect authority, remain loyal to ingroups, are suspicious of people who betray social norms, and wish to keep the drawbridge up to keep their family and friends safe—and who are willing to sacrifice a small amount of harm/care and fairness in order to be sure to also respect authority, purity, and loyalty.

You then have a second group of people who care about harm and fairness to the exclusion of almost everything else, who believe that you need to challenge authority in order to enact social progress, that social norms are often restrictive and hampering of creativity and people's individualized experiences, and who wish to let the drawbridge down to be open to diverse others who might also need our care.

You end up with a nation of people who can't understand each other at all, and who talk (and vote) in circles. And who all believe, as the stories-as-natural-thought psychologists Schank and Abelson we met in chapter 2 put it, that "there are good guys and bad guys, and the bad guys, using illegitimate methods, are trying to bring about an evil state of affairs. This can only be averted if the good guys mobilize their forces, recruit people from the sidelines (who are in danger of being seduced by the bad guys), and press forward to glorious victory."

We just differ on who we think the bad guys are.

REAPPRAISAL FOR SO-CALLED INTRACTABLE CONFLICTS

But even here, even among our most divisive conflicts, cognitive reappraisal might lend a hand. At Tel Aviv University in Israel, psychologist Eran Halperin is taking some of the ideas we've been discussing about how to change appraisals in order to influence emotion to some of the most thorny, most emotional tangles in the world—intractable problems like the Israeli-Palestinian conflict. Not only does he not shy away from difficult topics, he also doesn't shy away from difficult methods. He and his collaborators employ everything from pamphlets to video ads to virtual reality to test whether they can intervene to budge people on both sides of the conflict from their hardline us/them thinking. Let's visit just two examples of this powerful work.

In one intervention, Halperin and his colleagues employ something called paradoxical thinking. If you are arguing with someone with extremely entrenched views on an issue, it doesn't usually pay off to try to persuade them of the opposing views. No Red Sox fan is going to have his or her mind changed by someone in a Yankees cap extolling the many virtues of the competing team. However, Halperin found, if you instead do something like praise the Red Sox to an even more extreme degree than the person's own views, the person actually start's melting his or her rigidity a bit. It is almost like the Sox fan starts thinking, Well, the Red Sox are the best team ever, but c'mon now, even they have flaws. It opens the person's thinking a bit.

In a study testing whether such an approach might work with much more serious issues than sports teams, Halperin and colleagues had conservative Israelis watch a propaganda-style ad that depicted acts of state violence, presented with the argument that such tactics were not only just but that the conflict was probably necessary. Watching the video several times budged these thinkers—they started feeling that the conflict couldn't possibly be *needed*, which seemingly then opened them up to start considering alternatives to the conflict.[8]

In another line of research headed by Amit Golenberg,[9] Halperin's team stepped in at the level of collective beliefs about... well, collective beliefs. People vary in the extent to which they believe groups can easily change their minds. He and his colleagues reasoned that if one appraised group beliefs as generally static and difficult to budge, then if one were part of that group, one's views would similarly be pretty sticky. But if you instead believed that group beliefs were malleable, subject to change and influence from outside forces, then perhaps you'd be more open to shifting your own gears. Both perspective-taking and a group-malleability intervention were associated with benefits in attitudes, hope, and professed willingness to consider concessions.

Research by people other than Halperin's group confirms these basic messages for other sorts of divisive issues. For instance, a brief conversation that begins with discussing a time you felt vulnerable and judged by others, followed by information on transgender rights, yields surprisingly strong changes in transphobic beliefs, and these effects last over months.[10] Thinking about a time in which you were judged for being different seems to open your mind to the idea that we should support the rights of other people who are currently being judged for being different.

Collectively, this research suggests that by changing our stories, our appraisals, we may be able to come together on even some of the most contentious, divisive issues that face us. We can think of ourselves as one human hive, as capable of change, as able to take the perspective of people different from us.

It may be absolutely critical that we do so.

TWO CAVEATS: WHAT I'M NOT SAYING

By saying that the stories we choose shape our realities and that we can choose those narratives that yield the most prosocial, productive, humane emotions and outcomes, I am not saying that the power of positive thinking can magically create a world where there is no racism, homophobia, political partisanship, or massive class inequality. There are many injustices in our world that are baked into our systems of education, criminal justice, and health care, and only by confronting the ugly reality of those inequalities do we have any hope of carefully dismantling them.

What I *am* saying is that deciding on a narrative where human beings are destined for violence and resource hoarding, and hatred of people who don't look like them or vote like them, in some ways gives us permission to act violently and hoard resources and hate people who don't look or think like us. When people perceive there is no hope, as in the Israeli–Palestinian conflict, they feel resigned to the situation, which may result in people being less likely to try for change. As the lead author of a review of this research Smadar Cohen-Chen writes, "Those who believe such efforts can indeed change the course of the future are more inclined to walk the path of conflict resolution."[11] The stories we tell ourselves can open up possibility for change.

By saying that the stories we choose shape our realities and that we can choose those narratives that yield the most prosocial, productive, humane emotions and outcomes, I am not saying that we should be able to choose any story at all, to toss social norms out the window. We structure our social norms so that there is a socially dictated limit to the topics and viewpoints that can be publicly espoused without social recriminations, and those limits reflect our shared values. These limits are often conceptualized through something called the Overton window,[12] named after Joseph P. Overton, a think-tank leader and public policy expert. Overton was focused on politics and public policy, and so for him the window encapsulated those ideas or opinions that a politician could publicly endorse without being penalized in the court of public opinion. Since its popularization, the window is also used to depict the range of ideas that are generally thought to be acceptable based on the current zeitgeist or hivemind—acceptable to the mainstream populace, that is. Those ideas within the window are acceptable, those outside are considered fringe. As culture changes and shifts, so does the Overton window.

With a recent global rise in populism and softly focused, semi-flattering depictions of major white nationalist figures in the mainstream media, one might argue that there has been a shift in our Overton window regarding issues of race and identity. Consistent with this idea, hate crimes have spiked in the United States since 2016.[13] Research suggests that it isn't that new people are learning anew to hate but that major figures not being penalized for statements previously considered extreme may have signaled changes in social norms, allowing already-hating people to more openly express their views, to not fear censure.[14]★

I'm all in favor of social norms.

What I *am* saying is that social norms are not immutable laws, and they should be questioned by each new generation for their fairness, equity, and potential for harm.†

Speaking of norms, some of the most exciting research happening in the field of reducing prejudice and division has to do with directly targeting people's social norms through advertising, fiction, or other interventions.

NUDGING NORMS

Another body of research indicates that you might not even need to change the story of what people believe, their inner appraisal—which is admittedly a lot of effort and requires the cooperation of the person—you might also be able to nudge people by instead targeting their perception of social norms.

You might recall from chapter 2 that people are less influenced by what an average behavior or belief is and more influenced by their *perception* of the average behavior or belief. You might also recall that our fiction has an outsize influence on the morals of our collective hivemind. What if we could directly target these social norms using fictional narratives?

Social psychologist Betsy Levy Paluck has received a fellowship from the John D. and Catherine T. MacArthur Foundation (often called a MacArthur "genius grant") for just this line of

---

★ As a social scientist I must point out that these arguments are painted with an extremely broad brush, and that whether shifts in these abstract concepts are indeed causally linked would be nearly impossible to test.

† In case this isn't glaringly obvious by now, I took the blue pill.

work, suggesting that people's social norms can be nudged in a prosocial direction through deliberate interventions.

Like Halperin, Paluck didn't shy away from tough challenges or start small. In a field experiment in Rwanda, she partnered with a radio program and exposed people over a year's time either to a standard health program or to a serial soap opera.[15] The soap told the story of a Romeo-and-Juliet-style romance between members of the two major ethnic groups in the country. The characters acted out behaviors such as challenging norms, expressing dissent, and solving problems locally. Fascinatingly, but in line with the research we've reviewed thus far, the soap opera did little to change underlying *beliefs* about divisions between the ethnic groups—people who strongly felt that the ethnic groups were essentially different before listening to the soap opera still felt so afterward. But what it did profoundly affect was their perceptions of social norms and behavior, what it was proper to do and say about the ethnic differences.

In an interview with NPR, Paluck shared that people watching the soap opera would tell her, "This is clearly something that Rwandans are into. They're into this relationship on the soap. I may not personally believe in letting my daughter marry someone from the other ethnicity, but I'm going to let her—because that's what we as Rwandans are doing now."[16] The perception of the social norms and the behavior changed, came in line with the hivemind, even when the underlying feelings did not.

For we all silence those parts of ourselves that we suspect stand in contrast to our social others. German political scientist Elisabeth Noelle-Neumann wrote of a "spiral of silence," in which people who hold potentially controversial views hide their views, which leads to the general perception that such opinions are not held.[17] The spiral forces these maligned views ever inward until there is a possibility that such views cease to exist in a society over time. Such a spiral of silence can be prosocial (e.g., racists unwilling to state racist views in public) or antisocial (e.g., prior to the #metoo movement, the spiral of silence was one factor protecting powerful men from being held accountable for their crimes).

Paluck also has successfully taken social norms interventions into middle schools.[18] In one study, she recruited students into promoting antibullying initiatives. The selected students met with facilitators who helped them identify particular behaviors plaguing their particular schools and then devise activities to combat them. For instance, in one school the students handed out orange wristbands to mark students they observed engaging in prosocial or bullying-intervening behaviors. In another they developed hashtags targeting problem behaviors and put up posters throughout the school.

When are norms most likely to shift? When people closely identify with the source of the norm challenger—feeling comfort, friendship, and resemblance with the characters in so-called "edutainment" is important, as is the perceived status of the influencer. For instance, a Twitter bot study targeted people who were using racial slurs against black people, finding instances of users employing the n-word and replying with a condemnation and suggestion for change. The bot study was actually successful in statistically reducing the number of times the person targeted went on to use the slur, at least over a short period of time—with the most influential bots having a white male avatar and a high number of followers.[19]

Back in our Boston restaurant, Keith and I chat for a bit about the power of persuasive social others to nudge norms.

"Right after the election," Keith says, "I felt this powerful wave of—oh my god, what have I been doing? I've been wasting my life." He felt like he had been spending all of his time talking to open-minded audiences eager to learn about implicit bias and how to counter it when all along there was another whole group of people who not only didn't want to learn about subtle bias but who denied that there was such a thing as racial discrimination at all.

192

But then Keith realized that nothing he could say would sway someone on the far right of the political spectrum, the chasm is just too great. But if he could persuade the person one step to the right of him, then that person might influence the person one step to his or her right, and on and on down the line through the powers of social influence and contagion, taking advantage of allies who have access to people and conversations that he might not have. Then perhaps his work would have a larger impact on the world.

I tell Keith I agree with him completely, share with him that his argument is basically what this entire book is about, ideas and emotions and mental models spreading through the hivemind. That we are synchronizing, mirroring, influencing creatures held sway by a contagious sense of reality.

Then, with a glint in his eye, Keith asks me, "Are you open to the idea that people from 'the other side' could nudge *you*? Are you receptive to taking in conservative ideas?"

My resulting silence is so profound and elongated that later, transcribing the audio, I laugh out loud.

But then I press stop on the audio recording and sit back to think. I realize what it is I have to do next.

APPLYING REAPPRAISAL

But first, Heather joins us for the meal portion of the evening.

We spend most of the dinner in a frothy banter around in-jokes and stories of mutual acquaintances. This banter reminds me that many anthropologists claim that human beings use gossip as a form of "social grooming," that we replaced physical grooming that other apes bond over (picking mites out of fur) with a more language-based way of reaffirming our connections. Our banter does sort of emotionally feel like when my father would pull my toddler self onto his lap and pretend to search for mites in my hair, faux-nibbling his fingers as I shrieked and squirmed in delight.

Eventually I pull Heather and Keith around to one last bit of intellectual discussion. I ask them: How could they imagine their research findings someday being applied to real-world settings?

Heather is a bit taken aback. Ever a careful scientist, she notes that theirs is just one study.

"Well, look," she says, "I am proud of this work that we did and intrigued by what we found, but we will need to both replicate it and also do a lot more work teasing out the mechanisms before we can really conclude anything, let alone take it into the field."

That said, should subsequent experiments confirm and elaborate on the findings, she might start thinking about applications.

Heather was trained originally as a clinical psychologist, someone who does therapy. She learned in that context that you can try to help someone see the ways in which behavior change might be helpful and rewarding, but you are with that person for just the hour. After that, whether the person applies your discussions to his or her life and creates change is up to him or her.

"It's not as though you can follow people around in their daily lives...," she says.

Keith interrupts. "Why not?"

Heather gives Keith a quizzical head tilt.

Keith shrugs and says, "My phone nudges me when various apps think it is time for me to go for a run or meditate or stretch. Why not an app that nudges you—hey, remember you thought it might be a good idea to interact with someone a little different from you? Why not today? And then gives you a few tips for managing your anxiety about the interaction." He's ambivalent about whether such an app would actually be feasible or work. But he also notes that creativity involves thinking outside the box, being willing to entertain ideas that at first blush seem kind of wacky.

I mentally thank Keith for bringing us back around to one of the central theses in this book—social media and smartphones may create certain problems, but they're a tool, and a tool that can sometimes help us to live better lives. I feel the impatient tug of conversation away from things serious, so I release Heather and Keith from their interview obligations and let the social grooming over churros continue on its natural path.

Such are the services we provide for friends.

TEST-DRIVE: OUTSIDE MY COMFORT ZONE

To follow up on Keith's challenge to expose myself to uncomfortable ideas to see if I can be nudged, I first wrangle my friend Joe to attend a Republican fund-raiser for a local candidate with me. But the experience feels neither alienating nor particularly nudgy. My writer's group suggests I attend an evangelical event, but I'm aware of the good that religious groups can contribute to the world and so I don't think it would change my worldview much.

But then I realize what the solution should be—I should read a conservatively bent work of fiction. You may have noticed by this point in the book that I enshrine fiction a bit. I think that also there is something about the whole taking-someone-else's-brain-for-a-spin that makes it more likely for our view of the world to be a little bit different afterward compared to before. That argument is, after all, one of the central underpinnings of this book.

When contemplating what a work of conservative fiction might look like, I don't have to think longer than a few moments. Early twentieth-century philosopher Ayn Rand used the novel form to explore and illustrate her personal philosophy, and her fictional works have had an outsize influence on a number of political conservatives in the United States, including economist Alan Greenspan and congressman Paul Ryan. *The Fountainhead* is reportedly one of three fictional works Donald Trump has ever spoken about having read. The villain of *Dirty Dancing*,* an elitist country-club

---

* Possibly the best film ever made.

boy named Robbie, hands the book to the main character Baby after she gives him a hard time for impregnating and then abandoning her working-class friend. "Some people count, and some people don't," he tells her, handing her a copy of *The Fountainhead*, which he apparently carries copies of in his back pocket.

Thankfully, it isn't nearly as bad a read as my corner of the hivemind had led me to expect. I discover that the subject matter of her philosophy is a perfect fit for this book I am writing and you are reading. That is, how to resolve the tension between our dual natures—our collective aspects and our individual ones, the two faces of Homo duplex.

The central story concerns a redheaded architect named Howard Roark, who some readers believe was modeled after Frank Lloyd Wright. All around Roark, fellow architects and art critics rely on the hivemind's ideas about what dwellings should look like, and these ideas are all shaped around historical approaches. No one thinks for themselves, innovates, or considers contexts like the natural surroundings, the purpose of the building, or the characteristics of the people who live in it. No one, that is, except Roark, who stands out in his determination to produce grand works and to think for himself, outside the bounds of cultural mores and social norms. He routinely puts people off because he refuses to engage in small talk or flattery or indulge any social norms for polite behavior, and he will only accept contracts if he has complete freedom to operate as he will, with no input from any other party. He is an iconoclast. He utterly rejects the collective side of Homo duplex.

Roark is opposed at every turn by a cast of characters who vary in their degree of pettiness and villainy. Some, drained of any free thought by their relentless conformity to the collective opinion of their fellow society dwellers, dry up more and more over the years until they are mere husks of people. In long soliloquies, these people are characterized as "second-handers," people who do not have their own thoughts or ideas but merely borrow them from the collective. The mustache-twirling villain Ellsworth Tooley (nothing in the book is subtle) plays into humanity's worst instincts and tries to take down anyone with an individual spine or a new idea.

There is a love story, too, between Roark and one Dominique Francon, an icy, remote beauty who shares his disdain for social niceties. She believes Roark is so remarkable that his works have no place being beheld by ordinary mortals, that he should instead be destroyed. Their love story launches with a rape, where Roark comes to claim Dominique's body and she fights him like an animal: "He had thrown her down on the bed and she felt the blood beating in her throat, in her eyes, the hatred, the helpless terror in her blood." The true individual, the hero, takes what he wants, and when he wants to use a woman's body with no thought to her will or pleasure, it is no exception.

It surprises me a bit that *The Fountainhead* has such a strong and lasting following given its length, the centrality of fights over architecture—I have nothing against architecture, but it isn't typically the stuff of biting one's nails—and the tendency of the characters to go on unbroken pages-long philosophical rants, as unrealistic as the wry cultural commentary of the kids on *Dawson's Creek* was back in the day.

The philosophy Rand illustrates in her fictional works and exemplified in *The Fountainhead* she called Objectivism, and she summed it up as "the concept of man as a heroic being, with his own happiness as the moral purpose of his life, with productive achievement as his noblest activity, and reason as his only absolute."[20]

I'm not nudged by the idea that the world is filled with a handful of truly awake, truly important artists and thinkers, and underneath them is a sprawling mass of second handers. I find the implication gross and elitist. I'm also not persuaded by the idea that these true artists should not be held back by social norms at all, that they should blaze forward, ignoring all conventions, personal loyalties, and pesky things like consent to sexual intercourse. As we'll discuss at length in the next chapter, I also think that seeking your own happiness as the purpose of life is likely to do the very opposite of making you happy.

But what I did find compelling, and which I did find shaping my thinking a bit, was Rand's emphasis on the importance of retaining one's individual mind in the sea of the collective. How, in some ways, the very definition of creativity and innovation is an ability to think outside the hivemind. So much human progress involves questioning the contemporary hivemind's narrative, probing it for the ways in which it is outdated or incorrect.

Rand grew up in Communist Russia, direct witness to the dangers of enforced conformity, and this early experience clearly shaped her thinking about the world. In her nonfiction writing, she thinks of the collective side of human nature as dangerous and primitive, that we sacrifice individual rights on the altar of the tribe. She plants human progress solely in the purview of increasing individualism: "Supposing men were born social (and even that is a question)—does it mean that they have to remain so? If man started as a social animal—isn't all progress and civilization directed toward making him an individual? Isn't that the only possible progress?"[21]

In the next chapter we'll take this challenge of Rand's head-on. Rather than view the collective as savage and the individual as sacred, we'll examine evidence that following her mandate of increasing individualism may be part of why we feel so unhappy and disconnected in this modern age. I'll argue that instead, our collective social nature is something to be cherished.

We'll do so by considering research suggesting that human beings are so innately social that we extended our sociality to an entire other species.

Let's spend time with some furry friends.

SUMMER

Chapter Ten

Invisible Leashes

Gooseberry Island, Massachusetts

It is Father's Day, and my extended family has taken to our favorite stretch of sea. We're walking Gooseberry Island, a historic half mile of huge rocks, hundreds of bird species, and concrete World War II watchtowers that have since been taken over by lusty teenagers and graffiti artists, judging by the paintings and the debris. The day is perfectly sunny and crisp, and the weather has seemingly conspired for every flower on the island to have burst into bloom at once. The island is dotted with little white daisies, startlingly pink beach plum blooms, and more muted rose hip blossoms. I spent my childhood summers a little down the road in a teeny shack built by my grandfather, collecting mussels in buckets for adults to steam for dinner and chasing my brothers and numerous cousins in the waves. Something about the sharpness of the light and the salt in the air and the sound of the pulling tides imprinted on me—it is where I feel most alive.

Today a new family member has joined us. We have just adopted a ten-week-old yellow Labrador named Zaffy, a buttery ball of velvet ears and bright brown eyes and little golden eyelashes.

My niece Kiara is carrying Zaffy down the beach, and as we walk, we cause a ripple effect in the people who line the shore on their blankets and folding chairs. It reminds me of the

201

touch-sensitive plants my mother used to let me buy at fancy greenhouses, where you'd run your finger down the length of the leaf and spine by spine the plant would close itself up tight. Except that Zaffy is causing an opening rather than a closing—one by one as we pass them, people's eyes widen, mouths exclaim.

We have to stop every few steps to let people scratch her teeny ears and pet her tiny head, answer questions about her age, allow for pictures.

There is just something about dogs, and puppies in particular, that captures our delight.

And not just our delight—dogs are everywhere you look in human culture. As writer Jenna Woginrich reflects in a wonderful essay called "What Makes Dogs Different":[1]

> Dogs protect our livestock, homes, and children. They detect bombs, lead the blind, and track criminals and the stranded alike.... Some dogs pull sleds, taking us where we could never go alone. Others sniff out drugs, detect heart attacks, or listen to sounds in the forest we could never hear. Some dogs fill stewpots while luckier ones sit on cushions in royal halls. Look at any picture or literature of any class in the history of Man, and there is a dog. They are heroes and villains. They are lab rats and show stock. Some dogs go off to war for us, while others simply let us hold them until we can't cry anymore. They have helped us live, work, and eat, and in this relationship both of our species have exploded in populations and prominence.

Much like our discussion of romantic love earlier, this intertwining of our fates is likely the result of neither art nor fortunate accident, but rather of evolution. And it tells us more than a little about the importance of our collective selves.

DOMESTICATING EACH OTHER: THE COEVOLUTION OF HUMANS AND DOGS

Over the last decade, there has been a virtual explosion of research into the cognitive abilities of dogs and accompanying theorizing about their evolutionary roots. The story of this research, a narrative of reversals and new discoveries, has always enchanted me.

That story goes like this: Researchers attempting to probe animal cognition had focused most of their attention on chimpanzees, given their high degree of relatedness to humans, and on dolphins, given their high degree of sociality and intelligence. But a group of researchers began realizing that while sure, these are interesting candidate species to evaluate, might it not make more sense to focus on dogs? Like chimps and dolphins, they, too, are a highly social species. And while they don't share a high degree of relatedness with humans, what they *do* share is tens of thousands of years of coevolution with human beings. Tens of thousands of years of working together, living together, sharing campfires and hearths and even beds. Not to mention that in addition to the processes of natural selection working on us both, we also intentionally engaged in selective breeding of dogs, choosing to breed those with characteristics we appreciated and not to breed those with characteristics we didn't. This process of selective breeding almost surely augmented the social intelligence of these already social creatures.

Researchers set out to evaluate dogs and compare them to species such as chimps and dolphins. As hypothesized, dogs outperformed other species on many of the tasks used to assess social intelligence—intellectual attributes like understanding of gestures, ability to conceal and deceive, and perception of human emotion.

This was the story of this research I had picked up from the academic hivemind, reading and researching and teaching over the years. I also knew that one of the principal researchers in this area is Brian Hare out of Duke University. I show my classes video interviews with him, enjoy following him on Twitter, and sometimes assign his research articles for my upper-level students to read. When I decided to write about dogs and humans and their synchronization in this chapter, I picked up his book *The Genius of Dogs: How Dogs Are Smarter Than You Think*, cowritten with his wife, Vanessa Woods. In the book, Hare shares that people sometimes approach him in public and ask if he isn't "that dog guy." This bit made me laugh, because if I ended up on an airplane seated next to him, I, too, would have recognized him and asked him that question verbatim.

So I knew when I picked up the book how smart dogs were, and I knew that the discovery made for a good story, but I wasn't prepared for *how good* a story it is.

For one thing, a piece of the puzzle I didn't know was that Hare started his scholarly career working with none other than Michael Tomasello, one of our guides to the evolution of human sociality from chapters 2 and 3. Hare and Tomasello were working together on some of the research we reviewed on whether other animal species were capable of the sorts of shared intentionality that Tomasello believes shaped our human ultrasociality. The task they were using to test the animals involved hiding food under bins and then trying to use words and pointing and shared gaze to indicate to the animals which bin contained the food. As Hare tells it, they were working on these tasks in the lab and observing as chimpanzees failed test after test.

One day Hare casually mentioned to Tomasello that his dog Oreo could totally do this.

Tomasello was kind but skeptical, made a crack about how yes, everyone believes his dog is capable of calculus.

But Hare persisted—no, really. Oreo would blow these tasks out of the water.

Tomasello told Hare to collect some video recordings of Oreo and come back when he had actual data.

Hare did.

And Oreo could.

A flurry of tests followed that demonstrated that Oreo wasn't some wonder pup. Rather, dogs in general were quite skilled at using gestures and shared attention to intuit the intentions of their owners. Being scientists, Hare and Tomasello immediately began other tests that probed both the boundary conditions and the exceptions to this rule. Was it all the time dogs spent with humans? No, since human-socialized chimpanzees weren't all that much better than their wild counterparts, and puppies weren't really worse than adult dogs. It appeared to be inborn. How about wolves? Nope, they were similarly poor at these social sorts of tests, despite being quite smart in other ways.

Hare started traveling the world, pushing the research questions even further. He sought out some of the few wild dog species left on the planet, the New Guinea singing dogs and dingoes. Both species demonstrated great success on social cognition tests, despite not having been bred by humans and having little real-life contact with them.

In my favorite chapter of the book, Hare traveled to Siberia to meet some domesticated foxes. In a fascinating story in its own right, a Soviet researcher named Dmitri Konstantinovich Belyaev wanted to study evolution and genetics in an environment where both fields were forbidden by the Stalinist government and could have gotten him executed. He operated under the cover story of trying to develop the best possible silver fox pelts for commercial use. But what he really did was experiment on the foxes to see if he could observe domestication in real time. His experiment, like all good experiments, was a simple one. When a new litter of fox kits was born, he tested them for the degree to which they were aggressive with human beings, the extent to which they would willingly put up with human handling. Those judged to be more prosocial were put in one group and reared together. Another group of foxes were bred randomly, without this sort of selection, forming the control group. With successive generations, the social foxes grew increasingly social, until after thirty to thirty-five generations they were fully domesticated. In present-day form, these foxes will lie on people's laps and be petted, snuggle, and wag their tails. Like little fox-dogs.

Selecting for this one behavioral trait also seemed to be associated with a number of other traits that spread throughout the social foxes. Their craniums shrunk to a smaller, "feminized" size, their tails were more likely to be curly, their ears were more likely to flop down. They took on the physical traits of domestication. Even more intriguingly, when Hare tested them, the foxes were awesome at the pointing tests. Even better than the puppies. As Hare writes, "Domestication, selecting the friendliest foxes for breeding, had caused cognitive evolution."

All of this research led Hare and others to a remarkable hypothesis about dogs and humans. Perhaps human beings had not intentionally domesticated wolves, figured out that perhaps these wild beasts could be useful to us if we could tame them. Perhaps the domestication occurred naturally through the process of natural selection. According to this account, starving wolves during lean times might have started lurking around human campfires, sniffing around the free food that was sometimes scattered about—aka, our garbage. Those who were a little friendlier, a little more trusting, would have been the most likely to skulk around humans. These slightly friendlier wolves would have benefited from the scraps and had a higher rate of reproductive success. Over generations, just like the foxes, some of these wolves may have become protodogs, have gotten friendlier and friendlier. Given the tie between friendliness and cognition, they also might have become smarter and smarter (at least socially). Along the way, human beings may have realized that these creatures might be useful for chasing off predators and hunting together and pulling sleds.

In an even more remarkable hypothesis, Hare wonders if perhaps dogs domesticated us as well—or, at least, evolutionary pressures worked on humans that selected for humans who were partial to dog companionship. Human beings who were drawn to dogs, who were less fearful, less germ-phobic, more open to animal companionship would have had help hunting and protecting space and doing field work. They in turn might have had better reproductive success than their aloof contemporaries, and over time we may have been shaped through natural selection into a dog-loving species. The sort who might leave a twelve-million-dollar inheritance to a beloved Maltese, as Leona Helmsley did. Or who might follow @dog-rates on the order of millions.

In *The Story of Edgar Sawtelle*, a lauded book chosen by Oprah as one of her early book club selections, David Wroblewski creatively recast *Hamlet* on a contemporary farm, where a young mute man is the third generation to manage a dog breeding line begun by his grandfather. Much like Belyaev did with his foxes, the boy's grandfather began selecting dogs to breed based on an intuitive sense that the dog was remarkable in its attention to and care for human beings. He chose puppies who were especially cued into human emotions and signals, and successively over generations he created a breed of remarkably acute, emotionally attuned animals who had a level of socioemotional complexity to convincingly play the role of Ophelia or Horatio. The grandfather hoped to create a new line of evolved canines that, in his fond imagination, would one day be known as *canis posterus*—"next dogs."

Edgar and his dogs are fictional. But there are entire organizations dedicated to a similar mission, to breeding and training dogs to synchronize with their human owners. These dogs are achieving what Wroblewski created in his imagination: dogs exquisitely tuned in to their owners, creating for them new physical and emotion opportunities.

During my post-tenure sabbatical year, on Wednesday mornings I volunteered as a kennel attendant at NEADS: World Class Service Dogs. The organization trains service dogs from puppyhood to work with people who need assistance with the tasks of daily living. NEADS uses an innovative training program for their pups. The dogs spend their weekends with volunteers in their homes, gaining exposure to the community, but much of their training takes place in local prisons. Model residents at the correctional facilities apply to and then complete a rigorous training program to learn how to teach the puppies the skills they will need to work as service dogs.

The assistance the dogs provide varies by the needs of the new owners: people who are deaf or hard of hearing need a friend to alert them to ringing phones and knocks on the door, veterans suffering from post-traumatic stress disorder need a soothing life partner to help them through painful flashbacks and anxiety attacks, and people with a large variety of movement difficulties benefit from a dog to press elevator buttons and pick up dropped items.

While my volunteer job did involve scooping an awful lot of poop and other unglamorous tasks like scrubbing dog grease off the walls of the kennel, the dog time more than made up for it. Their ears were just so terribly soft and their brown eyes so full of hope and enthusiasm.

At my initial kennel volunteer orientation, the head kennel supervisor, Taverly, spoke of the head dog trainer, Kathy Foreman, in tones that bordered on awe. Kathy had been working at NEADS for decades and knew all the ins and outs of the program. Kathy had a near-magical ability to match clients with the perfect dogs for them. There seemed to be no end to the woman's positive traits in Tav's eyes—and over time, as I got to know other kennel personnel, I realized that everyone at NEADS felt similarly. So when I asked Tav whom I might be able to interview for the book and she told me Kathy was willing to talk with me, I was thrilled.

A STATE OF GRACE

The morning I arrive at NEADS for the interview, I walk into the building and am not terribly surprised to see a small bichon frise monitoring the reception desk. He stands with his back paws on the office chair and his small front paws on the desk, his head alert and his mouth open in a relaxed dog smile. He makes friendly eye contact with me as I enter and I laugh out loud. Manager of communications for NEADS Audrey Trieschmann rounds the corner and greets me. I kick myself for not getting my phone out of my pocket quick enough for a snap of the dog.

Audrey and I go upstairs to her office, passing the training room where I can see Kathy working with a black lab in a blue vest. I know the blue vest marks him as a puppy in training despite his large size, as the fully trained pups transition to red vests. The obedient dog is not distracted by us walking by. He retains his full, poised attention on Kathy's face.

While we wait for Kathy to finish up, Audrey and I chat for a while about her role monitoring the social media accounts for NEADS. She had worked at a previous nonprofit and observed very little interaction with her tweets and Facebook posts—an errant "like" here, a funny comment there. Transitioning to NEADS was startling. She posts a puppy image every morning and then just watches the notifications roll in, a seemingly unending stream of blue likes and red hearts.

Done with training for the moment, Kathy enters and we settle right down to the business of the interview. I start by telling her about the research at Duke and elsewhere evaluating canine ability to read human emotions and intentions. I ask Kathy to what extent she observes her dogs being able to pick up and be attentive to these unspoken cues.

Kathy tells us that she just started a new class at the prison, and as always, she began with her philosophy of dogs. She tells her budding trainers—she calls them hers, and I bet that over time they begin to see themselves as hers—that dogs evolved from wolves and share the same social structure. To survive, wolves evolved to have extremely strong social connections. Much like ourselves, without a pack they wouldn't be able to hunt, to raise their young, to defend their territory. Vocalization and body language are the main methods of interpack communication.

"If we want to communicate with these dogs," Kathy says, "we need to do so in a way that they can understand. I call it the invisible leash." This leash is an invisible channel of communication between dog and owner, a series of vocalizations, body language, and shared attention that binds them together and allows for mutual understanding.

In the wild, dogs and wolves connect with one another using high and low vocalizations. Kathy asks her prison trainers what they think the first discipline puppies receive is, and more often than not they answer correctly—a growl from their mother when they've transgressed. She feels that, for this reason, you have to pay a lot of attention to the tone of your voice when you talk to a dog. Is it high to encourage, or is it low like a growl?

She finds that most of the prisoners she works with have personas that are very neutral, probably a defense mechanism in the environment of the prison. They are reluctant to shed their carefully controlled outer shell.

"So," Kathy says, "I make them do their 'bebop' voice. I make them do their bebop voice in front of everyone because that is how they have to communicate with the dogs." It is so critical because the dogs sense when your heart isn't in it, when you're faking it or concealing something underneath. Kathy shares that she recently had an upsetting event in her life. She didn't believe she was showing any outward evidence that she was upset. She wasn't crying, or venting to a friend on the phone, or doing anything else that explicitly conveyed her dismay. But her dogs knew. They followed her around the house at her heels, nudging her and gazing into her face and trying to connect.

For this reason, she always tells her trainees, "When you're doing your bebop voice I want you to smile, because when you smile your body relaxes. I want that dog to look up at you, relaxing too, wagging its tail. I need it to want to be there." She says that over time, as they work with their dogs, she notices that the imprisoned trainers release some of their tight hold on their facial expressions. Their faces soften.

One of the men Kathy was working with in the prison wrote an essay about his experience training a NEADS puppy. In it, he said that having the puppy helped him keep his sanity in the alien, isolating environment of the prison. He wrote that the puppy gave him a sense of normalcy in a place he never wanted to accept as normal.

I can certainly imagine how introducing a furry little being, absent of all judgment, full of approval, brown eyes shining with admiration and eagerness for your guidance, could be a small ray of light in such a dehumanizing setting. A relationship, a goal to pursue, something to do well and do right.

No wonder their faces go soft.

For the dog-to-human channel, Kathy talks a lot about distance-increasing signals and distance-decreasing signals. Dogs are deeply connected to their humans along the invisible leash, but they also are aware that they are separate beings and sometimes want more space than other times. When they want distance, they growl, lower their head, stiffen their bodies. When they want to close the distance, they wag their tail, do a play bow.

They send clear signals, if you know what to look for, that communicate when they want to sync and when they want to be on their own.

This information is also carried in their faces, in whether they're relaxed and panting or pulling their lips back around their teeth, the degree to which their eyes are wide or narrow or relaxed, the extent to which their pupils are dilated. These are all signals that human beings also use to communicate and read emotions with other human beings.

"So, are they reading our faces?" Kathy asks. "Of course they are."

I ask Kathy about our need for companionship and social connection and the role dogs might play in fulfilling those specific needs. I think of a bit from Hare's book where a Stone Age skeleton is found buried with one hand on the skeleton of a tiny pup. Dogs have been part of our hearts for quite some time.

Kathy feels it is important to highlight that NEADS doesn't place companion dogs, but rather service dogs: highly skilled, highly trained animals to fulfill certain purposes for people whose lives have been altered by disabilities, disease, or paralysis. But while they are working dogs, they are also highly attuned to human emotions, and as such they offer unconditional love.

NEADS prides itself on its ability to match its dogs and clients to best serve both. During matching, the training staff and the client services manager, Katy Ostroff, scour profiles of both applicants and dogs. They try to judge how strong a presence each client has, their degree of comfort with dogs in general and managing the invisible leash in particular. The dog is also profiled—is he one that needs a confidence boost from his client? Or is she one who is always looking to move up the ladder of status and needs a firmer client? Some dogs just adore being petted, and so someone with movement restrictions might not be the best match, whereas other dogs prefer verbal praise, just love hearing

"Thatta boy. You're doing a great job." Some people want a goofy dog who makes everyone laugh, whereas other people like a dog who is more straightforward and analytical.

I remark that the matching process sounds a lot like dating, and Kathy agrees that there is definitely an element of ineffable chemistry to it. "When we walk in the room with the dog for the first time for you to meet it," Kathy says, "you have to have that warm, fuzzy feeling." It's got to click.

I ask Kathy if she has any match stories that particularly stand out to her.

She's been at this job for thirty-eight years, so it is a bit hard for her to choose just one. But then she does—a young man who was a competitive mountain biker. Let's call him Ben and his service dog Timber.

"Ben was working for a bike company in Europe and his bicycle hit a curb this big." Kathy holds up her hands, a mere few inches apart, shakes her head at the vagaries of life. Ben fell, hit his spine, and lost the use of his legs.

NEADS matched Ben with Timber, who was sort of goofy and easygoing. Timber would nudge Ben awake each morning. "Woo, woo, it's time to get up." A caregiver still had to help Ben out of bed each day—here Kathy pauses, lets it sink in that someone who once raced bicycles up and down mountains for a living couldn't swing his own legs down and get up for the day by himself—but with his dog, there was now a *reason* to get out of bed. There are several hours a day when Ben is alone with Timber. Since he has limited mobility in his hands and arms as well as being paralyzed at the waist, being at home with the dog gives him a sense of security.

But Kathy feels that the bigger contribution is that Timber has become the center around which Ben organizes his day, a being to care for.

"You want life to be about something outside of yourself," Kathy says. "We laugh, we smile, we worry—because of others, not ourselves. I think that really is what the dogs provide for so many of our clients. A new center to their universe."

Not only did Timber provide Ben with something other than his health to focus his days on, but the dog also provided him something to share with his caregivers. Rather than only endless needs and requests, he could share anecdotes, delights, and mutual plans. When he went out in public, the dog also provided a conversational point with strangers. "He said to me," Kathy says, "and so many of our clients say this to me: 'People see my dog first and my wheelchair second.'" The dog provides an icebreaker and a line of connection with strangers.

The dogs can also fill other empty gaps in people's emotional lives. One woman who entered the program was a mother to two children whose functioning was severely restricted. NEADS matched them with a service dog. Later, the mother told Kathy that she loved her children desperately and would always be there for them, but that given their limitations she knew they could never express any sort of gratitude to her.

"And their care is like you just wouldn't believe," Kathy says. She shakes her head in wonder. "The amount of time and effort it requires. You just don't know how some people cope. This woman's attitude is very accepting, very loving. But she told me, 'The dog makes me feel like he is thanking me. He is always wagging his tail and licking me. It makes me feel like there is someone who does appreciate me. Someone sees and feels grateful for all that I do.'"

Kathy routinely sees her dogs help her clients find the courage to live their lives with grace and resiliency, even in the face of great upheaval and challenges.

I can't help but think back to Hare's hypotheses about dogs and humans codomesticating each other, over tens of thousands of years choosing each other, again and again, forming mutual bonds of togetherness and companionship and attachment.

It reminds me, and not just a little, of romantic love.

A NEW CENTER TO OUR UNIVERSE

After reading Barbara Ehrenreich's book on group joy, I try to brainstorm how I might experience collective effervescence myself. I consider Burning Man, but it seems too expensive and complicated and I'm fairly certain I'm not cool enough for it. I sign up for event announcements for a program called Daybreaker, which makes me think of vampires but which is actually a morning yoga and dance party. It looks promising, but during the morning and without any mind-altering substances. I enjoy a good dance floor but mostly only in the context of weddings these days, and then only after a gin and tonic or two.

Instead, I join NEADS' fund-raising team of runners during the annual Falmouth Road Race on Cape Cod. The crowd has its anticipated effect. I run my fastest six to eight miles despite having barely trained—I think it is one part feeling like I don't want to let my little team down and one part the energy of the thousands of corunners and the throngs who have come out to cheer with bells, music, shouts, and orange slices. A young girls' dance troupe wears tutus and twirls and holds big signs that say, "If you get tired of running, try dancing!"

It is the first race I've run that prints your first name on the runner's bib as well as the number, and the effect is that the cheering crowds shout out our names. When I slow down at one point, someone shouts, "C'mon, Sarah, you can do it! Just two more miles!" For nearly twelve thousand runners, there are two thousand volunteers helping shepherd us onto shuttle buses, holding out water at water stations, and cheering.

I proudly wear a NEADS singlet, and everywhere I look I see shirts for other charities. ALS, Dana-Farber, Cops for Kids with Cancer. A man and his son with Down syndrome run next to each other with matching shirts that advocate for inclusivity and mental health. Many of the charity team shirts include a line "Running for _____" and a person's name. Many others have photographs of their running inspiration on their shirts. For a while I run behind a man who has an image of a premature infant on his back, all tiny limbs and multiple wires snaking in and out of her body. The trigger from my own past socks me in the stomach, and my pace stumbles for a bit before I recover. The announcer tells us that, collectively, the charity runners have raised millions of dollars.

The experience provokes that hivelike connective experience of feeling bigger than myself, one not just with the mass of people covering the seven miles with me but also with the people out in droves to support us. It also cements for me one of the lessons that all of these interviews and research articles and books have taught me.

We live for one another. One of the quotes from my interview with Kathy Foreman that stuck with me the longest is when she said, "You want life to be about something outside of yourself. We laugh, we smile, we worry—about others, not ourselves. I think that really is what the dogs provide for so many of our clients. A new center to their universe."

Kathy's sentiment is one that speaks strongly for the benefits of the wonderful program they offer. But the point here is bigger, I think. A dog can fill a gap in people's social support networks, provide someone to share the minutiae of daily living with—but the real crisis is that we don't have enough humans filling that space. We want to avoid blind conformity, and the processes of groupthink can lead us to divided, conspiracist, and dehumanizing thinking. But buying into a cult of individualism holds its own dangers.

In *Selfie: How We Became So Self-Obsessed and What It Is Doing to Us* journalist Will Storr traces a cultural history of the self and individualism from the sunny islands of Greece at the time of Aristotle to the tech bros of twenty-teens Silicon Valley.

Reviewing the literature and talking to a number of experts, he agrees with David Eagleman (and me, and apiarist Dan Conlon, and many others) about the nature of the self and consciousness: much of our decision making is based on unconscious motivations that our conscious selves then interpret into a pretty package or story. He argues that this confabulation is probably psychologically adaptive, for it can translate a lot of discord and chaos in our inner and outer experiences into a comforting feeling that we're in control of our own destinies—but he warns that it can also blind us to the true nature of reality.

Storr argues that we see ourselves as cast in an epic quest. "We feel as if we're the hero of the steadily unfolding plot of our lives," he writes, "one that's complete with allies, villains, sudden reversals of fortune, and difficult quests for happiness and prizes. Our tribal brains cast halos around our friends and plant horns on the heads of our enemies."

But rather than focusing like we have on our collective selves, the extent to which we form a hivemind, Storr is focused on the *other* side of Homo duplex—our individual natures. Much like Jesse Walker traced our paranoia about enemies and potential threats over eras and Vaughan Bell traced moral panics about social technology over centuries, Storr argues that the theme of emphasizing the perfectible individual self over the collective never leaves us, but that it does wax and wane with other cultural trends and important events.

Storr ends the book in Silicon Valley, where entrepreneurship is now a social value, start-ups invent gadgets and apps that make whole vocations obsolete with no thought to the human consequences, and there is wide-scale contempt for the value of the collective. This part of the book reminds me of a controversial blog post by self-styled "biohacker" Serge Faguet.[2] Faguet advocates for practices like eating only once a day to maximize efficiency, taking a variety of pharmaceutical agents to manage mood, focus, and sleep, and outsourcing one's sexual needs to paid sex workers who require no messy, time-consuming emotional investment. Most alarmingly of all, Faguet speaks fondly of a near future where there are two types of human beings—the superior ("enhanced") ones, who have engaged in this sort of biohacking, and the more basic sort of humans. These lowly basic humans "will (maybe) be taken care of well, but will have no real say in what happens."

Storr attributes many of these recent libertarian influences to the writings of our friend Ayn Rand. As we already know, her philosophy argues that human society will flourish when each individual follows his or her own self-interest and is not hobbled by the need to conform to social norms or governmental regulations. Ayn Rand famously claimed Aristotle, Storr's dubbed "father of individualism," as her only influence.

There are several problems with all of this enshrining of the self. First, it puts undue pressure on people to be perfect in form, temperament, and achievement. The effort required to both pursue these aims and monitor one's progress is taxing. Not just taxing, but depressing. When you reach midlife and haven't yet achieved your wildest dreams, and your midsection is soft, and your children resent you, and instead of happiness you are filled with self-doubt and self-criticism, you feel like you have failed. Failed not just because you haven't achieved maximum perfection but also because you feel sad about it when you should instead be perfectly mindfully accepting.

But secondly, in embracing the individual aspects of ourselves, we are neglecting the collective aspects. "When we defined ourselves, all those centuries ago," Storr writes, "as things that were separate from our environment and from each other, we turned our back on a truth that the descendants of Confucius knew well." Namely, that we are as much a collective as we are individuals, and that we may operate better, more intelligently, more altruistically, and more morally, when we care for and strive as a group than we do as individuals focused on self-perfection. That everything we do ripples out and affects others, even in ways that we cannot see, "no matter how convenient or seductive it might be to pretend otherwise and deny responsibility for anyone but our own sacred selves."

Sing it, Will Storr.

Returning full circle to chapter 1, Jonathan Haidt and Émile Durkheim argued that every society needs to work out how to balance the competing needs of individuals and groups. Haidt: "Most societies have chosen the *sociocentric* answer, placing the needs of groups and institutions first, and subordinating the needs of individuals. In contrast, the *individualistic* answer places individuals at the center and makes society a servant of the individual."[3] I believe that increasingly, American society has placed more emphasis on the individual to the detriment of the collective.

This sense of community—of being a part of a larger whole over space and time—may be critical for human happiness. It may also explain the perplexing finding that when major disasters strike, people very often report a bizarre sort of elation as their everyday lives are disrupted and the entire community draws together to solve problems. In her book *A Paradise Built in Hell: The Extraordinary Communities That Arise in Disaster*, Rebecca Solnit writes, "When all the ordinary divides and patterns are shattered, people step up—not all, but the great preponderance—to become their brothers' keepers. And that purposefulness and connectedness bring joy even amid death, chaos, fear, and loss." We are returned to a state of being more in tune with our ancestral past, and the result is a sense of profound meaning.

Large-scale studies find that involvement in religious communities predicts health, happiness, and longevity. These effects survive controlling for variables such as social support, meditation, and healthy lifestyle choices, as most religions have spoken or unspoken rules about behaviors like excessive alcohol use and sex with strangers who might carry sexually transmitted diseases.[4]

What religions provide is a ready-made system of shared social meaning, a strong narrative around which to center one's universe. They also provide, according to Haidt, an effective solution to a series of evolutionary puzzles: How do human beings justify and codify cooperation in the absence of genetic relationships? How do we encourage human beings to share and take care of one another and control their own selfish behaviors for the betterment of the collective, the hive? How do we incentivize generosity when behaving well holds no personal reward and doesn't prioritize one's kin? We may have solved these challenges in part by developing religions, and it may partially explain their lasting appeal.

For this reason, Haidt is unpersuaded by arguments that the future of mankind is secular:

> Asking people to give up all forms of sacralized belonging and live in a world of purely "rational" beliefs might be like asking people to give up the Earth and live in colonies orbiting the moon. It can be done, but it would take a great deal of careful engineering, and even after ten generations, the descendants of those colonists might find themselves with inchoate longings for gravity and greenery.[5]

Today's societal structure and intense focus on individualism may be betraying this need for connection and meaning that extends beyond the lifespan. It may explain our current woes a lot better than the fact that we spend too much time peering at our devices.

It also may explain, in part, why conspiracy theories have such an increasing hold on our public consciousness. As we discussed in chapter 6, part of the draw of conspiracy theories and cults is their appeal to our need for meaning, connection, and uncertainty reduction. Inducing a feeling of social ostracism increases superstition and belief in conspiracies,[6] and early work suggests that social motives play a strong role in the appeal of conspiracist thinking.[7] Involvement in social movements of many sorts begin less with fervent belief and more through the ordinary processes of seeking social engagement in the community[8]—as we also heard was part of how the 1920s Klan gained such a strong foothold.

Shoring up prosocial communities may not just enhance individual and collective well-being, it may also help undercut the appeal of fusion paranoia.

As a society, we more often focus on ways of being happier as individuals: What aspects of work and achievement do people need to be happy? What kinds of diets and fitness programs predict higher levels of well-being? Scour your local bookseller's advice section and you'll see book after book on how to hack your individual self into perfection. But we also need to consider the collective aspects of happiness. If we want people to flourish, we need to also ask whether people need to feel embedded in a larger group or society in which they share a common understanding of how the world works and which values to uphold.[9]

Variables that *decrease* reliance on social others tend to be associated with higher rates of suicide, even when these variables seem like they should make life easier—such as higher rates of wealth and achievement. Durkheim blames something he calls *anomie*, or formlessness. As social norms and rules for behavior diminish, people can follow their heart's desire and pursue hedonic happiness. Like the life-hacking blogger Faguet, we can swill pharmaceuticals to elevate our brain chemistry and shell out dollars to have sex with an endless parade of attractive mates who don't want to snuggle after. These activities may result in momentary pleasure, but they're unlikely to make us truly happy. And paradoxically, since there is no end marker for the amount of pleasure or wealth one can have, purely following one's desires leads one to chase an always-moving target.[10]

Extensive research in psychology on the paradoxical effects of seeking happiness underscore this point—trying to be happier through a variety of methods actually works against you, makes you *unhappier*. You can download apps and eat paleo and bone broth and insert Jade eggs in various intimate places,[11] but if you engage in these activities to chase happiness, happiness is not what you are going to find. One not-so-surprising exception to this rule? If you spend more time with the people you love in order to be happy, happier you might be.[12]

There is also quite a lot of evidence that self-focused mental processing leads to unhappiness. Rumination, a form of recurrent reflective thinking about what you could have done differently in life, is one of the most salient aspects of depression.[13] Mindfulness meditation trains one to routinely return one's attention to the present moment in part to reduce just these sorts of ruminative thoughts—worries, nagging concerns, self-evaluative thought. Popular interest in mindfulness in the United States has never been higher. In 2016, *TIME* magazine published a special issue on the degree to which the phenomenon had gripped our hive-mind consciousness.[14] More people than ever seem to be searching for meaning using these ancient practices.

All of this information from very disparate fields—happiness, depression, loneliness, service dogs, philosophy, psychology, religion—coalesces into something compellingly clear.

Living for ourselves, by ourselves, leads to unhappiness.

LONGING FOR BELONGINGNESS

Sixty feet above the ground and looking out at the tightrope in front of me, I feel my mouth abruptly go very dry. I am all geared up in a helmet and harness and pulleys and so am technically quite safe, but the ground still looks quite far away.

I'm not particularly afraid of heights but I am afraid of being trapped in social situations. Being halfway through a ropes course means that there is only one way out: forward over a rope and a few wobbly logs standing upright, looking impossibly far apart. It probably doesn't help my encroaching panic that it is nighttime, the dark pines swaying and whispering around me. I think longingly of the little yellow calming pills I sometimes take on long flights, which are back in my purse and tucked away in a locker. I take a long shaky breath and wonder whether the sting of shame is worth escaping this experience.

Then I look behind me.

Rounding up the last set of ropes is my cousin Elizabeth. She is calmly and rhythmically mastering the obstacles, the helmet causing her curls to escape from each side of her head in plumes that look like pigtails. She is humming the theme song to *Indiana Jones*.

I can't help but chuckle at the tune, and how quintessential it is for her to be humming it. My body calms. Like Jim Coan's hand-holders, I source courage from her relaxation, strength from her assured calm. We continue the climb together. My appraisals shift from ones of threat and entrapment to ones of safety and leisure. Suddenly the swaying dark pines seem well tempered by the cheerful white lights that sparkle around the greenery and obstacles, and the entire scene feels more charming fairy tale than ominous escape room. We end the course in an exhilarating zip-line down to a roaring bonfire where the rest of our party awaits with wine and Cheez-Its.

We are at our "womyn weekend," a biannual gathering that we launched back in our early twenties. My friend Julie and I had read an article in the magazine *Real Simple* about a group of women friends who designed their own retreat weekend. They rented a house and tapped into their various expertises: one friend led them in a yoga class, another cooked, another led meditations. We were young and low in funds, but my grandfather had built a little shack by the sea in Westport, Massachusetts, back in the 1970s when such things were possible for middle-class families, and I knew that we could commandeer it for a weekend. Julie and I each invited a relative and a friend or two to the weekend, described our idea, and decided to do some goal setting and crafts and swim and talk.

At the end of our first full day together as a group, we sat around the dinner table in the ocean breeze, discussing over flickering candlelight the intimate details of our lives with an openness that most of us had never experienced. Afterward we raced down to the shore, stripping off our garments as we ran, shrieking and laughing, and plunged into the cold moonlit sea. I surfaced with tears in my eyes, feeling more deeply grounded and connected than at any other time in my life.

We started meeting up twice a year, once in the summer and once in the winter. We set goals and nursed one another through happy times and hard. While we discussed and planned and problem solved, we colored, many years before the coloring book craze. A male caretaker who was fixing our cabin's woodstove once queried, confused: "Are those...adult crayons?"

The years slipped by, faster and faster. We started and ended relationships, we worried that we'd never find true love, we found true love, we got married, and we got divorced. We launched careers, we left careers, we entered and exited graduate programs. We struggled with infertility, got pregnant, lost pregnancies, had babies, and chose to remain child-free. Because we were grounded in this group, every threat felt less threatening, every problem felt solvable, every decision felt like a collective decision. When some new thorny dilemma would arise in my life, I approached it calmly, knowing that I'd figure it out at the next womyn weekend.

On our tenth anniversary we donned sparkly outfits and feather boas and wrote each and every milestone we'd achieved on little slips of paper. We tossed all of them into a velvet top hat and then took turns reading them and toasting them with champagne. In between we danced in front of a roaring fire.

I sometimes wonder if I wrote this book because both the topics we've considered and starting womyn weekends sourced from the same internal impulses and curiosities, or rather because nearly two decades of growing and living and thriving in this group collective shaped my thinking about the world and how to best live in it.

All around you are people eager for connection, longing for belongingness. You are not alone—you were never alone. Reaching out and building communities may be critical for health and happiness. Yours. Theirs. *Ours.*

This basic principle echoes back to the very first ideas of this book—that we evolved as much to be a collective species as we did to be an individualistic one. Writing in the *Rumpus*, Mandy Len Catron advises a letter writer that we don't need to follow one set path in life to end up at happiness: "To have a good life, you don't need kids or a husband or a picket fence. You just need to find people who matter and keep walking toward them."[15]

Ignoring our collective selves not only denies our true nature, but it also sets us up for loneliness and grasping at health fads and conspiracy theories to find meaning.

We've come full circle and are ready to consider some of the lessons this year has taught us.

Chapter Eleven

Bee Lessons

Bethel, Maine

I recently turned forty years old.

To celebrate I headed up to the mountains with my brothers and their broods and my cousin Elizabeth and hers. We hauled the kids out for a steep, buggy hike up Mount Will.

When we returned to my uncle's home, I saw that my sister-in-law Kathie had transformed the dining room. She had strung up little white lights and decorative fans, and everywhere I looked were colored paper hearts with messages typed on them. She explained that she had used Facebook to reach out to forty of my closest friends and asked them to express what they loved about me in a single sentence so that I would be surrounded by their affection on my birthday.

One love note for every year of my life.★

The notes were from my best friend in kindergarten and my postdoctoral mentor and my mother—people from every stage of life, from every degree of intimacy. Naturally, I cried. That night as I stretched out on a cot across from my cousin, her dog snoring at my feet, I flipped through the stack of hearts and reread them. I fell asleep in a cocoon of love.

★ Yes, this is the same sister-in-law who worries she is a f$cking asshole.

I later found out that Kathie put all this together in the two days before my birthday. In no time in our past would such a thing be possible, an act of care performed so easily and smoothly, people's thoughts from literally across the globe summoned and presented in such a short period of time.

Psychologist Sherry Turkle writes, "We make our technologies, and they, in turn, shape us. So of every technology we must ask, Does it serve our human purposes?"[1]

Rather than delete all of our profiles and bin our smartphones, I think we need to ask of social technology a related question, which is *How* can we shape our technologies (or our usage of them) to *best* serve our human purposes?

Lesson #1: Use Social Media for Connection: Enhance, Don't Eclipse. Dial Down the Outrage, Dial Up the Empathy, and Create Room for Mistakes.

Over and over again as I interviewed experts and scrutinized research and read other people's books, I ran into the sentiment that social media possesses great potential for drawing us together and expanding our intellect and creativity and capacity for empathy—but that this potential has gone largely unfulfilled. We can certainly find case studies like Rana LaPine and Teri Clarke and the young people launching social movements on Facebook where that potential has been realized. But most of the friends and family I talked with in the course of writing this book seem pretty convinced that the effects of social media on their lives and that of their children are mostly negative.

Perhaps this will strike you as naive, but I think that social media's potential still exists, and that it isn't too late to maximize it. To do so, we'll have to approach our personal use from a meta-cognitive perspective (applying our antidote of reappraisal) and our collective use from one of social policy.

We need a lot more research on the effects of social media and technology on people's well-being, particularly that of our young people. But my best reading of the data so far suggests that it matters quite a bit *how* you use social media. We need to use social technology first of all to enhance, not eclipse, our existing social connections. Use social media actively, prosocially, and in ways that reinforce your face-to-face relationships. Don't allow a heart on Instagram to substitute for a lunch date. For "social network sites may . . . open the door to loneliness if they are used for 'social snacking,' or temporary but illusory fulfillment of social needs."[2] Don't ignore the person with the sparkling eyes across the dinner table from you in order to check in with your Fantasy Football team. Do post in-joke memes to your friends' timelines, do share a Timehop memory of your cousin's wedding a decade ago for your extended relatives to enjoy, do text your great-aunt the ridiculous thing your toddler just said to brighten her day.

When using social media, we need to dial down the outrage a bit, dial up the empathy, and create room for people to make mistakes. Back in Charlottesville, I asked Jim Coan how he saw social media fitting in with his Social Baseline Theory and the degree to which it does or doesn't amplify the processes of mirroring and empathy. Jim thinks that social media and technology could be amazing tools to connect us and draw us together, but the culture that has grown up around how we use them has resulted in more drawbacks than benefits. But ever the optimist, he *also* feels that we could develop new social norms governing how we utilize these tools.

"One of my least favorite tropes in television and movies," Jim said, "is when two characters are having an intense conversation and one character says this devastating remark and then walks away. Why do they walk away? And why doesn't the person follow them and say, hey, wait . . . defend themselves, ask for an explanation. It drives me nuts! Twitter is like that—*haha! and then leave*—over and over and over again." He shook his head. "I think solving the social media problem is some sort of Venn diagram of improving the tools, addressing our crappy, messed-up contemporary culture, and tolerating negative feelings. Right in the middle of those overlapping circles is increasing our tolerance for dumb things that we've done and other people have done."

We need to enforce social norms of equality and empathy and treating each other well, but we also have to stop shutting down conversation lines and playing into the hot emotions of meme culture. We need to stop saying devastating things and walking away like we're sitcom characters. We need to, as Keith Maddox and Heather Urry's research suggested, regulate our emotions and have the difficult conversations that are our first step to a better world. Push yourself to find the nuance where your disagreements live.

In terms of how *much* to be on online, the digital landscape is just a new arena where many of the same rules we developed in other areas of life apply. Adults can employ many of the same lessons we've learned about limiting meaningless television or scarfing Goldfish crackers in how we spend our digital time. Goal setting, intentional rewards, structuring environments of low temptation are all relevant strategies.

Adolescents and younger children need boundaries and good models to follow in order to learn—but parents can provide these with a light touch, avoiding the "juvenoia" we discussed in Salt Lake City. Psychologist Candice Odgers writes that "the design of a digital world that is safe, inclusive, stimulating, and nurturing for all requires that we resist fear-based reactions,"[3] and instead emphasize the importance of quality time with our children, positive relationships, and reasonable limits. We don't want to infect our children with trickle-down anxiety; we want to help them develop the tools and confidence to navigate a complicated digital world.

You can start with your own behavior, modeling moderation

in your own screen use. Set up digital habits in your home that everyone follows. In establishing rules about how often and how much to be online, we can approach screens like we do nutrition. Few parents would hand their child a key to a candy store and allow the child unlimited access—similarly, handing your child a smartphone with no restrictions is unlikely to be a good idea. Each family should develop its own "media ecology," as Devorah Heitner calls it in her book *Screenwise: Helping Kids Survive (and Thrive) in Their Digital World*. Setting up media rules that adults follow as well as children is most likely to be effective.

Process the digital world with your children. Kristelle Lavallee, content strategist at the Center on Media and Child Health, suggests setting up systems with your children where you don't surveil every action they take online but where you do dip in now and then—and strike up conversations about what you see when you do. Kristelle and her colleagues at the Center advocate for parenting in every single domain, that you can't draw lines between media and technology and real life: "All of it is reality," Kristelle says. "Digital life is also your real life."

Finally, if you were persuaded by arguments that teens are so drawn to their devices because we've increasingly taken away their other publics, sources of autonomy, and control in their everyday lives (and that these changes could be driving more anxiety and depression than the screens in their hands), then check out the great #freerangekids movement, started by Lenore Skenazy.[4] Allow your children, especially your teens, the freedom to wander on their own, to explore. Dip into their digital lives so that you can help them navigate challenges and minimize risks, but don't stalk them. Set up opportunities for them to gather with their friends outside of the gaze of their parents. Shut down the impulse to helicopter and bulldoze. Honor their digital citizenship.

None of this work will be easy. As Siva Vaidhyanathan observes, "norm-building is so much harder than technology development."[5] But it is critically important that we do it, and do it well.

Lesson #2: Embrace the Power of the Collective but Temper It with Dissent and Innovation.

I structured my high school valedictorian speech around the following quote from Ralph Waldo Emerson: "It is easy in the world to live after the world's opinion; it is easy in solitude to live after our own; but the great man is he who in the midst of the crowd keeps with perfect sweetness the independence of solitude."

Two decades later, I must take issue with both Ralph and seventeen-year-old me. All of the research, reading, writing, and conversations that led to the completion of this book have led me to conclude that this quote is incomplete. It *is* important to keep your head when everyone about you is losing theirs. Thoughtless obedience to authority is dangerous. As writer Philip Gourevitch has observed, "genocide, after all, is an exercise in community building."[6] We have to openly examine our own biases, challenge the structural inequalities in our society, and innovate. Without challenge to existing norms and social strictures, society would remain stagnant. As Frederick Douglass once wrote, "If there is no struggle, there is no progress. Those who profess to favor freedom, and yet depreciate agitation, are men who want crops without plowing up the ground. They want rain without thunder and lightning. They want the ocean without the awful roar of its many waters."[7] The people we laud as artists and heroes are those who strike out on their own, who buck the hive, who resist. We need to be individuals.

But at the same time, an over focus on one's narcissistic self leads to unhappiness. We crave community, togetherness, and working together on goals. Multiple scholars have landed on the same essential take-home message: human beings crave collective experiences and systems of shared meaning, and in our capitalistic, competitive, industrial, nuclear-family world, these experiences are dwindling and could be contributing to systemic mental health problems such as those we are observing in our teens.

In journalist and writer Johann Hari's book *Lost Connections*, he concluded that the common thread across all of *his* expert interviews was that the true path to happiness "comes from dismantling our ego walls—from letting yourself flow into other people's stories and letting their stories flow into yours; from pooling your identity, from realizing that you were never you—alone, heroic, sad—all along." We need to abandon the ancient story of an individual hero on a mighty quest with angelic allies, fighting enemies on all sides. Instead we need to see ourselves in a shared battle for a better world, with people to help up on our horse left and right. Especially those who started the battle with fewer resources.

If we look to our young people, we may see a good model for coexisting communally while avoiding undue conformity. We love to look down our noses at our youth. For as long as there have been generations, older generations have criticized the newer for their lack of discipline and dangerous irreverence for the values of the past, how things ought to be done. Social media and the think-piece-o-sphere seem to have raised this perennial habit to a fever pitch, with millennials being blamed for the decline of everything from golf to fabric softener to home ownership. But as sociologist Charles Horton Cooley reminds us, our youth are probably the best among us at thinking independently, outside the hivemind of the collective: "The will of middle age is stronger in the sense that it has more momentum, but it has less acceleration, runs more on habit, and so is less capable of fresh choice."[8] We become mired in our grooves and increasingly cautious of tiptoeing outside of what we perceive as socially acceptable behavior. We become rigid in our beliefs, less diverse in our experiences, and more cautious about upsetting the norms that keep us in the inner circle, safe from the enemies outside and within. We should listen to our young people and allow them greater voice.

We can intervene in our own appraisals in order to resist the power of the crowd—to be aware of its influence and consciously act to resist it. In his book *Situations Matter: Understanding How Context Transforms Your World*, psychologist and Tufts University professor Sam Sommers reviews all of the ways in which the social setting we're in influences our choices, behaviors, and even our very perception. Much of the advice sections of his book focus on how to keep your head when in the midst of a crowd—how to intervene in emergency situations rather than assume that someone else in the crowd will leap to the charge, how to understand that our collective society has loaded us up with automatic biases regarding marginalized social groups and to consciously combat the associations and stereotypes they give us, and how to risk embarrassment in order to behave morally.

Be a creative individual who is simultaneously deeply connected with your community.

Lesson #3: Take the Antidote: Regulate Your Emotions.

Hopefully I have convinced you of the many powers of reappraisal to prosocially shape the emotions and behaviors of both individuals and groups. Which emotions are likely to be the most productive, the most rewarding, lead us to both a better society and a better life?

First, let's avoid fear. A gift I can offer you: People *always* think that contemporary living is a time of upheaval, of rapid change, of the ground shifting beneath their feet. They look to the past with nostalgia and affection, thinking that things were more secure then, more stable, less chaotic.* As just one example,

---

* At least, this is how the people shaping the narrative feel. This nostalgia might be a marker of privilege.

in 1895 philosopher of crowds Gustave Le Bon wrote, "The present epoch is one of these critical moments in which the thought of mankind is undergoing a process of transformation. Two fundamental factors are at the base of this transformation. The first is the destruction of those religious, political, and social beliefs in which all the elements of our civilisation are rooted. The second is the creation of entirely new conditions of existence and thought as the result of modern scientific and industrial discoveries."[9] He saw in his contemporary society a burning down of old traditions and too-rapid transformation based on sudden changes to technology and social movement. My point is not that he was wrong, but rather that it is the nature of the hivemind to look to the past and see a linear narrative begot by history books and films and essays and to conclude that it was a simpler time, one of long observed traditions and slow, gradual progress. Not so to the people living it.

We are living in unprecedented times, but that doesn't mean that the sky is falling. Philosopher Martha Nussbaum writes that fear is related to our desire to control others, to avoid uncertainty and vulnerability.[10] It constricts, it pulls in, it squinches its eyes shut, and it crouches.

Certain fears, of course, are realer than others, and certain social groups have much more reason to fear than others—particularly those who belong to identities that are likely to be scapegoated by the dominant group when the tides of paranoia and persecution rise. But the narrative of fear in the current hivemind—about screen time, about immigration, about a cultural civil war, about enemies above, below, outside, and within—dominates, divides, and does little to contribute to progress.

Elevate hope. In sharp contrast to the narrowing of fear, hope opens, hope encourages, and hope expands.

Hope need not be naive cheerleading. As historian Rebecca Solnit writes, "Hope is an embrace of the unknown and the unknowable, an alternative to the certainty of both optimists and pessimists. Optimists think it will all be fine without our involvement; pessimists adopt the opposite position; both excuse themselves from acting."[11]

I've often described the content of this book to other people as "Everything is horrifying—but don't be afraid." That sounds like a contradiction but is not. We need neither pessimists or optimists. We need agents of change who quell fear, who hope, and who act. All the better if these thoughtful problem solvers use all of the tools at our disposal, including digital media.

One such pioneer is educator and writer Bonnie Stewart, who has launched a grassroots movement that she calls Antigonish 2.0. The movement is named after a group of priests and scholars in Antigonish, Nova Scotia, at the turn of the twentieth century who began their own grassroots effort to build social and economic community. Watching global populism and political polarization spread across the globe with a wary eye, Stewart banded together a group of intrepid scholars interested in spreading a competing wave of digital literacy and civic engagement, using the original Antigonish model of nested groups spreading influence. So far the organization has conducted free online courses, hosted four-word storytelling sessions on Twitter, and held web chats.

These are the sorts of creative ideas we need to work toward solving some of these dilemmas—and I love that this effort leverages the same social technologies that can contribute to the problems, now used for good rather than ill.

Use anger, but don't burn out on it. Anger is a curious emotion. Most negative feelings involve withdrawal or avoidance. Fear inspires you to run away, disgust leads you to recoil, shame encourages you to hide your face. Positive emotions, on the other hand, encourage approach—an extended hand of friendship, an embrace of affection, a leap into new opportunities.

The surprising thing about anger is that most people find it unpleasant, yet it pushes us toward approach, not avoidance. You want to lunge forward, to strike, to right a wrong. You experience a surge of adrenaline, a boost in motivation. Interestingly, when you perceive you have been wronged, whether you feel anger instead of a withdrawal emotion such as fear or disgust depends on how in control of the situation you feel.[12] Moreover, research suggests that anger may serve a utilitarian purpose, benefiting performance in confrontational games or negotiations.[13]

Anger and outrage are critical elements in addressing wrongs and social injustices, and so we do not want to regulate away anger. At the same time, part of what feels so toxic about the current polarized political climate is the unmitigated nature of our collective anger. There feels like there is no escape from it. A friend recently posted on Facebook that she was in Wegmans after the Kavanaugh hearings and got so angry that she briefly contemplated taking every jar of pickles she saw and smashing it against the floor.*

We need anger but should use it judiciously, not letting it dominate or rule us.

Choose the prosocial emotions: gratitude, compassion, and pride. Psychologist David DeSteno, author of *Emotional Success: The Power of Gratitude, Compassion, and Pride*, argues that our rational selves and self-control are sharply limited, and that we would do better to shore up prosocial emotions like the ones listed in his subtitle. These so-called character emotions motivate behaviors that lead us to reach out to one another, to behave prosocially, and to reinforce community. They also encourage healthy behaviors that benefit your future self by delaying gratification and building social capital.

In sum: reappraise and regulate your emotions. Avoid fear and

---

* Because she happened to be in the pickle aisle, not for any Freudian reasons.

practice hope, gratitude, compassion, pride, and maybe add a dash of anger here and there when you need to pursue social justice.

Which leads us to another important reappraisal.

Lesson #4: Build More Inclusive Ingroups: We Are More Bonobo Than Chimp, More Honeybee Than Honey Badger.

For centuries, scientists couldn't conceive of a female creature with great power within her species, and so assumed (with varying levels of true belief versus willful ignorance) that the honeybee queen was actually a honeybee king.[14] Even in the halls of science, where objectivity is prized above all, the effects of hivemind appraisals can be blinding—they shape the questions we think to ask, the methods we use to assess, and the conclusions we draw.

I think that we have focused too much on the idea of humanity as inherently tribal, prone to selfish competition and violent, clashing ingroups. Back in chapter 1, Jonathan Haidt said we were 90 percent chimp and 10 percent bee. While of course this is a metaphor and those percentages do not actually relate to any biological measurement of species interrelatedness, I'd nonetheless propose that we dedicate a much greater percentage to the collective side of Homo duplex.

Dwelling on the idea that we are deeply tribal may be actively working against us. A chorus of experts we talked to or read about—among them Kimberly Norris Russell, Sarah Blaffer Hrdy, Patrick Clarkin, Frances de Waal, and Jim Coan—underscore the same point: we may not have evolved to be as prone to outgroup hostility as we've been led to believe. We may be more bonobo than chimpanzee, more like the scores of hunter-gatherer tribes that are largely egalitarian (remember Sea Cow and Wild Pig?) than the few that are violently parochial. Alloparenting may have shaped our early societies more than hunting or war.

Even if these experts are wrong and our tribal tendencies

outweigh our hiveish ones, the grandest aspect of our humanity is our infinite adaptability and the flexibility with which we define who is "Us" and who is "Them." We may not be able to escape our ultrasociality or our tendency to form ingroups, but we *can* train ourselves to be more sensitive to whom we invite into our circles. You can experimentally manipulate people's sense of ingroups and change their biases by doing so—for instance, in one study randomly assigning people to mixed-race teams of Lions versus Tigers yielded greater levels of outgroup bias against the opposing felines than members of the outgroup race. Think of humanity as a giant hive of cooperating honeybees rather than an amalgam of warring clans, and allow the reappraisal to include all human beings in your ingroup.

You can do this without releasing the solidarity you share with your ingroups. Being great at ingroups doesn't have to translate automatically into being hostile to outgroups. As author and activist Audre Lorde once wrote, "How can we use each other's differences in our common battles for a livable future?"[15] For we are going to need all of the tools at hand, and as apiarist Dan Conlon reflected back in chapter 1, the healthiest hives are the most diverse.

In his remarkable book *Tattoos on the Heart: The Power of Boundless Compassion*, Father Greg Boyle asks us to imagine circles of compassion: "Imagine no one standing outside of that circle, moving ourselves closer to the margins so that the margins themselves will be erased. We stand there with those whose dignity has been denied. We locate ourselves with the poor and the powerless and the voiceless. At the edges, we join the easily despised and the readily left out. We stand with the demonized so that the demonizing will stop."

Speaking of demonizing, don't allow yourself to use dehumanizing language—if you find yourself slipping into it, shut it down.

Lesson #5: Remember That You're Not the Da Vinci Code Guy.

At some point along the way, the hivemind began to equate critical thinking and skepticism with a disenchantment with experts. But part of working as a hive is trusting the other bees who are skilled in a task to do that task—let the scouting bees chime in on scouting, let the nurse bees do the nursing.

During an online course I took called Engagement in an Era of Polarization,[16] Mike Caulfield, director of blended and networked learning at Washington State University Vancouver and head of the Digital Polarization Initiative of the American Democracy Project, commented that we all love to think we're the guy from the popular book and movie *The Da Vinci Code*. We think that there is a great mystery hovering around the edges and that we're going to be the ones to crack the code and unveil the truth. But really, most of the time we should consult the experts, the people who have dedicated their lives to studying a phenomenon. I wouldn't trust my mechanic to perform my root canal or my dentist to fix my carburetor. When it comes to stories that have a whiff of conspiracy about them, you should trust Snopes.com over your brother-in-law who spends too much time on reddit.

Another thing Caulfield says that I find persuasive is that many approaches to digital literacy are incredibly laborious—they ask you to work through a complicated checklist for nearly every fact you encounter. This is not how human beings work, especially during their leisure time. He instead encourages us to rely on one another, to take advantage of the hivemind through a method he has published in a free online book called *Web Literacy for Student Fact-Checkers . . . and Other People Who Care About Facts.*

Imagine you stumble upon a meme or an internet rumor. Let's take one example from both the left and the right of the political spectrum—say, that Pope Francis endorsed Trump during the campaign (false), or that sometime in the 1990s Trump said if he ran for president it would be for the Republican Party because they were so dumb they'd believe anything (also false). Here are the steps: (1) check to see if you can find someone who has already done a lot of the work debunking the claim, (2) go "upstream" to the source—try to find the original appearance of the quote, photograph, or claim, (3) read laterally—what do other respected voices say about this source, this website, this journalist? Is this person widely respected, and if yes, how diverse are his or her fans? and (4) circle back—if you don't have your answer yet, you've probably still learned a lot from the first tour round and can start again with better search terms and strategies.

I love this proposal because it is grounded in a deep understanding of the hivemind—we can't know everything individually, but collectively we know quite a lot.

As we learned from the storage center in the mountains of Salt Lake City, some things that sound like conspiracy theories are true. And as we have heard ad nauseum in the last few years with varying levels of accuracy, sometimes news that appears to be true ends up being fake. We're never going to know everything for sure, and we have to get comfortable with that. We have to embrace the ambiguity but train ourselves not to assume the worst.

In Jesse Walker's book on the history of US paranoia that we reviewed extensively in chapter 6, he reflects on the lessons of our endless preoccupation with paranoia:

> The conspiracy theorist will always be with us, because he will always be us. We will never stop finding patterns. We will never stop spinning stories. We will always be capable of jumping to conclusions, particularly when we're dealing with other nations, factions, subcultures, or layers of the social hierarchy. And conspiracies, unlike many of the

monsters that haunt our folklore, actually exist, so we won't always be wrong to fear them. As long as our species survives, so will paranoia.

Yet we can limit the damage that paranoia does. We can try to empathize with people who seem alien. We can be aware of the cultural myths that shape our fears. And we can be open to evidence that might undermine the patterns we think we see in the world. We should be skeptical, yes, of people who might be conspiring against us. But we should also be skeptical—deeply, deeply skeptical—of our fearful, fallible selves.

This is also critical: we have to embrace said ambiguity without just deciding that nothing at all is true, or nothing matters. Because unprecedented levels of technological, economic, and climate change mean that desperately important issues are at stake, and we need all hands on deck. We cannot let consensus reality shatter. Splintering into irreconcilable tribes could lead to devastating consequences.

Lesson #6: Listen to People's Stories, Real and Fictional.

We are really good at mind reading, at mental simulation, at theory of mind. But we are also terrible at these same things. We use our personal experience as a measure of how the world works. If we don't experience or see racism in our daily lives, we assume racism is no longer a problem. If we can go for a dark morning run without a thought to our own personal safety (as you might if you are a man), we assume that everyone enjoys such a sense of personal safety moving through the world (which you might not if you are a woman).

We need to listen to people's stories. *Especially* stories from people who are different from us in race, ethnicity, gender, class, sexual orientation, gender identity, or political perspective. The great Madeleine L'Engle: "Because we fail to listen to each other's stories we are becoming a fragmented human race."

Researchers have successfully developed empathy-building interventions that attempt to immerse people in the experiences of others. These range from asking able-bodied college students to use a wheelchair around campus to requiring medical students to listen to an audio hallucination that mimics the experiences of their schizophrenic patients to having sex offenders engage in role-play exercises to develop understanding of the consequences of their actions on their victims—and these interventions work (at least in the short term).[17] I would argue that novelists, film-makers, and other storytellers have been working on empathy-building interventions for centuries. If you don't have access to a psychology lab, you can always read and view and share diverse novels and short stories and films and television shows.

Fiction may not only encourage us to empathize with people different from us, it may also hold the power to encourage social change for good. Henry Jenkins, principal investigator of the Civic Imagination Project at the University of Southern California, defines civic imagination as the ability to visualize a different version of contemporary society, to think outside the hivemind to a world where culture, politics, economics, and social norms are other than the current conditions. His research suggests that to activate civic imagination, and for such speculations to bear fruit, several related factors must converge:[18]

> The ability to imagine what a better world might look like, to construct a model of change-making, to see one's self as a civic agent, to feel solidarity with others whose perspectives differ from one's own, and to belong to a larger collective with shared interests...

Jenkins suggests that one compelling way that civic imagination is evoked is through the fictional stories of popular culture. These stories unite people in a shared vision. They take what may be one person's view of what the world could be, and make it many people's view.

Jenkins uses the Marvel superhero film *Black Panther* as an illuminative example. The movie directly pits scenes of contemporary racialized poverty and violence in Oakland, California, against a utopian alternative in the form of Wakanda, a mystical city in Africa that operates outside, but parallel to, the rest of civilization. The black citizens of Wakanda have never experienced colonization or been enslaved, they have access to superior technology but do not abandon their connection to their rich cultural heritage, and competing factions coexist peacefully. In a sort of meta-utopia, the fact that the film is almost entirely populated by black actors playing every type of character—warrior and pacifist, cleric and tech geek, medic and politician—illustrates the power of true representation on-screen. The protagonist, the prince and then king T'Challa, provides a gripping example of how one might become an agent of social change. The filmmakers explore the tension behind more adaptive and less adaptive approaches to change-making with the film's primary antagonist. Killmonger is not presented as a typical straightforward villain but rather as someone whose perspective differs from T'Challa's in important ways but who shares similar goals. At the end of the film, characters with divergent perspectives come together under T'Challa's leadership and pursue collective change—not just with their fellow Wakandans, but with the black communities in the rest of Earthen civilization.

Black Panther was one of the most critically acclaimed and commercially successful films of all time. Whether it inspired a wave of civic action in the real world would be difficult to evaluate, but

Jenkins's model of civic imagination as inspiring collective action suggests the possibility.

Lesson 7#: Build and Support Architectures of Serendipity.

As we increasingly separate ourselves into ideological, geographical, and economic silos, we lose opportunities to grow and change, to be nudged out of our narrow ways of thinking. Numerous scholars we checked in with over the course of the book have proposed ways to address this daunting problem.

Cass Sunstein, the legal scholar and author of *#Republic* from chapter 4, believes we need government and community programs that intentionally bring together diverse people—town halls, community festivals, or shared social events.* The challenge will be overcoming the fact that our towns and communities are increasingly segregated along ideological lines.

Siva Vaidhyanathan suggests that we need to support institutions designed for deep thought, such as libraries, public higher education, museums, and scientific communities, that we need to create support for careful, thorough journalism, and that we need regulation of tech companies, especially when it comes to how they intentionally curate our experience and narrow our ability to see diverse opinions and material outside what we think we want to know. We need our social media to expose us to the world as it is, not the world as we search for it. For our "inability to think through our problems collectively threatens our lives collectively," and these institutions and regulations are designed for just that sort of collective thought.

Most provocatively, philosopher Martha Nussbaum advocates a mandatory program of national service for our youth, in which all high schoolers would engage in community service (elder

---

* We need to create architectures of manufactured serendipity.

care, child care, infrastructure work, depending on their skills and future career intentions) for a period of three years. Critically, they would be forced to engage in this service in a part of the country that was very different from their own—geographically, ethnically, politically. Jim Coan and Sebastian Junger both highlighted the military as a diverse community that similarly breaks down demographic silos.

I think we need to do a better job supporting and selling the idea of higher education for the sake of this exposure to people and ideas from different backgrounds. We need something like a large-scale college dorm experience, where people are forced to engage with differently minded others. Higher education has huge structural issues that need fixing, but it is also one of the only places left in our society where you get manufactured serendipity, where you listen to people's stories in the form of history and literature and sociology, and where you form a community who will travel with you for life. It is also one of the only mechanisms by which people better their life conditions in terms of jobs and income and security, have a shot at changing the hand they were dealt when they were born.* Of course I'm biased—it is my life's work, after all—but I would love a world where every student had a shot at a college degree that didn't just disseminate "work skills" but also "being a human being in this complicated world" skills.†

One day way back in the mid-nineties, I arrived home from school to find a letter from my soon-to-be college roommate at Boston University. It listed her name (Kate) and also her phone

---

* This promise is often oversold, especially by higher education institutions looking to profit off their students—see Tressie McMillan Cottom's excellent book *Lower Ed: The Troubling Rise of For-Profit Colleges in the New Economy.*

† See Cathy Davidson's excellent work on how really, "being a human being in this complicated world" skills *are* work skills, in her book *The New Education: How to Revolutionize the University to Prepare Students for a World in Flux.* Also, support free college.

number and home address, should I wish to contact her. Excited, I sat down and penned a letter. I viewed college as a fresh start after my extremely homogenous parochial education, an exciting new world of diverse people and ideas and experiences. My letter planted a stake in the ground—I proudly proclaimed my intentions to get involved in social activism and avant-garde theater troupes on campus, my atheism, my love of science fiction and fantasy and heavy metal music, and my aversion to athletics.

A few days later, my future roommate read my letter and then cried for an hour on her mother's shoulder. She was at the time a conservative Christian, a cheerleader, a popular girl who liked popular music and popular fiction, and her intended major was athletic training.

After a long talk with her mother about keeping an open mind, she rang me up. Her voice conveyed kindness and enthusiasm, but all of her questions about living together threw me for a loop. She asked if I planned on bringing distilled water for our iron, and did I have a good iron or should she bring hers? Taking the call in my childhood bedroom, I eyed my floor strewn with crinkly hippie skirts and animal rights T-shirts and honestly had no idea what to say. She asked if I was bringing a shoe rack. I similarly eyed my single pair of Keds and said no, I didn't currently have a shoe rack. Was it okay that her best friend might be sobbing in our room for hours because of a separation from her high school sweetheart? I sighed.

This isn't a love-at-first-sight story—it took Kate and me some time to get to know each other and realize that our outward differences masked other deep commonalities. We both were huge nerds, extremely close with our families, and loved to write. We discovered a common musical ground in Alanis Morissette, who had just released *Jagged Little Pill*, and became mutually obsessed with the dramatic antics of the characters on the television show

Party of Five. A few years later at my wedding, I called Kate to the dance floor to twirl together to the show's theme song.

We also learned that some of our differences complemented each other well. Kate's bubbly, warm extroversion drew me out of my introverted shell. When I refused to stand up for myself, she'd get fiery and steel-backboned on my behalf. I had never in my life exercised, but Kate convinced me that it was worthwhile, dragging me out to the gym and to step aerobics classes and to hit the pavement jogging.

It didn't take long for me to realize Kate was unusually strong and resilient for someone so young. She had lost her father to cancer in high school. She nursed her mother through multiple sclerosis all through college, returning home on weekends to fight with health insurance companies and clean and grocery shop for her little brother, who was still in high school. We were woken early one morning our junior year in college to the news that she had lost her mother as well. I witnessed her recover from that loss, marry, raise an amazing daughter, end her marriage, find love again, and fight her way through two bouts of breast cancer. The day of her oceanside wedding to her new love, I watched with tears in my eyes as during the middle of her second round with cancer, she break-danced to her brother's band in a strapless wedding gown. It was the most beautiful, life-affirming, bad-ass act I had ever seen a human being commit.

I visited Kate a few days before her death. She was in and out of consciousness. I told her that I believed that she was one of the most remarkable human beings I had ever met and meant it.

Kate was one of the great loves of my life, and we never would have become friends if it were not for manufactured serendipity. Had the shuffling and random assignment of names in the BU system not paired us up, we would never have done the work of digging through our differences to build the affection, respect,

Acknowledgments

Of all the arguments in this book that we operate as a hivemind, probably the most convincing one is that the book you hold in your hands was written at all. All of the ideas and much of the writing was the collective effort of many people.

First, I would like to thank my literary agent Jessica Papin of Dystel, Goderich, & Bourret, and my editor Leah Miller. I am so grateful to Jessica for reading my initial query so long ago on a snowy afternoon and deciding to take a chance on me, for calmly shepherding me through each stage of finding a publisher and creating the book, and for her responsiveness and great sense of humor.

This would be a very different book had Leah Miller not provided such wonderful edits along the way—some of my favorite sentences in the book are more hers than mine. She could see more clearly than I could the core of the narrative and helped shape the book to reflect it. I am particularly grateful to her for never pressuring me to write a superficial polemic, indeed pushing me even further to consider nuance and complexity.

The experts I interviewed throughout the book were so generous with their time and intellect, and for this I thank them deeply: Dan Conlon, Kimberly Norris Russell, Patrick Clarkin, Rana LaPine, Teri Clarke, Jim Coan, Kelly Baker, Nnamdi Pole, Kristelle Lavallee, Anne Collier, Keith Maddox, Heather Urry, and Kathy

Foreman. Time is our most precious resource, and you shared it with me. A special thanks to the experts who had not shared any personal or digital connection with me beforehand, for responding to my out-of-the-blue request to travel to you, buy you food, and tour around inside your brain for a little while.

I am indebted to my two writing collectives. First, to Keith Maddox, Ayanna Thomas, and Heather Urry for regular writing blocks together, always with the promise of hijinks to come. Second, to my writer's group Mike Land and Jim Lang, who tolerated reading much of this work while it was not just doughy but often mere yeast and water. Particularly grateful to Mike for appreciating all of my sci-fi references, and to Jim for his talent for taking the messy circular thoughts in my brain and helping me to lay them in some semblance of a linear narrative.

Of course, thank you to my family: My parents Rosemary and William Cavanagh for creating the first and most important collective of my life—that of our family—and for their lifelong support and affection. My brothers Andy and Dan for not giving me trouble for always whining about how much writing I had to do (oh wait...). My most significant other Brian Chandley, time guardian and coparent and metaphysical partner, who created the space and time for this work to be completed. My daughter Noelle Margery Chandley for our many writing blocks together as she worked on her supernatural romance novel (watch for it), followed always by ramen noodles and *Doctor Who*. My sister/ cousin Elizabeth Jane Cavanagh and sister/sister-in-law Kathie Crivelli, who emerged as accidental main characters in the book just because they're by my side supporting me through so much of my life. My aunt and godmother Aunt Deirdre for allowing me to print her beautiful painting at the start of the book, for sharing her ideas with me, and for being a role model since I was very small.

To my womyn Elizabeth Cavanagh, Laura Phillips, Julie Sargent, and Kathleen Sargent: without you, life would be a paler version of itself. Thank you for helping me to be flexible and flowing, for supporting and brainstorming and reminding me to play, and for knowing I had this book in me. Thank you, too, to the women who joined us for part of the journey.

I am grateful to all of my generations of students. Teaching is my very favorite thing in the world and has always felt like this amazing privilege where we open up our brains and let our thoughts dance together. I have learned so much from all of you. Gratitude to the students who worked with me on various aspects of the book: Kaitlyn Doucette, Luke Gustavson, Julia Merchant, and Tyshawn Thompson. Most especial thanks to my first and closest mentees Erin Fitzgerald and Ryan Glode—I am so proud of the people you have become.

Finally, I would like to thank Twitter. As many feel about their family members, I think you are deeply flawed and often incredibly annoying, but I love you so. At least half of the thoughts in this book were shaped by conversations, articles, books, and authors I found through you. Plus, you have @darth.

Notes

PREFACE

1. Alan C. Kerckhoff and Kurt W. Back, *The June Bug: A Study of Hysterical Contagion* (New York: Appleton-Century-Crofts, 1968).
2. Elaine Showalter, "Scratching the Bin Laden Itch," *New Statesman* 131, no. 717 (2002): 12–13.
3. Susan Dominus, "What Happened to the Girls in Le Roy." *The New York Times Magazine*, March 7, 2012.
4. Jenna L. Clark, Sara B. Algoe, and Melanie C. Green, "Social Network Sites and Well-Being: The Role of Social Connection." *Current Directions in Psychological Science* 27, no. 1 (2018): 32–37.
5. Charles Horton Cooley, *Human Nature and the Social Order* (Abingdon-on-Thames, UK: Routledge, 2017).
6. Kelly J. Baker, *The Zombies Are Coming!: The Realities of the Zombie Apocalypse in American Culture* (New York: RosettaBooks, 2013).
7. Tressie McMillan Cottom, "In an Age of Wicked Problems, Beware of Simple Solutions," *Huffington Post* (2018).

CHAPTER ONE: Welcome to the Hivemind

1. E. J. Masicampo, "Conscious Thought Does Not Guide Moment-to-Moment Actions—It Serves Social and Cultural Functions," *Frontiers in Psychology* 2013: 1–5.
2. Jonathan Haidt, *The Righteous Mind: Why Good People Are Divided by Politics and Religion* (New York: Vintage, 2012).
3. Christian Von Scheve and Sven Ismer, "Towards a Theory of Collective Emotions," *Emotion Review* 5, no. 4 (2013): 406–413.
4. Margaret Thaler Singer, and Janja Lalich, *Cults in Our Midst* (San Francisco: Jossey-Bass, 1995).
5. Sandra Manninen et al. "Social Laughter Triggers Endogenous Opioid Release in Humans." *Journal of Neuroscience* 37, no. 25 (2017): 6125–6131.

6. Ruth Feldman, "The Neurobiology of Human Attachments," *Trends in Cognitive Sciences* 21, no. 2 (2017): 80–99.

7. Carsten K. W. De Dreu, Lindred L. Greer, Gerben A. Van Kleef, Shaul Shalvi, and Michel J. J. Handgraaf. "Oxytocin Promotes Human Ethnocentrism," *Proceedings of the National Academy of Sciences* 108, no. 4 (2011): 1262–1266.

8. Weihua Zhao, Shuxia Yao, Qin Li, Yayuan Geng, Xiaole Ma, Lizhu Luo, Lei Xu, and Keith M. Kendrick, "Oxytocin Blurs the Self-Other Distinction During Trait Judgments and Reduces Medial Prefrontal Cortex Responses," *Human Brain Mapping* 37, no. 7 (2016): 2512–2527.

9. Miho Nagasawa, Shouhei Mitsui, Shiori En, Nobuyo Ohtani, Mitsuaki Ohta, Yasuo Sakuma, Tatsushi Onaka, Kazutaka Mogi, and Takefumi Kikusui, "Oxytocin-Gaze Positive Loop and the Coevolution of Human-Dog Bonds," *Science* 348, no. 6232 (2015): 333–336.

10. Giacomo Rizzolatti, Luciano Fadiga, Léonardo Fogassi, and Vittorio Gallese, "Resonance Behaviors and Mirror Neurons," *Archives Italiennes de Biologie* 137, no. 2 (1999): 85–100.

11. Giacomo Rizzolatti and Laila Craighero, "The Mirror-Neuron System," *Annual Review of Neuroscience* 27 (2004): 169–192.

12. V. S. Ramachandran, *The Tell-Tale Brain* (New York: W. W. Norton & Company, 2011).

13. Much of this content was sourced from my interview with neuroscientist James Coan (see chapter 5, "Selfing and Othering") and his Circle of Willis podcast interview with Marco Iacoboni.

14. Marco Iacoboni, Roger P. Woods, Marcel Brass, Harold Bekkering, John C. Mazziotta, and Giacomo Rizzolatti, "Cortical Mechanisms of Human Imitation," *Science* 286, no. 5449 (1999): 2526–2528.

15. Simone G. Shamay-Tsoory, Nira Saporta, Inbar Z. Marton-Alper, and Hila Z. Gvirts, "Herding Brains: A Core Neural Mechanism for Social Alignment," *Trends in Cognitive Sciences* 23, no. 3 (2019): 174–186.

16. Elaine Hatfield, John T. Cacioppo, and Richard L. Rapson, "Primitive Emotional Contagion," *Review of Personality and Social Psychology* 14 (1992): 151–177.

17. Christian Von Scheve and Sven Ismer, "Towards a Theory of Collective Emotions," *Emotion Review* 5, no. 4 (2013): 406–413.

18. Lauri Nummenmaa, Juha Lahnakoski, and Enrico Glerean, "Sharing the Social World via Intersubject Neural Synchronization," *Current Opinion in Psychology* (2018).

19. M. Tomasello, *The Natural History of Human Thinking* (Cambridge, MA: Harvard University Press. 2014).

20. Richard Dawkins, *The Selfish Gene (30th Anniversary Edition—with a New Introduction by the Author)* (New York: Oxford University Press, 2006).

21. L. Coviello, Y. Sohn, A. D. I. Kramer, et al., "Detecting Emotional Contagion in Massive Social Networks," *PLOS ONE* 9, no. 3: e90315–e90316, doi: 10.1371/journal.pone.0090315.

22. Adam D. I. Kramer, Jamie E. Guillory, and Jeffrey T. Hancock, "Experimental Evidence of Massive-Scale Emotional Contagion Through Social Networks," *Proceedings of the National Academy of Sciences* 111, no. 24 (2014): 8788–8790.

23. Y-R Lin and D. Margolin, "The Ripple of Fear, Sympathy and Solidarity During the Boston Bombings," *EPJ Data Science* 3, no. 1 (2014): 1–28, doi:10.1140/epjds/s13688-014-0031-z.

24. G. Shteynberg, J. B. Hirsh, E. P. Apfelbaum, J. T. Larsen, A. D. Galinsky, N. J. Roese, "Feeling More Together: Group Attention Intensifies Emotion," *Emotion* 14, no. 6 (2014): 1102–1114, doi:10.1037/a0037697.

25. John Brownlee, "This Massive Twitter Brain Visualized the News of David Bowie's Death in Real Time," *Fast Company,* February 2016.

26. Jasper H. B. de Groot, Monique A. M. Smeets, Annemarie Kaldewaij, Maarten J. A. Duijndam, and Gün R. Semin, "Chemosignals Communicate Human Emotions," *Psychological Science* 23, no. 11 (2012): 1417–1424.

27. Jasper H. B. de Groot, Gün R. Semin, and Monique A. M. Smeets, "I Can See, Hear, and Smell Your Fear: Comparing Olfactory and Audiovisual Media in Fear Communication," *Journal of Experimental Psychology: General* 143, no. 2 (2014): 825.

28. J. H. B. de Groot, M. A. M. Smeets, M. J. Rowson, et al. "A Sniff of Happiness." *Psychological Science* 26, no. 6 (2015): 684–700, doi: 10.1177/0956797614566318.

CHAPTER TWO: Our Fiction, Ourselves

1. D. R. Johnson, B. L. Huffman, and D. M. Jasper, "Changing Race Boundary Perception by Reading Narrative Fiction," *Basic and Applied Social Psychology* 36, no. 1 (2014): 83–90, doi:10.1080/01973533.2013.856791.

2. Maria Eugenia Panero, Deena Skolnick Weisberg, Jessica Black, Thalia R. Goldstein, Jennifer L. Barnes, Hiram Brownell, and Ellen Winner, "Does Reading a Single Passage of Literary Fiction Really Improve Theory of Mind? An Attempt at Replication," *Journal of Personality and Social Psychology* 111, no. 5 (2016): e46.

3. Panero, et al., "Does Reading a Single," e46.

4. Joe O'Connor, "Shark Phobia: The Memory of *Jaws* Continues to Scare Swimmers Away from the Ocean," *National Post,* 2013.

5. Daniel Kahneman, "Maps of Bounded Rationality: Psychology for Behavioral Economics," *American Economic Review* 93, no. 5 (2003): 1449–1475.

6. World Health Organization, *Eliminating Virginity Testing: An Interagency Statement*, no. WHO/RHR/18.15, World Health Organization, 2018.

7. Elizabeth Levy Paluck, "What's in a Norm? Sources and Processes of Norm Change," *Journal of Personality and Social Psychology* (2009): 594.

8. Michael Tomasello, *A Natural History of Human Morality* (Cambridge, MA: Harvard University Press, 2016).

9. Tomasello, *A Natural History.*

10. Matthew D. Lieberman, *Social: Why Our Brains Are Wired to Connect* (Oxford University Press, 2013).

11. Lieberman, *Social.*

12. D. Centola, J. Becker, D. Brackbill, and A. Baronchelli, "Experimental Evidence for Tipping Points in Social Convention," *Science* 360 (2018) (6393): 1116–1119.

13. E. Yong, "The Tipping Point when Minority Views Take Over" *Atlantic*, June 2018.

14. Yong, "The Tipping Point."

15. R. B. Cialdini, L. J. Demaine, B. J. Sagarin, D. W. Barrett, K. Rhoads, and P. L. Winter, "Managing Social Norms for Persuasive Impact," *Social Influence* 1, no. 1 (2006): 3–15, doi:10.1080/15534510500181459.

16. R. Schank and R. Abelson, *Knowledge and Memory: The Real Story*, lead article in *Knowledge and Memory: The Real Story*, edited by Robert S. Wyer, Jr. (Hillsdale, NJ: Lawrence Erlbaum Associates, 1995).

17. Brian A. Nosek, Frederick L. Smyth, Jeffrey J. Hansen, Thierry Devos, Nicole M. Lindner, Kate A. Ranganath, Colin Tucker Smith, et al., "Pervasiveness and Correlates of Implicit Attitudes and Stereotypes," *European Review of Social Psychology* 18, no. 1 (2007).

18. Denise Sekaquaptewa, Penelope Espinoza, Mischa Thompson, Patrick Vargas, and William von Hippel, "Stereotypic Explanatory Bias: Implicit Stereotyping as a Predictor of Discrimination," *Journal of Experimental Social Psychology* 39, no. 1 (2003): 75–82.

19. D. Smith, P. Schlaepfer, K. Major, et al., "Cooperation and the Evolution of Hunter-Gatherer Storytelling," *Nature Communications* 8, no. 1 (2017): 1–9.

20. E. Giugni, R. Vadalà, and C. De Vincentiis, "The Brain's Default Mode Network: A Mind 'Sentinel' Role?" *Functional Neurology* 25, no. 4 (2010): 189.

21. Diana I. Tamir, Andrew B. Bricker, David Dodell-Feder, and Jason P. Mitchell, "Reading Fiction and Reading Minds: The Role of

Simulation in the Default Network," *Social Cognitive and Affective Neuroscience* 11, no. 2 (2015): 215–224.

22. Véronique Boulenger, Olaf Hauk, and Friedemann Pulvermüller, "Grasping Ideas with the Motor System: Semantic Somatotopy in Idiom Comprehension," *Cerebral Cortex* 19, no. 8 (2008): 1905–1914; Simon Lacey, Randall Stilla, and Krish Sathian, "Metaphorically Feeling: Comprehending Textural Metaphors Activates Somatosensory Cortex," *Brain and Language* 120, no. 3 (2012): 416–421.

23. Scherer, Klaus R., Angela Schorr, and Tom Johnstone, eds. *Appraisal Processes in Emotion: Theory, Methods, Research* (Oxford University Press, 2001).

CHAPTER THREE: Thresholds of Inclusion

1. David Foster Wallace, *This Is Water: Some Thoughts, Delivered on a Significant Occasion, About Living a Compassionate Life* (London: Hachette, 2009).

2. J. Warner, "A Million Thoughts on 'The Coddling of the American Mind,'" *Inside Higher Education*, September 2019.

3. Sara Goldrick-Rab, *Paying the Price: College Costs, Financial Aid, and the Betrayal of the American Dream* (Chicago: University of Chicago Press, 2016).

4. Patrick Clarkin, "Thresholds of Inclusion." *kevishere*, July, 2016.

5. Frans de Waal, *Primates and Philosophers: How Morality Evolved* (Princeton, NJ: Princeton University Press, 2009).

6. Sasha Y. Kimel, Rowell Huesmann, Jonas R. Kunst, and Eran Halperin, "Living in a Genetic World: How Learning About Interethnic Genetic Similarities and Differences Affects Peace and Conflict," *Personality and Social Psychology Bulletin* 42, no. 5 (2016): 688–700.

7. Carolyn Parkinson, Adam M. Kleinbaum, and Thalia Wheatley, "Similar Neural Responses Predict Friendship," *Nature Communications* 9, no. 1 (2018): 332.

8. Janice Chen, Yuan Chang Leong, Christopher J. Honey, Chung H. Yong, Kenneth A. Norman, and Uri Hasson, "Shared Memories Reveal Shared Structure in Neural Activity Across Individuals," *Nature Neuroscience* 20, no. 1 (2017): 115.

9. L. Munoz, "Shared Neural Activity for Shared Memories," *DeepStuff .org*, 2017.

10. Lauri Nummenmaa, Enrico Glerean, Mikko Viinikainen, Iiro P. Jääskeläinen, Riitta Hari, and Mikko Sams, "Emotions Promote Social Interaction by Synchronizing Brain Activity Across Individuals," *Proceedings of the National Academy of Sciences* 109, no. 24 (2012): 9599–9604.

11. Stephen C. Levinson, "Turn-Taking in Human Communication—Origins and Implications for Language Processing," *Trends in Cognitive Sciences* 20, no. 1 (2016): 6–14.

12. Lauri Nummenmaa, Juha Lahnakoski, and Enrico Glerean, "Sharing the Social World via Intersubject Neural Synchronization," *Current Opinion in Psychology* (2018).

CHAPTER FOUR: Building Us Up and Taking Us Down

1. Jenna L. Clark, Sara B. Algoe, and Melanie C. Green, "Social Network Sites and Well-Being: The Role of Social Connection," *Current Directions in Psychological Science* 27, no. 1 (2018): 32–37.

2. P. Verduyn, O. Ybarra, M. Résibois, J. Jonides, and E. Kross, "Do Social Network Sites Enhance or Undermine Subjective Well-Being? A Critical Review," *Social Issues and Policy Review* 11, no. 1 (2017): 274–302, doi:10.1111/sipr.12033.

3. Dohyun Ahn and Dong-Hee Shin. "Is the Social Use of Media for Seeking Connectedness or for Avoiding Social Isolation? Mechanisms Underlying Media Use and Subjective Well-Being," *Computers in Human Behavior* 29, no. 6 (2013): 2453–2462; Eveline Teppers, Koen Luyckx, Theo A. Klimstra, and Luc Goossens, "Loneliness and Facebook Motives in Adolescence: A Longitudinal Inquiry into Directionality of Effect," *Journal of Adolescence* 37, no. 5 (2014): 691–699.

4. M. K. Burke and R. E. Kraut, "The Relationship Between Facebook Use and Well-Being Depends on Communication Type and Tie Strength," *Journal of Computer-Mediated Communication* 21, no. 4 (2016): 265–281, doi:10.1111/jcc4.12162.

5. N. B. Ellison, C. Steinfield, and C. Lampe, "The Benefits of Facebook 'Friends': Social Capital and College Students' Use of Online Social Network Sites," *Journal of Computer-Mediated Communication* 12, no. 4 (2007): 1143–1168, doi:10.1111/j.1083-6101.2007.00367.x.

6. Clay Shirky, *Here Comes Everybody: The Power of Organizing Without Organizations* (New York: Penguin, 2008).

7. David G. Myers and Helmut Lamm. "The Group Polarization Phenomenon," *Psychological Bulletin* 83, no. 4 (1976): 602.

8. John Suler, "The Online Disinhibition Effect," *Cyberpsychology & Behavior* 7, no. 3 (2004): 321–326.

9. John Suler, "The Online Disinhibition Effect," 321–326.

10. L. Rösner and N. C. Kramer, "Verbal Venting in the Social Web: Effects of Anonymity and Group Norms on Aggressive Language Use in Online Comments," *Social Media + Society* 2, no. 3 (2016).

11. Elias Aboujaoude, Matthew W. Savage, Vladan Starcevic, and Wael O. Salame, "Cyberbullying: Review of an Old Problem Gone Viral," *Journal of Adolescent Health* 57, no. 1 (2015): 10–18.

12. M. J. Crockett, "Moral Outrage in the Digital Age," *Nature Publishing Group* 1, no. 11 (2017): 1–3, doi:10.1038/s41562-017-0213-3.

13. M. J. Crockett, "Moral Outrage," 1–3.

14. M. J. Crockett, "Moral Outrage," 1–3.

15. W. J. Brady, J. A. Wills, J. T. Jost, J. A. Tucker, and J. J. Van Bavel, "Emotion Shapes the Diffusion of Moralized Content in Social Networks," *Proceedings of the National Academy of Sciences.* 2017;114(28): 7313–7318. doi:10.1073/pnas.1618923114.

16. T. Sawaoka and B. Monin, "The Paradox of Viral Outrage," *Psychological Science* 29, no. 10 (2018): 1665–1678, doi:10.1177/0956797618780658.

17. A. Waytz and K. Gray, "Does Online Technology Make Us More or Less Sociable? A Preliminary Review and Call for Research," *Perspectives on Psychological Science* 13, no. 4 (2018): 473–491, doi:10.1177/1745691617746509.

CHAPTER FIVE: Selfing and Othering

1. Charlottesville Critical Incident Review 2017, https://www.police foundation.org/wp-content/uploads/2017/12/Charlottesville-Critical-Incident-Review-2017.pdf.

2. James A. Coan and David A. Sbarra, "Social Baseline Theory: The Social Regulation of Risk and Effort," *Current Opinion in Psychology* 1 (2015): 87–91.

3. James A. Coan, Hillary S. Schaefer, and Richard J. Davidson, "Lending a Hand: Social Regulation of the Neural Response to Threat," *Psychological Science* 17, no. 12 (2006): 1032–1039.

4. Robert B. Zajonc, "Attitudinal Effects of Mere Exposure," *Journal of Personality and Social Psychology* 9, no. 2 pt.2 (1968): 1.

5. A. Waytz and N. Epley, "Social Connection Enables Dehumanization," *Journal of Experimental Social Psychology* 48, no. 1 (2012): 70–76, doi:10.1016/j.jesp.2011.07.012.

6. Jeff Greenberg and Spee Kosloff. "Terror Management Theory: Implications for Understanding Prejudice, Stereotyping, Intergroup Conflict, and Political Attitudes." *Social and Personality Psychology Compass* 2, no. 5 (2008): 1881–1894.

7. As cited in Barbara Ehrenreich, *Dancing in the Streets: A History of Collective Joy* (New York: Macmillan, 2007).

8. As cited in Ehrenreich, *Dancing*.

9. Dr. Robert Jay Lifton *The Nazi Doctors: Medical Killing and the Psychology of Genocide* (New York: Basic Books, 2017), http://phdn.org/archives/holocaust-history.org/lifton/LiftonT021.shtml.

10. Johanna K. Turunen, *In the Face of Violence: Identity, Justification and the Individual in Rwanda* (University of Eastern Finland, 2012).

11. Nour Kteily, Emile Bruneau, Adam Waytz, and Sarah Cotterill, "The Ascent of Man: Theoretical and Empirical Evidence for Blatant Dehumanization," *Journal of Personality and Social Psychology* 109, no. 5 (2015): 901.

12. S. S. Wiltermuth, Synchronous Activity Boosts Compliance with Requests to Aggress, *Journal of Experimental Social Psychology* 48, no. 1 (2012): 453–456, doi:10.1016/j.jesp.2011.10.007.

13. S. Wiltermuth, Synchrony and Destructive Obedience, *Social Influence* 7, no. 2 (2012): 78–89, doi:10.1080/15534510.2012.658653.

14. M. Cikara and Elizabeth Levy Paluck, "When Going Along Gets You Nowhere and the Upside of Conflict Behaviors," *Wiley Online Library* 7, no. 8 (2013): 559–571.

15. Elizabeth Levy Paluck and Donald P. Green, "Deference, Dissent, and Dispute Resolution: An Experimental Intervention Using Mass Media to Change Norms and Behavior in Rwanda," *American Political Science Review* 103, no. 4 (2009): 622–644.

16. Lasana T. Harris and Susan T. Fiske, "Social Groups That Elicit Disgust Are Differentially Processed in mPFC," *Social Cognitive and Affective Neuroscience* 2, no. 1 (2007): 45–51.

17. Don A. Vaughn, Ricky R. Savjani, Mark S. Cohen, and David M. Eagleman, "Empathic Neural Responses Predict Group Allegiance," *Frontiers in Human Neuroscience* 12 (2018).

18. Greg Toppo, "Education for All.... Even a 'Nazi'?" *Inside Higher Education,* (September 2018).

19. Orrin Johnson, "Why Free Speech is Society's Immune System," TEDx University of Nevada, February 2018. https://www.youtube.com/watch?v=o9KzMWdHLhQ.

CHAPTER SIX: The Enemy Inside

1. Jesse Walker, *The United States of Paranoia: A Conspiracy Theory* (New York: Harper, 2013).

2. Kelly J. Baker, *The Zombies Are Coming!: The Realities of the Zombie Apocalypse in American Culture,* (New York: RosettaBooks, 2013).

3. Kelly J. Baker, *Gospel According to the Klan: The KKK's Appeal to Protestant America, 1915–1930* (Lawrence, Kansas: University Press of Kansas, 2011).

4. Janja Lalich, "Cults Today: A New Social-Psychological Perspective," *Cult Research* (January, 2017).

5. Susan M. Reverby and Henry W. Foster. "Examining Tuskegee: The Infamous Syphilis Study and Its Legacy" *Journal of the National Medical Association* 102, no. 2 (2010): 148–150.

6. United States Congress, Senate Select Committee on Intelligence, and Stephen Foster, *The Project MKULTRA Compendium: The CIA's Program of Research in Behavioral Modification*, Lulu. com, 2009.

7. Krishnadev Calamur, "Ferguson Documents: Officer Darren Wilson's Testimony," National Public Radio Online (2014).

8. John M. Curtis and Mimi J. Curtis. "Factors related to Susceptibility and Recruitment by Cults," *Psychological Reports* 73, no. 2 (1993): 451–460.

9. Michaela Pfundmair, "Ostracism Promotes a Terroristic Mindset," *Behavioral Sciences of Terrorism and Political Aggression* (2018): 1–15.

10. Michael A. Hogg, Christie Meehan, and Jayne Farquharson, "The Solace of Radicalism: Self-Uncertainty and Group Identification in the Face of Threat," *Journal of Experimental Social Psychology* 46, no. 6 (2010): 1061–1066.

11. Michael A. Hogg, "From Uncertainty to Extremism: Social Categorization and Identity Processes," *Current Directions in Psychological Science* 23, no. 5 (2014): 338–342.

12. Lawrence Wright and Morton Sellers, *Going Clear: Scientology, Hollywood, and The Prison of Belief* (New York: Vintage Books, 2013).

13. Curtis and Curtis, "Factors," 451–460.

14. Latson, Jennifer. "The Jonestown massacre, remembered." *TIME*, November, 2014.

15. Doris Lessing, *Prisons We Choose to Live Inside* (Toronto: House of Anansi, 1992).

16. Janja Lalich, *Bounded Choice: True Believers and Charismatic Cults* (Berkeley: University of California Press, 2004).

17. Michael Barkun, "Conspiracy Theories as Stigmatized Knowledge." *Diogenes* (2016): 0392192116669288.

18. Richard Hofstadter, *The Paranoid Style in American Politics* (New York: Vintage, 2012).

19. Heikki Peltola, Annamari Patja, Pauli Leinikki, Martti Valle, Irja Davidkin, and Mikko Paunio, "No Evidence for Measles, Mumps, and

Rubella Vaccine-Associated Inflammatory Bowel Disease or Autism in a 14-Year Prospective Study," *Lancet* 351, no. 9112 (1998): 1327–1328.

20. Falz Siddiqui and Susan Svrluga, "N.C. Man Told Police He Went to D.C. Pizzeria with Gun to Investigate Conspiracy Theory," *Washington Post*, December 5, 2016.

21. Tracy Clark-Flory, "Inside the Terrifying, Twisted Online World of Involuntary Celibates," *Salon*, May 2014.

CHAPTER SEVEN: Hacked

1. Lisa M. Shin, Christopher I. Wright, Paul A. Cannistraro, Michelle M. Wedig, Katherine McMullin, Brian Martis, Michael L. Macklin, Natasha B. Lasko, Sarah R. Cavanagh, Terri S. Krangel, Scott P. Orr, Roger K. Pitman, Paul J. Whalen, and Scott L. Rauch, "A Functional Magnetic Resonance Imaging Study of Amygdala and Medial Prefrontal Cortex Responses to Overtly Presented Fearful Faces in Posttraumatic Stress Disorder," *Archives of General Psychiatry* 62, no. 3 (2005): 273–281.

2. Sarah R. Cavanagh, Lisa M. Shin, Nasser Karamouz, and Scott L. Rauch, "Psychiatric and Emotional Sequelae of Surgical Amputation," *Psychosomatics* 47, no. 6 (2006): 459–464.

3. Olivia Solon, "Facebook Is Hiring Moderators. But Is the Job Too Gruesome to Handle?" *Guardian,* 2017.

4. Jonah Engel Bromwich, "Logan Paul, YouTube Star, Says Posting Video of Dead Body was 'Misguided.'" *New York Times*, 2018.

5. Yasmeen Serhan, "'I Don't Want You to Get Shooted,'" *Atlantic,* June, 2017.

6. Jean M. Twenge, "Have Smartphones Destroyed a Generation?" *Atlantic*, September 2017.

7. T. Vigen, *Spurious Correlations* (New York: Hachette Books, 2015).

8. Amy Orben and Andrew K. Przybylski, "The Association Between Adolescent Well-Being and Digital Technology Use," *Nature Human Behaviour* (2019): 1.

9. Andrew K. Przybylski and Netta Weinstein, "A Large-Scale Test of the Goldilocks Hypothesis: Quantifying the Relations Between Digital-Screen Use and the Mental Well-Being of Adolescents," *Psychological Science* 28, no. 2 (2017): 204–215.

10. https://twitter.com/JonHaidt/status/1093535204692684800.

11. J. M. Twenge, T. E. Joiner, G. Martin, and M. L. Rogers, "Amount of Time Online Is Problematic If It Displaces Face-to-Face Social Interaction and Sleep," *Clinical Psychological Science* 6, no. 4 (2018): 456–457.

12. Andrew K. Przybylski, Kou Murayama, Cody R. DeHaan, and Valerie Gladwell, "Motivational, Emotional, and Behavioral Correlates of Fear of Missing Out," *Computers in Human Behavior* 29, no. 4 (2013): 1841–1848.

13. Jenna L. Clark, Sara B. Algoe, and Melanie C. Green. "Social Network Sites and Well-Being: The Role of Social Connection," *Current Directions in Psychological Science* 27, no. 1 (2018): 32–37.

14. Anthony Robinson, Aaron Bonnette, Krista Howard, Natalie Ceballos, Stephanie Dailey, Yongmei Lu, and Tom Grimes, "Social Comparisons, Social Media Addiction, and Social Interaction: An Examination of Specific Social Media Behaviors Related to Major Depressive Disorder in a Millennial Population," *Journal of Applied Biobehavioral Research* (2019): e12158.

15. Robinson et al., "Social Comparisons," e12158.

16. Melissa G. Hunt, Rachel Marx, Courtney Lipson, and Jordyn Young, "No More FOMO: Limiting Social Media Decreases Loneliness and Depression," *Journal of Social and Clinical Psychology* 37, no. 10 (2018): 751–768; Christina Sagioglou and Tobias Greitemeyer, "Facebook's Emotional Consequences: Why Facebook Causes a Decrease in Mood and Why People Still Use It," *Computers in Human Behavior* 35 (2014): 359–363.

17. Siva Vaidhyanathan, *Antisocial Media: How Facebook Disconnects Us and Undermines Democracy* (Oxford University Press, 2018).

18. Robert R. Morris, Stephen M. Schueller, and Rosalind W. Picard, "Efficacy of a Web-Based, Crowdsourced Peer-to-Peer Cognitive Reappraisal Platform for Depression: Randomized Controlled Trial," *Journal of Medical Internet Research* 17, no. 3 (2015).

19. A. Waytz and K. Gray, "Does Online Technology Make Us More or Less Sociable? A Preliminary Review and Call for Research," *Perspectives on Psychological Science* 13, no. 4 (2018): 473–491, doi:10.1177/1745691617746509.

20. Vaughan Bell, "Don't Touch That Dial! A History of Media Technology Scares, from the Printing Press to Facebook," *Slate,* February 15, 2010.

21. Nelli Bowles, "A Dark Consensus About Screens and Kids Begins to Emerge in Silicon Valley," *New York Times,* October 26, 2018.

CHAPTER EIGHT: Walking Amygdalas

1. danah boyd, *It's Complicated: The Social Lives of Networked Teens* (New Haven, CT: Yale University Press, 2014).

2. D. Finklehor, "The Internet, Youth Safety and the Problem of 'Juvenoia'" Crimes Against Children Research Center, 2011.

3. Robert M. Sapolsky, *Why Zebras Don't Get Ulcers: The Acclaimed Guide to Stress, Stress-Related Diseases, and Coping-Now, Revised and Updated* (New York: Holt Paperbacks, 2004).

4. Sonia Livingstone, Lucyna Kirwil, Cristina Ponte, and Elisabeth Staksrud, *In Their Own Words: What Bothers Children Online?* (EU Kids Online Network, 2013).

5. Raisa Bruner, "Meet the Teen Who is Pushing for an End to 'Period Poverty,'" *TIME*, January 9, 2019.

CHAPTER NINE: Antidote

1. Kevin N. Ochsner and James J. Gross, "Cognitive Emotion Regulation: Insights from Social Cognitive and Affective Neuroscience," *Current Directions in Psychological Science* 17, no. 2 (2008): 153–158.

2. James J. Gross, "The Extended Process Model of Emotion Regulation: Elaborations, Applications, and Future Directions," *Psychological Inquiry* 26, no. 1 (2015): 130–137.

3. Sarah R. Cavanagh, Erin J. Fitzgerald, and Heather L. Urry. "Emotion Reactivity and Regulation Are Associated with Psychological Functioning Following the 2011 Earthquake, Tsunami, and Nuclear Crisis in Japan," *Emotion* 14, no. 2 (2014): 235.

4. Keith B. Maddox, "Perspectives on Racial Phenotypicality Bias," *Personality and Social Psychology Review* 8, no. 4 (2004): 383–401.

5. Heather L. Urry, "Seeing, Thinking, and Feeling: Emotion-Regulating Effects of Gaze-Directed Cognitive Reappraisal," *Emotion* 10, no. 1 (2010): 125.

6. Jennifer R. Schultz, Sarah E. Gaither, Heather L. Urry, and Keith B. Maddox, "Reframing Anxiety to Encourage Interracial Interactions," *Translational Issues in Psychological Science* 1, no. 4 (2015): 392.

7. S. Iyengar, G. Sood, and Y. Lelkes, "Affect, Not Ideology," *Public Opinion Quarterly* 76, no. 3 (2012): 405–431.

8. Boaz Hameiri, Roni Porat, Daniel Bar-Tal, Atara Bieler, and Eran Halperin, "Paradoxical Thinking as a New Avenue of Intervention to Promote Peace," *Proceedings of the National Academy of Sciences* 111, no. 30 (2014): 10996–11001.

9. A. Goldenberg, S. Cohen-Chen, J. P. Goyer, C. S. Dweck, J. J. Gross, E. Halperin, "Testing the Impact and Durability of a Group Malleability Intervention in the Context of the Israeli-Palestinian Conflict," *Proceedings of the National Academy of Sciences* 115, no. 4 (2018): 696–701, doi:10.1073/pnas.1706800115.

10. David Broockman, and Joshua Kalla, "Durably Reducing Transphobia: A Field Experiment on Door-to-Door Canvassing," *Science* 352, no. 6282 (2016): 220–224.

11. S. Cohen, R. J. Crisp, and E. Halperin, "A New Appraisal-Based Framework Underlying Hope in Conflict Resolution," *Emotion Review* 9 (2016): 208–214.

12. Joseph Lehman, "A Brief Explanation of the Overton Window," (Mackinac Center for Public Policy, 2012).

13. "FBI: US Hate Crimes Rise for Second Straight Year," BBC, November 13, 2017.

14. Elizabeth Levy Paluck and Michael Suk-Young Chwe, "Confronting Hate Collectively," *PS: Political Science & Politics* 50, no. 4 (2017): 990–992.

15. Elizabeth Levy Paluck and Donald P. Green, "Deference, Dissent, and Dispute Resolution: An Experimental Intervention Using Mass Media to Change Norms and Behavior in Rwanda," *American Political Science Review* 103, no. 4 (2009): 622–644.

16. Maanvi Singh, "'Genius Grant' Winner Used a Soap Opera to Prove a Point About Prejudice," NPR, October 2017.

17. http://noelle-neumann.de/scientific-work/spiral-of-silence/.

18. Elizabeth Levy Paluck and Hana Shepherd, "The Salience of Social Referents: A Field Experiment on Collective Norms and Harassment Behavior in a School Social Network," *Journal of Personality and Social Psychology* 103, no. 6 (2012): 899.

19. Kevin Munger, "Tweetment Effects on the Tweeted: Experimentally Reducing Racist Harassment," *Political Behavior* 39, no. 3 (2017): 629–649.

20. Ayn Rand, *For the New Intellectual: The Philosophy of Ayn Rand* (New York: Penguin, 1963).

21. Ayn Rand and Leonard Peikoff, *The Journals of Ayn Rand* (New York: Penguin, 1999).

CHAPTER TEN: Invisible Leashes

1. Jenna Woginrich, "What Makes Dogs Different," *Orvis,* July 2013.

2. Serge Faguet, "How to Biohack Your Intelligence?—?with Everything from Sex to Modafinil to MDMA," Medium.com, 2018.

3. Jonathan Haidt, *The Righteous Mind: Why Good People Are Divided by Politics and Religion* (New York: Vintage, 2012).

4. Kevin S. Seybold and Peter C. Hill, "The Role of Religion and Spirituality in Mental and Physical Health," *Current Directions in Psychological Science* 10, no. 1 (2001): 21–24.

5. Jonathan Haidt, *The Righteous Mind: Why Good People Are Divided by Politics and Religion* (New York: Vintage, 2012).

6. Damaris Graeupner and Alin Coman, "The Dark Side of Meaning-Making: How Social Exclusion Leads to Superstitious Thinking," *Journal of Experimental Social Psychology* 69 (2017): 218–222.

7. Karen M. Douglas, Robbie M. Sutton, and Aleksandra Cichocka, "The Psychology of Conspiracy Theories," *Current Directions in Psychological Science* 26, no. 6 (2017): 538–542.

8. Ziad W. Munson, *The Making of Pro-Life Activists: How Social Movement Mobilization Works* (Chicago: University of Chicago Press, 2010).

9. Jonathan Haidt, J. Patrick Seder, and Selin Kesebir, "Hive Psychology, Happiness, and Public Policy," *Journal of Legal Studies* 37, no. S2 (2008): S133–S156.

10. Iris B. Mauss, Maya Tamir, Craig L. Anderson, and Nicole S. Savino, "Can Seeking Happiness Make People Unhappy? Paradoxical Effects of Valuing Happiness," *Emotion* 11, no. 4 (2011): 807.

11. Gunter, Jen. "Dear Gwyneth Paltrow, I'm a GYN and your vaginal jade eggs are a bad idea," *Dr. Jen Gunter*, 2017.

12. Julia M. Rohrer, David Richter, Martin Brümmer, Gert G. Wagner, and Stefan C. Schmukle, "Successfully Striving for Happiness: Socially Engaged Pursuits Predict Increases in Life Satisfaction," *Psychological Science* 29, no. 8 (2018): 1291–1298.

13. S. Nolen-Hoeksema, B. Wisco, and S. Lyubomirsky, "Rethinking Rumination," *Perspectives on Psychological Science* 3, no. 5 (2008): 400.

14. Kate Pickert, "The Mindful Revolution," *TIME*, February 3, 2014: 34–48.

15. Mandy Len Catron, "Mixed Feelings: Two Roads Diverged at a Picket Fence," *Rumpus*, November 19, 2018.

CHAPTER ELEVEN: Bee Lessons

1. Sherry Turkle, *Alone Together: Why We Expect More from Technology and Less from Each Other* (London: Hachette UK, 2017).

2. Moira Burke, Cameron Marlow, and Thomas Lento, "Social Network Activity and Social Well-Being," in *Proceedings of the SIGCHI Conference on Human Factors in Computing Systems* (ACM, 2010): 1909–1912.

3. Candice Odgers, "Smartphones Are Bad for Some Teens, Not All," *Nature,* February 21, 2018.

4. http://www.freerangekids.com/.

5. Siva Vaidhyanathan, *Antisocial Media: How Facebook Disconnects Us and Undermines Democracy* (Oxford University Press, 2018).

6. Philip Gourevitch, *We Wish to Inform You that Tomorrow We Will Be Killed with Our Families* vol. 24 (Basingstoke, UK: Pan Macmillan, 2015).

7. Frederick Douglass, "West India Emancipation Speech," delivered August 3, 1857.

8. Charles Horton Cooley, *Human Nature and the Social Order* (Abingdon-on-Thames, UK: Routledge, 2017).

9. Gustave L. Bon, "The Crowd: A Study of the Popular Mind" (1896).

10. Martha C. Nussbaum, *The Monarchy of Fear: A Philosopher Looks at Our Political Crisis* (Oxford University Press, 2018).

11. Rebecca Solnit, "Hope Is an Embrace of the Unknown," *Guardian*, July 15, 2016.

12. Dacher Keltner, Deborah H. Gruenfeld, and Cameron Anderson, "Power, Approach, and Inhibition," *Psychological Review* 110, no. 2 (2003): 265.

13. M. Tamir, B. Q. Ford, M. Gilliam, "Evidence for Utilitarian Motives in Emotion Regulation," *Cognition and Emotion* (2012): 1–9; J. J Van Bavel, and W. A. Cunningham, "Self-Categorization with a Novel Mixed-Race Group Moderates Automatic Social and Racial Biases," *Personality and Social Psychology Bulletin* 35, no. 3 (2008): 321–335.

14. Sophia Swinford, "The Curious Feminist History of Queen Bees," *Aleteia*, 2018.

15. Rudolph P. Byrd, Johnnetta Betsch Cole, and Beverly Guy-Sheftall, *I Am Your Sister: Collected and Unpublished Writings of Audre Lorde* (New York: Oxford University Press, 2009).

16. https://www.edx.org/course/engagement-time-polarization-davidsonx-davnowxpolarization.

17. Erika Weisz and Jamil Zaki, "Empathy Building Interventions: A Review of Existing Work and Suggestions for Future Directions,"in *The Oxford Handbook of Compassion Science* (Oxford University Press 2017), pp. 205–217.

18. Henry Jenkins, "What *Black Panther* Can Teach Us About Civic Imagination," Global-e, 2018.

Hivemind Reading List

Alter, Adam. *Irresistible: The Rise of Addictive Technology and the Business of Keeping Us Hooked*. New York: Penguin, 2017.

Atwood, Margaret. *Oryx and Crake*. Vol. 1. Toronto: Vintage Canada, 2010.

Baker, Kelly J. *Gospel According to the Klan: The KKK's Appeal to Protestant America, 1915–1930*. Lawrence, Kansas: University Press of Kansas, 2011.

Baker, K. J. *The Zombies Are Coming!: The Realities of the Zombie Apocalypse in American Culture*. New York: Rosettabooks, 2013.

Bayard, Pierre. *How to Talk About Books You Haven't Read*. New York: Bloomsbury Publishing, 2007.

Bergner, Daniel. *What Do Women Want?: Adventures in the Science of Female Desire*. Edinburgh: Canongate Books, 2013.

Blaffer Hrdy, Sarah. *Mothers and Others: The Evolutionary Origins of Mutual Understanding*. Cambridge: Belknap, 2009.

Bon, Gustave L. *The Crowd: A Study of the Popular Mind*. 1896.

boyd, danah. *It's Complicated: The Social Lives of Networked Teens*. New Haven, CT: Yale University Press, 2014.

Boyle, Greg. *Tattoos on the Heart: The Power of Boundless Compassion*. New York: Simon and Schuster, 2011.

Brooks, Kinitra, Linda D. Addison, and Susana Morris. *Sycorax's Daughters*. San Francisco: Cedar Grove Publishing, 2017.

Catling, Brian. *The Vorrh*. New York: Vintage, 2015.

Catron, Mandy Len. *How to Fall in Love with Anyone: A Memoir in Essays*. New York: Simon and Schuster, 2017.

Caulfield, Mike. *Web Literacy for Student Fact-Checkers*. Monteal: Pressbooks, 2017.

Christakis, Nicholas A., and James H. Fowler. *Connected: How Your Friends' Friends' Friends Affect Everything You Feel, Think, and Do*. New York: Back Bay Books, 2009.

Cooley, Charles Horton. *Human Nature and the Social Order*. Abingdon-on-Thames, UK: Routledge, 2017.

Cottom, Tressie McMillan. *Lower Ed: The Troubling Rise of For-Profit Colleges in the New Economy*. New York: The New Press, 2017.

Davidson, Cathy N. *The New Education: How to Revolutionize the University to Prepare Students for a World in Flux*. London: Hachette UK, 2017.

DeSteno, David. *Emotional Success: The Power of Gratitude, Compassion, and Pride*. New York: Houghton Mifflin Harcourt, 2018.

Eagleman, David. *Incognito: the Secret Lives of the Brain*. New York: Vintage, 2012.

Ehrenreich, Barbara. *Dancing in the Streets: A History of Collective Joy*. New York: Macmillan, 2007.

Freeman, Jacqueline. *Song of Increase: Listening to the Wisdom of Honeybees for Kinder Beekeeping and a Better World*. Louisville, Co: Sounds True, Inc., 2016.

Gazzaley, Adam, and Larry D. Rosen. *The Distracted Mind: Ancient Brains in a High-Tech World*. Cambridge, MA: MIT Press, 2016.

Goldrick-Rab, Sara. *Paying the Price: College Costs, Financial Aid, and the Betrayal of the American Dream*. Chicago: University of Chicago Press, 2016.

Haidt, Jonathan. *The Righteous Mind: Why Good People Are Divided by Politics and Religion*. New York: Vintage, 2012.

Hare, Brian, and Vanessa Woods. *The Genius of Dogs: How Dogs Are Smarter Than You Think*. New York: Penguin, 2013.

Hari, Johann. *Lost Connections: Uncovering the Real Causes of Depression—and the Unexpected Solutions*. New York: Bloomsbury Publishing, 2018.

Harris, Lasana T. *Invisible Mind: Flexible Social Cognition and Dehumanization*. Cambridge, MA: MIT Press, 2017.

Heitner, Devorah. *Screenwise: Helping Kids Thrive (and Survive) in Their Digital World*. Abingdon-on-Thames, UK: Routledge, 2016.

Hoffer, Eric. *The True Believer: Thoughts on the Nature of Mass Movements*. New York: Mentor, 1961.

Hunt, Lynn Avery. *Inventing Human Rights: A History*. New York: W. W. Norton & Company, 2007.

Junger, Sebastian. *Tribe: On Homecoming and Belonging*. New York: Twelve, 2016.

King, Stephen. *On Writing*. New York: Simon and Schuster, 2002.

Lalich, Janja. *Bounded Choice: True Believers and Charismatic Cults*. Berkeley, CA: University of California Press, 2004.

L'Engle, Madeleine. *A Wrinkle in Time*, 50th anniversary commemorative edition. Vol. 1. New York: Macmillan, 2012.

Lieberman, Matthew D. *Social: Why Our Brains Are Wired to Connect.* Oxford University Press, 2013.

Livingstone, Sonia, and Julian Sefton-Green. *The Class: Living and Learning in the Digital Age.* New York: NYU Press, 2016.

Lukianoff, Greg, and Jonathan Haidt. *The Coddling of the American Mind: How Good Intentions and Bad Ideas Are Setting Up a Generation for Failure.* New York: Penguin, 2018.

Mandel, Emily St. John. *Station Eleven: A Novel.* New York: Vintage, 2014.

Martin, George R. R. *A Game of Thrones.* New York: Bantam, 2011.

McNeill, William H. *Keeping Together in Time.* Cambridge, MA: Harvard University Press, 1997.

Mitchell, David. *The Bone Clocks.* London: Hachette UK, 2014.

Nagoski, Emily. *Come as You Are: The Surprising New Science That Will Transform Your Sex Life.* New York: Simon and Schuster, 2015.

Nussbaum, Martha C. *The Monarchy of Fear: A Philosopher Looks at Our Political Crisis.* Oxford University Press, 2018.

Ramachandran, V. S. *The Tell-Tale Brain.* New York: W. W. Norton & Company 2011.

Rutherford, Adam. *A Brief History of Everyone Who Ever Lived: The Human Story Retold Through Our Genes.* New York: The Experiment, 2018.

Sapolsky, Robert M. *Why Zebras Don't Get Ulcers: The Acclaimed Guide to Stress, Stress-Related Diseases, and Coping—Now Revised and Updated.* New York: Holt Paperbacks, 2004.

Shirky, Clay. *Here Comes Everybody: The Power of Organizing Without Organizations.* New York: Penguin, 2008.

Solnit, Rebecca. *A Paradise Built in Hell: The Extraordinary Communities That Arise in Disaster.* New York: Penguin, 2010.

Sommers, Sam. *Situations Matter: Understanding How Context Transforms Your World.* New York: Riverhead Books, 2012.

Storr, Will. *Selfie: How We Became So Self-Obsessed and What It's Doing to Us.* New York: The Overlook Press, 2018.

Sunstein, Cass R. *#Republic: Divided Democracy in the Age of Social Media.* Princeton, NJ: Princeton University Press, 2018.

Thompson, Clive. *Smarter Than You Think: How Technology Is Changing Our Minds for the Better.* New York: Penguin, 2013.

Tolkien, J. R. R. *The Lord of the Rings: Fellowship of the Ring.* 1954.

Tomasello, Michael. *A Natural History of Human Morality.* Cambridge, MA: Harvard University Press, 2016.

Tomasello M. *A Natural History of Human Thinking.* Cambridge, MA: Harvard University Press. 2014.

Turkle, Sherry. *Alone Together: Why We Expect More from Technology and Less from Each Other.* London: Hachette UK, 2017.

Twenge, Jean M. *IGen: Why Today's Super-Connected Kids Are Growing Up Less Rebellious, More Tolerant, Less Happy—and Completely Unprepared for Adulthood—and What That Means for the Rest of Us.* New York: Simon and Schuster, 2017.

Vaidhyanathan, Siva. *Antisocial Media: How Facebook Disconnects Us and Undermines Democracy.* Oxford University Press, 2018.

Walker, Jesse. *The United States of Paranoia: A Conspiracy Theory.* New York: Harper, 2013.

Wright, Lawrence, and Morton Sellers. *Going Clear: Scientology, Hollywood, and the Prison of Belief.* New York: Vintage Books, 2013.

Wroblewski, David. *The Story of Edgar Sawtelle.* Toronto: Anchor Canada, 2009.

Yanagihara, Hanya. *A Little Life.* Basingstoke, UK: Pan Macmillan, 2016.

Index

About the Author

Sarah Rose Cavanagh is a psychologist, professor, and associate director of the D'Amour Center for Teaching Excellence at Assumption College. Her research considers whether the strategies people choose to regulate their emotions and the degree to which they successfully accomplish this regulation can predict trajectories of psychological functioning over time. Her most recent research project, funded by the Davis Educational Foundation, focuses on whether giving students tools for emotion regulation at the start of class can improve their same-day and semester-long learning. Sarah's first book, *The Spark of Learning: Energizing the College Classroom with the Science of Emotion*, was published in 2016. She gives keynote addresses and workshops at a variety of colleges and regional conferences, blogs for *Psychology Today*, and writes essays for the *Chronicle of Higher Education*. She lives with her family and friends in Massachusetts, where she can be close to both pumpkin patches and the sea. She's also on Twitter too much, at @SaRoseCav.